BOMBAY IN THE DAYS OF GEORGE IV

BOMBAY IN THE DAYS OF GEORGE IV

MEMOIRS OF SIR EDWARD WEST

Chief Justice of the king's court during

its conflict with the East India company

WITH HITHERTO UNPUBLISHED DOCUMENTS

F. DAWTREY DREWITT, M.A., M.D

GYAN

Published by

Gyan Publishing House
5, Ansari Road
Daryaganj, New Delhi-110002
Phone: 011-47034999, 9811692060
E-mail: books@gyanbooks.com

Distribution Network
gyanbooks.com
India, USA, Canada, UK, Australia, France

ISBN: 978-81-212-8917-7 (PB)
First Published, 1907

2nd Impression 2023

Printed at: Gyan Press, Delhi.

BOMBAY IN THE DAYS OF GEORGE IV

AUTHOR: F. DAWTREY DREWITT

BOMBAY IN THE DAYS OF GEORGE IV

Walter L. Colls Ph. Sc.

Lady West
from a miniature by Pastorini. 1822.

BOMBAY IN THE DAYS OF GEORGE IV

MEMOIRS OF SIR EDWARD WEST

Chief Justice of the King's Court during its conflict with the East India Company

WITH HITHERTO UNPUBLISHED DOCUMENTS

BY

F. DAWTREY DREWITT, M.A., M.D.

FELLOW OF THE ROYAL COLLEGE OF PHYSICIANS

WITH ILLUSTRATIONS

LONGMANS, GREEN, AND CO.

39 PATERNOSTER ROW, LONDON

NEW YORK, BOMBAY, AND CALCUTTA

1907

PREFACE

THE greater part of this necessary vindication of the acts of one, whose reputation has been at the mercy of his opponents, was written some time ago. It has no relation to present vexed questions. Whatever enchantment distance of time may lend, Bombay in the days of George the Fourth can have no more resemblance to modern Bombay, than a "Collector" in the time of Thackeray, to the scrupulous and efficient India Civil Servant of to-day.

Nor is it intended in any way to depreciate the great work—taken as a whole—accomplished by England in India. England's ideals are high, and she criticises her actions with severity; but, if her rule in that vast Empire be compared, not with that of an ideal Government, in a perfect world, but with such as exist, or are known to have existed, on the earth, fair-minded people must agree that the British nation has been worthy of its sovereignty.

There is no perfectly even advance in human affairs. All true progress seems to be as intermittent as the ebb and flow of a steadily advancing tide on a sandy seashore; and nations, like individuals, ought to be judged by the sum of their highest, not their least successful achievements—as painters by finished pictures, not by imperfect studies. The greater Anglo-Indians have far more than atoned for the lesser.

In ages to come—may they be far distant—when the strength, mental and physical, necessary to the nation who holds India shall fail—when blindness shall overtake the seer—and want of wisdom the wise—and England shall no longer know the things that pertain to her good—when the unchanging decree shall at last go forth that wheresoever the carcase is there shall the eagles be gathered together—then, in that dread day, may the just administration of her great Empire by the best of her silent, toiling sons be not forgotten!

CONTENTS

CHAPTER I

CHAPTER II

CHAPTER III

CHAPTER IV

CHAPTER V

CHAPTER VI

CHAPTER VII

CHAPTER VIII

CHAPTER IX

CHAPTER X

CHAPTER XI

CHAPTER XII

CHAPTER XIII

CHAPTER XIV

CHAPTER XV

CHAPTER XVI

CHAPTER XVII

CHAPTER XVIII

ILLUSTRATIONS

INTRODUCTION

Sir Edward West lived, and died, a champion of judicial integrity.

He brought to the service of India neither military skill nor subtle diplomacy, but that moral force by which England holds her vast Empire.

An able and just "King's Judge," sent to India by the Crown, he upheld on behalf of Parliament British honour and fair play against greed and injustice.

His faith, that what was morally wrong could not by any means be politically right, helped to keep the reputation of his country sweet in the rather close atmosphere of the Company's rule at Bombay.

Yet so little has been made public of Sir Edward West's life in India that the Dictionary of National Biography knows him only as a political economist, and devotes but a single sentence to his life as an Indian Judge.

The Johns Hopkins University Press at Baltimore, in a reprint of Sir E. West's Essay on "The Application of Capital to Land," quotes a short notice of its author in the "Annual

Biography." But Dr. Jacob Hollander in the preface to the Essay says truly: "Bare details of West's personal life have come down to us . . . it is at least interesting to conjecture that had his life been prolonged, West's influence upon the development of English economic thought would have been considerable."

A memoir of him—a small pamphlet, signed "Scaevola," and probably written by Sir Charles Chambers—was published in Bombay soon after his death. Of this there is no copy in the British Museum or India Office libraries.

Mention, too, is made of Sir E. West in the biographies of Mountstuart Elphinstone, and of Sir John Malcolm. These notices betray so much bias on the side of the East India Company, and against the King's Judge, as to give false impressions.

An account of Sir Edward West and his times, though with obvious limitations, can be obtained from the newspapers and magazines of the period. Files of Indian Journals and like literature furnish materials for an interesting and continuous history of the social and political growth of British India. In them—in their daily record of events, letters to the Editor, extracts from Parliamentary and India House debates, in their very advertisements—a dead world of which England knows little, lives again. In the following pages use has been made of these sources of information.

Like other judges sent to India under the Regulating Act to check the irregularities of the Company, Sir Edward West soon died at his task. His death was immediately followed by that of his wife, and of his brother judge, Sir Charles Chambers. A daughter aged two years was the only member of his family left; and thus opponents and their biographers have been—with little fear of contradiction—enabled to deal as they pleased with the dead judge's memory.

On the death of her parents, Sir Edward and Lady West's little daughter was brought to England, and afterwards married Colonel R. G. Wale, son of General Sir Charles Wale, K.C.B., Governor of Martinique until its restoration in 1815. Many documents which belonged to the Chief Justice, together with Lady West's Journal, have been lent to the author by Sir Edward West's granddaughters, Miss Fanny Lucretia, and Miss Mildred Wale. Mrs. Lane, to whom letters from Sir Edward and Lady West are addressed, was Sir E. West's sister, and wife of Capt. C. Lane. Their only daughter, who married R. D. Drewitt, died in 1860. The letters long since passed into the possession of the author—Mrs. Lane's grandson.

Neither letters, diary, nor memoranda have been previously published. They are printed as they were written, and the old spelling of Asiatic names has been retained throughout.

The writing of this short memoir has involved the expenditure of time and trouble, but there must be many, who, like the writer, have discovered that the pleasure of putting handbooks of history aside, carefully exploring some small spot in the great human past; and seeing vividly one moment of "yesterday, its aim and reason," is in itself compensation for the trouble, and for the consciousness of imperfection in the result.

Lady West's letters and journal, written hastily, and without thought of publication, contain the usual mingling of events serious and trivial. To omit the trivial would be to rob the story of some of its pathos, and to render it less like life.

The Author is indebted to the courtesy of the India Office for the use of documents, and also to Mr. F. G. Stokes and other friends who have kindly examined proofs.

BOMBAY IN THE DAYS OF GEORGE IV

CHAPTER I

India eighty years ago—Suttee—Thuggee—The East India Company's government—The King's Law Courts—Unenviable position of the King's Judges—Sir James Stephen on the "Regulating Act"—The King's Judges of Bombay—Sir James Mackintosh as Recorder: his conflict with the Company—Sir Alexander Anstruther—Sir William Evans—Excessive mortality among the King's Judges: Sir J. W. Kaye's comment.

INDIA—the land, whose story fills so large a volume of English history—the grave for the strongest of our race—must ever be so full of interest for us that no record of its past should be lost.

For this reason alone the letters contained in the following pages from Sir Edward West, Lady West, and Sir John Peter Grant,[1] the memoranda made by Sir Edward West, together with Lady West's Diary, kept throughout her few years in Bombay, seem worthy of preservation. They tell a story full of pathos. They throw light on the social life of our predecessors in India, and they

[1] Sir E. West's fellow judge—Sir John Peter Grant of Rothiemurchus, well known to readers of "Memoirs of a Highland Lady."

bring before us the antagonism of the East India Company, with which all King's Judges had to contend, during the years immediately preceding those great reforms which range themselves round the coming of Lord William Bentinck in 1828, and the renewal of the Company's charter in 1833.

It was this opposition of the old order of society in India, especially in Bombay, with its old standards of public morality, which made the position of a King's Judge who remembered his oath, a difficult one; and it is for this reason that the story of the short lives of Sir Edward and Lady West, of their devotion to what they believed to be their duty, of their early deaths, is of historical importance, though possibly not more pathetic than that of countless others.

For, through many generations, England has paid her yearly tribute of young lives to the East. On that hard condition the children of the dominant race, nursed in their island home, have gained, and still maintain, the mastery; maintain it—let us not forget—as much by high honour, and English love of fair play to all men, as by the sword. And justice should be done to those—whether King's Judges, or members of that small band among the shareholders and office-holders of the Company—who in the dark days at the close of the first quarter of the nineteenth century worked with higher aim than that of collecting gold in a poverty-stricken land.

More than a generation has now passed since India was at last taken out of the hands of the Company, to receive "her Magna Charta." Every year it becomes more difficult for us to realise the conquered, but ungoverned, India of the early part of the last century—the India through which bands of professional assassins moved with impunity[1]—in which thousands of wretched women, some leaving orphan children behind them, some mere children themselves, were burned alive under the warrant of the English magistrate, while the district police-officer looked on, and the Brahmin priest and the wretched woman's relations divided her jewels. It is difficult to imagine an India in which the majority of the East India Company were making their final attempt to keep out fellow-countrymen, and to escape criticism by abolishing the freedom of the press, and transporting at pleasure newspaper editors whom they disliked[2]—an India in which a local Governor could threaten to attack and deport the Commander-in-Chief of the King's troops if he should attempt to enforce the writ of the King's Judges;[3] in which the oppressive taxes of newly-annexed

[1] The Thugs, an association of men of various religions and castes, taught from childhood to consider robbery with murder their hereditary calling, were causing many hundreds of deaths at this time. See chapter xviii.

[2] See chapter vi.

[3] After the death of Sir Edward West and Sir Charles Chambers, Sir John Malcolm made arrangements to seize and deport Sir Thomas Bradford, Commander-in-Chief at Bombay, on his preparing to enforce the writ of Sir J. Peter Grant, the surviving King's Judge.—"Life of Malcolm," p. 525. See also chapter xvii.

States were collected by torture;[1] in whose unhealthy prisons men awaiting trial, innocent and guilty alike, were kept in chains for months, herded with convicted criminals, and on whose juries no Indian, no Eurasian, however well educated or respected, could serve.

The exiled Englishman in the India of those days, with no Simla[2] as a refuge, without quinine,[3] without ice,[4] could have found little relief from the heat, the sickness, the dull stifling monotony of the land. Small wonder that the hurried making of money became the aim of many; and that little thought was taken for the conquered Indian.[5]

[1] "Report of the Administration of the Bombay Presidency," 1892. Published by Bombay Government. See also p. 120.

[2] In 1830, Lord William Bentinck bought the greater part of the hill of Simla, and made it a summer health resort.

[3] Quinine had been extracted from Cinchona bark in 1820, but had not come into use. In 1639 the Countess of Cinchona, wife of the Viceroy of Peru, introduced Cinchona bark into Spain. The live tree was not brought from the Andes until two hundred years afterwards. Many explorers tried, and failed, to obtain it. One was murdered. Jussieu, the French botanist, who on a voyage from Syria shared his daily allowance of half a glass of water with his young Cedar of Lebanon, procured plants in 1739. They were destroyed in a storm. In 1835, Dr. Royle and other doctors of medicine petitioned the East India Company to introduce the tree into India, without any success. In 1860 Sir Clements Markham brought plants from the Andes to the coast, but the custom-house officials detained them, while patriotic Peruvians poured boiling water on their roots. In 1862 he landed plants alive in India, and now happily, forests of Cinchona flourish in the Neilgherries. Quinine is within reach of all, and deaths from malaria have diminished 60 per cent.

[4] The first ice was brought to Bombay in 1836. The coolies complained that it "burned" their backs.

[5] Bombay society could nevertheless be generous to fellow-countrymen. Subscriptions announced in the *Bombay Gazette* in 1824, towards the relief of starving English Colonists at the Cape, amounted to 9014 rupees. During the previous year a large portion of the 70,000 rupees subscribed in India towards the distressed Irish fund came from Bombay.

But if they were dark years, those years following the Mahratta wars, the darkness was only that which precedes the dawn. Wherever there are English men and women, some will be found working for justice, for freedom, and for the good of their fellow-men. It was at this very time, when the Mahratta war had been brought to a close, when the Peshwa's territories had been occupied, and the three Presidencies of Bengal, Madras, and Bombay had been united by continuous British possessions and dependencies,[1] that the national conscience asserted itself, and an increasing number of our countrymen began to feel that it would be a nobler thing to govern India for the good of her swarming millions than for gold and glory.

Within a few years of the close of the period covered by this short history — thanks to Sir Charles Forbes, Joseph Hume, Silk Buckingham, and others at home, and to the few who bravely faced unpopularity in India, and prepared the way for the great work of Sir William Bentinck —widow-burning had been suppressed; the Thug bands had been hunted down and annihilated;[2]

[1] "The Mahratta war, undertaken upon grounds of very doubtful policy, has ended in establishing the uncontrollable influence of England from Lahore to Cape Comorin. Your map will help your memory to form some idea of the immensity of this Empire."—Sir James Mackintosh, "Life," vol. i. p. 226.

[2] Between 1830 and 1835, 2000 Thugs, in whose existence the Company's magistrates had disbelieved, had been arrested.—Wilson's "History," vol. ix. p. 304. See last chapter of this book.

the Company's Provincial Courts of Appeal and Circuit proverbial for dilatoriness and incapacity had been abolished; natives had been admitted to juries, to judgeships, and to many offices of State; the cruel system of appointing unsupported King's Judges as buffers between the Company and the Crown had been changed; and a new legal member, independent of the Company, had been added to the Council. The barbarous and insanitary jails of Bombay had been rebuilt; the heavy taxation of Mahratta Territory, resulting almost in depopulation, had been lessened. The Company, though granted a new lease of life, had for ever lost its monopoly; Englishmen were no longer excluded from England's most important possessions; a new order had begun; and in future the governing race was destined to govern India, not for gold, but for the good of the governed.

The King's Judges—notably Sir Edward West, the last of the Recorders and the first Chief Justice of the Supreme Court of Bombay—were among the pioneers of the coming change, and seem to have met that fate which awaits reformers, the advance guards of our growing civilisation, on whose memories we now lightly trample, having found them stepping-stones to a more enlightened rule.

Decent justice has never been done to these Recorders of Bombay, and other King's Judges, who were sent out from England to undertake the thankless task of protecting the natives of India against the Company, and who died at their posts one after another, to be followed to their hastily-dug graves by the ill-will, not only of evil-doers, but of many an official.

The history of the creation of the King's Courts is well known. At the end of the eighteenth century, under the Company, justice in India was most imperfectly administered. Magistrates there were, who, in spite of the difficulty of their task, did their duty: but the average Company's law-court was almost useless. Not only had the magistrates larger districts than they could administer, but as men they seem to have been inferior to magistrates at home.[1] They were sent to India as mere boys, grew up without the higher training, the restraints, and the unconscious acquirement of knowledge, and of good feeling, which come to those who live among equals in England. Their vanity flattered by subservient Indians, their weaknesses studied and indulged, they naturally fell into the hands of unscrupulous native officials, who, as their master's energy diminished, used their power over their fellow-countrymen for every form of blackmail and corruption. Native spies were trusted who lived

[1] "A system which allowed the veriest dolts to be sent out to India to discharge duties of the highest importance had a large share in bringing about these scandals."—Sir T. Colebrooke in "Life of Elphinstone," vol. i. p. 79.

by sacrificing innocent people; one informer alone being thus able to cause the imprisonment by his magistrate of a hundred and ninety-two innocent persons.[1] "The Provincial courts, too, proved inadequate to the demands of public justice, and while the causes had been suffered to fall into almost hopeless arrear, the periods fixed for the regular gaol deliveries had been protracted beyond the legal limits, and persons had been detained in confinement without trial for a length of time which was equivalent to the punishment, even although undeserved."[2]

This was the court of law with which Mountstuart Elphinstone was best acquainted. He had been in Provincial India since boyhood, and he was fond of telling a story illustrating the reputation of the local courts, and the dread they inspired among the natives. During the progress of our conquests in the north-west the inhabitants were observed to be flying in considerable numbers from the territory we had acquired. "Is Lord Lake coming?" was the eager inquiry: "No," was the reply, "the Adawlut" (the Company's law court) "is coming, which is ten times worse!"[3] In 1773, after much opposition from the Directors of the Company and to the consternation of many of them, an Act for introducing "Regulations

[1] Sir H. Strachey, Judicial Records, 70.

[2] Wilson, "History of British India," ix. p. 260.

[3] The story is given in Colebrooke's "Memoir of Elphinstone," "Life of Elphinstone," and in Cotton's "Elphinstone."

for the better Management of the affairs of the Company" was passed. A Supreme Court of duly qualified judges, appointed by the Crown itself, was established in the town of Calcutta, and subsequently, in Madras; and in 1799, a Recorder's Court, consisting of Sir William Syer and a mayor and aldermen, took the place of the old Mayor's Court of Bombay, where the magistrates were too closely connected with the trade of the country to act as any sort of check on doubtful commercial transactions.[1]

The jurisdiction of the King's Courts was thus limited to the inhabitants of the Presidency towns and to those who had dealings with them. In the Provinces anarchy remained and grew.

As might have been expected, the position of a judge sent out from England by the Crown—a "King's" judge, as opposed to the judge or magistrate of the East India Company—was not an enviable one. The King's Judges were appointed to act as a check on the East India Company, and a protection to the natives of India against oppression and extortion, and they took an oath to administer justice without favour. Naturally enough the Company regarded them with suspicion and dislike, and did all that was possible to restrict their powers and limit their jurisdiction. Their

[1] Sir William Syer arrived in Bombay in 1799, and died in 1802; he is said by Sir James Mackintosh to have presided over the Court with "much integrity and skill." He is not mentioned in the "Dictionary of National Biography," nor is much known of his life.

instructions, too, were intentionally ill-defined, and parliamentary support was uncertain. The Crown, in fact, acted as the absentee landlord of British India, not quite sure of the extent of its title to the great estate; and it sent to each of the three Presidency towns the King's Judge as its agent to enforce English justice and fair dealing on its powerful tenant, the East India Company; saying in effect to the judge, "Go and do what you know to be right. We must give you rather vague instructions, and when the East India Company, whom we wish to control, turns on you, we may possibly be able to give you our support." The lot of a King's Judge was a singularly hard one!

The late Sir James Stephen[1] states the case clearly with reference to the Calcutta judges: "The East India Company," he says, "as a corporation, and its leading servants, both civil and military, were disposed to regard the sovereignty of India as their own private property, and to resent all interference with it by Parliament as an unwarrantable invasion of their rights. . . . The policy of Parliament was to assert the rights of the King of England and to establish in India institutions by which those rights might be maintained. This policy was, however, adopted in a way characteristically vague and imperfect. . . . The vagueness of the language of the Act arose[2]

[1] "Story of Nuncomar," vol. ii. p. 125.
[2] Ibid., vol. ii. p. 129.

from the fact that its authors did not wish to face the problem with which they had to deal. They wished that the King of England should act as sovereign, but they did not wish to proclaim him to be so. . . . It is not surprising that the proceedings of the Court should have given the greatest offence to the Government and Council of India. . . . The difficulties in the interpretation of the Regulating Act were shown by the Select Committee which collected materials for the Charter Act of 1833."

Under such conditions, at a time when the administration of both civil and criminal law was defective, it was impossible for judges who did their duty without regard to personal comfort not to come into collision with those who represented the old traditions of the Company.

But if the lot of the three King's Judges at Calcutta was a hard one, that of the single King's Judge at Bombay was infinitely harder. Each Calcutta judge had at least the support and advice of his fellow judges; the Recorder of Bombay had no such help, and with the European community against him, and with no moral support from independent public opinion, he stood at times alone for the laws he had sworn to enforce. Never did judges do their duty under harder conditions. Never were they under greater temptation to time-serving.

A complete history of this period has not been

—probably never can be—written, for the judges died at their posts, more or less suddenly, one after another, and the authorised version of their doings has been chronicled by the admirers and biographers of their longer-lived opponents—governors and officials of the Company—who retired to England and were able to tell their story without fear of contradiction.

The rapidly succeeding deaths of the King's Judges of Bombay during the first twenty-eight years of the last century make painful reading. With the exception of Sir James Mackintosh, who threw up his appointment of Recorder and returned to England, broken-hearted at the treatment he had received from Bombay "society," apparently not one King's Judge—from Sir William Syer, who died in 1802, to Sir Edward West, and Sir Charles Chambers, who died in 1828—lived to return to England; and the average length of their lives in Bombay seems to have been about three years and ten months. And these were men strong and active, in mind and body, some of England's best.

Hitherto from Sir James Mackintosh alone has it been possible to obtain some idea of the life of a King's Judge in Bombay. Mackintosh was a man of well-known ability, kindliness of heart, and love of justice—in India untainted by any greed, in spite of the money-making scramble around him; in England a member (with "Bobus"

Smith, Sydney Smith, Lord Holland, Jeffrey, and Ricardo) of the "King of Clubs"; and a welcome guest at Holland House.—Of Mackintosh Sydney Smith wrote:[1] "Sufficient justice has not been done to his political integrity: not rich, . . . invited by every party upon his arrival from India, he remained steadfast to his friends, never mentioned his sacrifices or his services. . . . A high merit in Sir James Mackintosh was his real and unaffected philanthropy . . . he had a genuine love of human happiness."

Mackintosh wrote of Bombay:[2] "There is languor and lethargy . . . here to which I never elsewhere saw any approach. . . . Every Englishman who resides here very long has, I fear, his mind either emasculated by submission or corrupted by despotic power. . . . The constitution of the Anglo-Indian Government is founded in opposition to the most demonstrated principles of political science, and its measures are in perfect unison with its original principles." . . . "This Government is too needy to listen to any proposal for mitigating the fate of their subjects: all that they can get is not enough for them. We have . . . a people beggared by imposition. . . . The Act for vesting the trade and territory in an exclusive company ought to have been entitled 'An Act for Preventing the Progress of Industry in

[1] "Works of Sydney Smith." Longmans, 1859, vol. ii. p. 304.
[2] "Life of Sir J. Mackintosh," by his Son, 1836, vol. i. p. 212.

India.'"[1] Mackintosh was determined, if possible, to sentence no one to death, and he was able to carry out his determination till within a few weeks of leaving India. An attempt was, however, made to assassinate him. "When I accepted office," he wrote, "I knew that I ought to despise unpopularity and even death; thank God, I do despise them."

Throughout his recordership there was difficulty in enforcing ordinary justice. In 1810 a servant of the Company, high up in the service, together with the clerk and the cash-keeper of the police, were found guilty of taking bribes, to prevent a trial for attempted murder. Mackintosh sentenced the guilty parties, and made enemies for life.

At another time when the Customs Master, a respected servant of the Company, receiving a salary of 5000 rupees a month, was found to be taking bribes from natives, to allow clandestine exportation of grain during a famine,[2] the jury for a long time refused to convict; and when at last the head of the customs was fined 17,000 rupees, the news was received with universal consternation. "And then," writes Mackintosh,[3] "I was treated in the grossest manner. There was no liberal public opinion to support me, and no firm Government to frown down indecent reflec-

[1] "Life of Sir J. Mackintosh," 1836, vol. i. p. 385.
[2] Ibid., p. 271. [3] Ibid., p. 272.

tions on the administration of justice. All this disgusted and almost silenced me for a time. . . . I shall always feel the consequences of this act of duty." . . . With a solitary judge "there is no advice in difficulty, no encouragement against clamour, no protector and witness against calumny, no successor in case of death. . . . I should prefer Botany Bay, if I were appointed Governor and Chief Justice, with assurance of support from home; I could at least rescue the children from brutality."[1]

Mackintosh retired to England, and carried with him to his grave the scars of his single-handed struggle for justice. His successor, Sir Alexander Anstruther, arrived in Bombay in 1812, and lived until 1819.

Sir A. Anstruther was succeeded by Sir William Evans, Vice-Chancellor of the Duchy of Lancaster, a lawyer of great promise, "distinguished in his writings of law by vigour and independence of judgment." He arrived in 1820, and died suddenly the following year; a short life in Bombay even for a King's Judge.

Sickness and death were rife in India at this time, and many a man serving in the Army and Company's Civil Service, from sunstroke, fever, cholera, and limited knowledge of the laws of temperance and health, died in India, or left it damaged in mind or body. But high as was the

[1] "Life of Sir J. Mackintosh," vol. i. p. 342.

death-rate in the Army and in the Company's Civil Service, the mortality among King's Judges was higher; and was destined, as will be seen later on, to become higher still. No attempt has been made to explain this. Kaye, in his Life of Sir John Malcolm, who succeeded Elphinstone as Governor of Bombay, writing of the King's Judges (whom Malcolm styled "quill-driving lawyers"), makes the not very sympathetic or scientific comment that "there was a rot among them."[1] Their deaths were generally sudden. Burial the next day was compulsory. Medical men were few, and medical knowledge slight, and little reliance can be placed on most statements as to the cause of death.

[1] Kaye's "Life of Malcolm," vol. ii. p. 505.

HILLINGTON HALL, NORFOLK.

From a Drawing by Col. R. G. Wale, 1850.

CHAPTER II

Birth and parentage of Sir Edward West—Childhood at Hillington—Harrow—Honours at Oxford: Fellow of University College—Writes "A Treatise of the Law and Practice of Extents"—His eminence as an early writer on Political Economy recognised in the United States—Death of Sir Martin Ffolkes—Edward West on Circuit—Family correspondence—A contested election in 1822—Marriage of Edward West and Lucretia Ffolkes—He is appointed Recorder of Bombay—Knighthood.

ON news of the death of Sir William Evans reaching England, Edward West was appointed Recorder to the King's Court of Bombay.

Edward West, a son of Balchen West, who had been Receiver-General for Hertfordshire, was born in 1782. Balchen West had died early in life, and the son, Edward, was brought up at Hillington Hall, near King's Lynn, in Norfolk, by his uncle, Sir Martin Browne Ffolkes, F.R.S., a nephew of Martin Ffolkes, one of the first Presidents of the Royal Society, and friend of Isaac Newton.

Edward West's grandfather—Temple West—had been Admiral of the White in the French War; his grandmother being a daughter of the memorable old sea-dog, Admiral Sir John Balchen, who in 1744, after more than half a century of sea-going and sea-fighting, went down with all his crew in the Flagship *Victory*,[1] returning damaged from the rescue of some store ships from the French. Monuments of both Admirals are in Westminster Abbey. Temple West's father was Archdeacon Richard West, D.D., Prebendary of Durham, who married Maria Temple, Lord Cobham's sister.

Frances, Edward West's sister, married Captain Lane of the 47th Regiment of Foot, and to Mrs. Lane most of the accompanying letters are addressed.

At Hillington, West profited by his uncle's guardianship. After leaving Harrow he went to University College, Oxford. Here, to quote his brother judge,[2] "In taking his Arts' degree he arrived at the highest honour the University could bestow, after the present system of examination was adopted . . . he was placed in the first class of those distinguished both in classical and mathematical attainments. In order to acquire distinction in mathematical learning he pursued a course quite consistent with the natural energy of his character. Finding that the University of Oxford did not possess competent instructors for the more abstruse parts of mathematics, he placed himself for a time under the tuition of Mr. Friend in London." West was elected a Fellow of his

[1] A name later on to be transferred to another battleship on which a still greater admiral, a cousin of Lady West, was to die.

[2] It is here taken for granted that the anonymous memoir printed at Bombay was written by Sir Charles Chambers.

college. In 1814 he was called to the Bar at the Inner Temple, and rose rapidly. He was a man of unusual ability, and of unflinching integrity and courage. His brother judge says: "As a practical lawyer he belonged to the highest class of his profession. His knowledge was accurate and deep, and his judgment sound; and in that quality which ought to be the brightest ornament of an English barrister he was pre-eminent—disinterestedness. . . . His mind was set on the highest objects. It could not therefore stoop to low gains, nor be contaminated by the baseness which always attends an appetite for them. . . . The only legal work which he published was his work on 'Extents.'[1] It is, however, a standard work, and placed Sir Edward West's reputation for learning and acumen on the firmest basis." This work on "Extents"[2] helped greatly to reform abuses in the Court of Exchequer. However desirable it may have been that such a man should have been sent to Bombay at this time, it can scarcely be wondered at that his reforming energy should have aroused opposition.

In 1815 West wrote an important "Essay on

[1] An Extent is an "Execution at the suit of the Crown."

[2] "A Treatise of the Law and Practice of Extents in Chief and in Aid with an Appendix of Forms of Writs, Affidavits for Extents, Pleadings and Extents, Rules of Court, and Table of Fees. By Edward West, of the Inner Temple, Esq., Barrister-at-Law." London: Printed for J. Butterworth & Son, 1817. [8vo, pp. i-xv, 1-336, 1-152.]

the Application of Capital to Land,"[1] showing the "impolicy of any great restriction on the importation of corn." Mr. Ricardo, in the preface to his "Principles of Political Economy," says that "Mr. Malthus, and the author of the 'Essay . . .' presented to the world, nearly at the same moment, the true doctrine of rent." The pamphlet, by the advice of Brougham, was published anonymously. "No publication," says his brother judge, "since the great work of Adam Smith, has been of greater service to the science of political economy than the few pages of that essay." Adam Smith had considered the fall of profits in the production of corn as society advances to be due to accumulation of capital and to competition. West showed the true cause to be the increased cost of production. "Nor can it be considered a slight triumph of his judgment and acuteness that the erroneous notions of Adam Smith had been adopted by all previous writers, by Mr. Malthus, Mr. Say, and others."[2]

In 1825, Sir Edward West sent home from India a pamphlet on the "Price of Corn and Wages of Labour."[3] In this tract he "sug-

[1] "Essay on the Application of Capital to Land, with Observations shewing the Impolicy of any great Restriction of the Importation of Corn, and that the Bounty of 1688 did not lower the price of it. By a Fellow of University College, Oxford." London: Printed for T. Underwood, 1815. [8vo, pp. 1-69.]

[2] Anonymous memoir.

[3] "Price of Corn and Wages of Labour, with Observations upon Dr. Smith's, Mr. Ricardo's, and Mr. Malthus's Doctrines upon those

gested the precise plan upon which Mr. Canning's corn bill was framed." All the measures he recommended seem to have been moderate and considerate.

Within a few years essays and writer were forgotten; and only lately has it been pointed out by economists[1] that Sir E. West was "the first of the Ricardian School," and that "it is impossible to read his pamphlet without seeing that the form in which the law of diminishing returns" (*i.e.* of the produce of land in proportion to capital expended on it) "was subsequently taught and the phraseology in which it was expressed are far more due to him than is imagined."[2]

In 1903 the Johns Hopkins University of Baltimore republished Sir E. West's original pamphlet with a facsimile title-page, and Dr. Jacob Hollander in his preface to the reprint says, "Bare details of his life have come down to us . . . had his life been prolonged . . . West's influence upon the development of economic thought would have been considerable."

His own country's ignorance of his name is

Subjects; and an Attempt at an Exposition of the Causes of the Fluctuation of the Price of Corn during the Last Thirty Years." By Sir Edward West, late Fellow of University College, Oxford, and author of "An Essay on the Application of Capital to Land." London: John Hatchard & Son, Piccadilly, 1826. [8vo, pp. i–viii, 1–150; with a Chart of the Price of Wheat, 1774–1821.]

[1] Preface to American reprint of "Application of Capital to Land."

[2] Cannan, "History of the Theories of Production and Distribution," p. 279. London, 1893.

well shown by the fact that in the British Museum Catalogue the "Edward West" of the work on "Extents," and the "Edward West" of the two works on Political Economy, are treated as distinct persons.

Nor is there any pictorial record of his features. When appointed to the King's Court at Bombay, West declined an invitation from the Fellows of University College, Oxford, to sit for his portrait. And after his death, when the natives of Bombay had subscribed for a picture of the Englishman who had befriended them, it was found that there was not even a sketch of which a copy could be made.

From an Indian newspaper of the time we learn that Sir E. West was "well proportioned," "rather below middle height," with "light grey eyes," "high, broad forehead," and "countenance pleasing and attractive"; that the "contour of his head was particularly striking, giving an elevated and distinguished expression to his face."[1] As the following history will show, he seems to have been sensitive to any slight or injustice. His countenance "betrayed a considerable degree of susceptibility; where his mind was in the least degree excited his sensations appeared like lightning on his countenance."[2]

Edward West's uncle and guardian, Sir

[1] *Bombay Gazette*, August 1828. [2] Ibid.

Martin Ffolkes,[1] had married in 1775 Fanny, daughter and co-heir of Sir John Turner, Bart., of Warham.[2] Lady Ffolkes had died in 1813, and Sir Martin in December 1821, leaving a son, William, and two daughters, Anna and Lucretia. Early the following spring the letters show us the old home broken up; Hillington Hall in process of rebuilding; Sir William Ffolkes living with his young wife in the dower house at Congham, and standing as Whig candidate for King's Lynn in his father's place; and the two sisters taking, as daughters still do when country homes are broken up, a house in London. They show us Lucretia unhappy at the loss of parents, and at some rift in an old attachment to Edward West; inclined to be critical, but warm-hearted to friends, earnest and active; living in the world, on visits to her friends, but devoted always to the memory of her parents and her Norfolk home. We see, too, Edward West on circuit, and all of them unconscious of the fact that news of the death of Sir W. Evans, Recorder of Bombay, who had so lately left England, was slowly finding its way round the Cape; and that Edward West and Lucretia Ffolkes were about to marry and leave for India. We see in them, too, the passing of

[1] Sir W. Ffolkes and members of his family signed their surname with two small ff's. The modern spelling of the name—a capital and small f—has been adopted in this book.

[2] Sir Charles Turner, his father, was Nelson's maternal grandfather.

the cloud; the engagement at Dunraven Castle; and the return to receive congratulations from his cousins and sister at Glympton.

Pleasant looking and intelligent Lucretia Ffolkes seems to have been; like Edward West, free from personal vanity; interested in others rather than in herself; and ever mindful of home. One never-failing entry appears in the diary each year of her exile: "February 14th, Lynn Mart proclaimed,"—recalling the time when England was still an agricultural country—when cultivated people frequented their country towns, and no one dreamed that, under Victorian statesmen, changing economic conditions would drive from the country all but the aged, and the infirm in mind and body; and empty the only nursery for strong Englishmen—for such as fought at Waterloo or sank beneath the waves off Trafalgar. "One of the gloomy features of village life," wrote Dr. William Ogle in 1877, "is the absence of young men and women from the scene. So soon as children have passed school age they are drafted off in large numbers to the towns."[1] The gloom has deepened since 1877.

The letters, too, show us Edward West and his fellow passengers in January of the year 1822 taking a full ten hours on the journey from

[1] Dr. William Ogle, late Superintendent of Statistics, Registrar-General's Office, in "St. George's Hospital Reports," p. 701. 1877.

A. E. Purdy, King's Lynn, Photo.

HILLINGTON HALL, NORFOLK, 1907.

London to Oxford—Lucretia Ffolkes canvassing for her brother against Colonel Walpole for the ancient town of Lynn—the excitement of a contested election—the enthusiasm in the country for Queen Caroline, and the "sale of the contents" of the great houses of Wanstead and Fonthill.

From EDWARD WEST *to his Sister*, MRS. LANE, *Glympton Park*, *Woodstock*, *Oxon*.

TEMPLE, *Jan.* 5, 1822.

MY DEAR FANNY,—You were I dare say surprised that I did not call at Glympton on my way to the Sessions, as I had intended. The fact was that I left London on Saturday at two o'clock, thinking that I might have reached Glympton by nine or ten o'clock in the evening and have passed part of Sunday with you. But, unfortunately, I had taken my place in so slow a coach that I did not reach Oxford till twelve o'clock at night. . . .

From LUCRETIA FFOLKES, *afterwards* LADY WEST, *to* LADY FFOLKES, *Congham Lodge*, *Lynn*.[1]

(Franked by Sandford Graham.)

LONDON, *June Twenty*, 1822,
MANSFIELD STREET, *Thursday*.

Anna wrote so voluminously yesterday that I fear that I have but little more to say to you, my dearest Charlotte, except thanks for your kind letter just received, and our delight to hear that you get on so prosperously, and my anxious hope that ffolkes will go to a Poll . . . besides, I think you will frighten the Walpoles, and they will give up, as I cannot think that the Corporation will be generous enough to pay the contest. Nothing could be so kind as the Pratts. Old Mr. Pratt says that he and Jermyn would attend the Committee here all day, and if you can give them

[1] The three following letters have been kindly lent by Miss Ffolkes.

any names in Norfolk or here, they will either write or canvass personally. I am going to send Edward this morning to Mr. Coke[1] with your address, to hear what he says, and whether he can give you His Presence. The young Pratts all will. After the post was gone yesterday, Mr. Dominick Browne[2] sent us all the handbills, which are I think very good, and the three letters. We immediately sent off George Martin to Islington, and Joseph with the others—the Baker's friend's name is Brooks. He lives at Lynn. He has written to him, and is sure of his vote. A sailor named Drury Gathercole came yesterday evening from Deptford to say that he had received a letter from our party, and had been yesterday personally canvassed for Col. Walpole, but that he had told them nothing should prevent him voting for a ffolkes, our dear father had always been so kind to him. I gave him a glass of wine, and requested him to look after other voters, which he promised he would do. He said the other party were very alert, and that the election would be the end of next week. We have sent Poulton to Taylor the Hatter, who says he knows some voters, and will write to them instantly. We heard of Jacomb the Butcher in Mary-le-bone Street, who has two votes. I have sent Lord Bridport[3] and Mr. Pratt to them, but have not yet had their answers. Has ffolkes written to Mr. Harry Bird, as we have had a letter to know whether ffolkes stands, having had an application from Messrs. Everard, Baggs and Hogg; but of course he "shall ever vote for a ffolkes." We shall answer it to-day to say that he does stand.

Lord Bridport has just been in with Mr. Sandford Graham, who is so extremely anxious about ffolkes' success. He entreats you to send up a list of the voters, and he will go and canvass them all instantly, and look sharp after

[1] Thomas William Coke, afterwards Earl of Leicester, Member for Norfolk for many years between 1776 and 1832. Consistent follower of Fox; reformer of agriculture in Norfolk; and believed by some to have been the benefactor of thousands who never heard his name, by the introduction of the William Coke (Billy cock) hat.

[2] Of Castle M'Garrett, Ireland—represented Co. Mayo in seven parliaments; afterwards Lord Oranmore—brother of Lady Ffolkes.

[3] Samuel, second Lord Bridport, who married Nelson's niece, Duchess of Brontë. Admiral Hood, first Lord Bridport, had married the daughter of the Rev. Richard West, Prebendary of Durham, great-grandfather of Sir E. West and Lucretia Ffolkes.

them. He says you ought to depute some lawyer to manage for you here, and to have a place of rendezvous. He heard yesterday that it is thought here that ffolkes will succeed, and that whatever the cost he ought to stand to be certain of success next time. The Writ was moved for yesterday, and the Election is talked of next Thursday. Since I have written this, Mr. Parry has been here, and brought ffolkes' note. I am delighted to hear that ffolkes positively stands. I urged him to be quick, and told him of the activity of the Walpoles. Here is Mr. Crackenthorpe. He says that you must have a Committee, or nothing will be done to a purpose. Pray send the list of voters, and let me know where I can send to Mr. Parry as I may want him. *I* am now going to call on Mr. Coke to shew him ffolkes' address, and that he stands. We have also sent the address to the *Morning Chronicle* and the *Times*. Pratt's brother-in-law is at Lynn, Muggridge, apply to him. Mr. Pratt really thinks you will run them so hard, he almost hopes for your success. James Hales has been here. He tells me he has written to ffolkes and will go to Lynn if he can do any good. His Norwich voter will go whichever way Raven and King go. I have not time to eat, drink, or think of anything but ffolkes. We begged Mr. D. Browne to send us franks by the second post.

I cannot think of news, but Marcia Duffield says that Miss Locke of Norbury Park is to marry Lord Walscourt, and Mr. Locke, the brother, another of the Lady Beauclerks. Mr. Duffield and Hester go to-day, and the others on Monday, and Anna has promised to make our first visit to them when we leave London. Of course we shall stay here to receive ffolkes when he comes up to take his seat in the House of Commons. . . .

I am now going to Mr. Coles . . . yr. truly attached Sister,

L. G. B. FFOLKES.

James Hales says the writ will be at Lynn to-morrow night. Pray send the list of Voters and have a Committee formed here with an active leader.

I see an advertisement from Col. Walpole to say the day of election, and to send the voters to a Mr. Hine in Essex Court, Temple. Lord Bridport and I have just been to visit Mr. Osbert Hampton, the person who works for Whippy the saddler. He was out, but I saw his wife, and talked so prettily to her, that I hope he will decide for you to-morrow. Edward Pratt is going to him, Mr. Keppel[1] told Lord Bridport he would do so also. Mrs. Elwes told Lord B. that her father meant to vote for you, which rather surprises me with his relationship and intimacy with the Baggs.

From Lucretia Ffolkes *to* Lady Ffolkes, *Congham Lodge, Lynn.*

(Franked by Dominick Browne.)

London, *June twenty-seven*, 1822.

. . . The account of your triumphal entré is quite beautiful, indeed it must have been a splendid exhibition, and your seeing Her Majesty[2] quite delightful. How truly gratified you must have been at the extraordinary popularity evinced to your good husband, and to the memory of our ever to be lamented Father: I am not surprised at the lamentations of the Corporation; they must be so astonished and angry at ffolkes proving the weakness of their forces, and have only to thank themselves for it, as they have occasioned it all by their offering a seat to the Portland family, and will rue the day in which they invited a stranger. Selfes are poor, and are looking to the Corporation for help. I am astonished at their activity, it is so completely against their principles. It is ridiculous for me to send a frank of your brothers; I shall honestly make it a single letter in case of its being charged.

Joseph tells me that he saw a Lynn man yesterday, just come up, who says that Lynn was never known so full, and he reports that brickbats were flying thickly at the Corporation. Joseph hopes that you will send us up some Colors. He quite cried when I told him of ffolkes' glorious reception at Lynn. Mr. Blaauw went to Wanstead[3] on Tuesday to bid for a staircase carpet, but it was out of the question, as it sold for 18 shillings a yard. We drink tea

[1] Afterwards Lord Albemarle, author of "Fifty Years of my Life."

[2] Queen Caroline. A sense of unfair treatment aroused extraordinary enthusiasm for the Queen throughout the country.

[3] Wanstead House, near Epping, bought by Sir Josiah Child, Chairman of East India Company and millionaire. Rebuilt in great splendour by his son, Lord Tylney, in 1713. William Tylney Long Wellesley, fourth Lord Mornington, ran through the fortune of his wife, heiress of Wanstead, and the house was dismantled.

at the Bridports to-night; she goes out every evening in the Phaeton, and now we shall drive out most days with the Blaauws. The Sneyds wish us to go to the Opera on Saturday. I have made every possible excuse, as I do not feel in spirits for such a scene. Font Hill[1] is to follow the example of Wanstead; the Catalogue, 1 guinea for each person; his West India property is nothing, and he is otherwise ruined. Mr. Beckford . . . has lived for years in retirement and unknown. I hope you will enjoy the Swaffham races. Lord Nelson is more kind and affectionate than ever; and disappointed at not seeing us. Anna has, I suppose, told you that Miss Sparrow is to marry Lord Mandeville, the Duke of Manchester's son; a nice match, as she gains rank and he money. Maria West has just been here. Hales was, I hear, to be with you today; he has been canvassing at Bury; the Reynardsons have been also to enquire. It is now ½ past 5, I am going airing with Lady Bridport. Hastily but most affecly., Yours and ffolkes. LUCRETIA.

From part of a letter in the handwriting of ANNA MARTINA FFOLKES *to* LADY FFOLKES.

June 1822, *Thursday.*

MY DEAR CHARLOTTE,—As we mean to get a frank tomorrow to send some enclosures I shall indulge in beginning a little manuscript and thanking you for your entertaining letter. We had a long day yesterday with Maria Hadsley. We visited the Bazaar, Panorama, half the silversmiths in the purlieus of the Haymarket and Strand, and finished by calling upon the Invalid at Brompton. Poor Lady Brownlow bears strong marks of the anxiety she has gone through. . . . We have written all our proposals to our friends, first for being at Wood, and on Monday remov-

[1] William Beckford, a man of extravagant Oriental imagination, inherited Fonthill in Wiltshire, together with a hundred thousand a year from property in Jamaica, and a million of ready money. He twice pulled down and rebuilt Fonthill; and surrounded the grounds with a high wall to exclude visitors. Here he lived with one or two friends, his books, and an enormous collection of bric-à-brac. During the year 1822 Fonthill and the greater part of its contents were sold for £330,000.—"Dictionary of National Biography."

ing to the Ways, being at Flaxley Abbey about the 30th for two or three days, and reaching Dunraven about the 5th of next month, but I begin to think there will be some demur in our first visit, as since I saw Marcia on Sunday, she had had such alarming accounts of her eldest niece's dangerous state, that I cannot see how the Duffs can receive us. She has just called with an account that the Physician has announced to the Crutchleys he sees no hope of her recovery, a most rapid decline.[1] She is just fourteen, which will make her loss deeply felt by her parents. Lu[2] has engaged herself to tea at neighbour Blaauws. We are going again this eve to the Bridports, to-morrow to the Astleys, and Saturday to Mr. Moore's. Lu is passing this morning in Wimpole Street; she is seldom at home. Lu begins to recover her spirits; I once thought of her renewing the old flame with Sir Edward,[3] but he seems to fight quite shy of us. We have seen nothing of him since Sunday.

Friday. It is decided that a frank is not to be got till to-morrow. Yet I shall proceed with my gossip. We went yesterday to see the Plate, and what think you of that indelicate Countess shewing it off herself. It is really very handsome, and had we not supplied ourselves we might have bought many things at a very cheap rate, as the embossed is 7 shillings, and the plain 6 shillings an ounce. Mr. Meyrick has taken the Apostle spoons, and all the spoons and modern articles of Plate. The Kettle and Lamp is to be sold, but I really am too poor to buy it; you should have it for the bottom of your Breakfast Table.

From Lucretia Ffolkes *to* Lady Ffolkes.

Flaxley Abbey, Gloucester,
Monday, July 29, 1822.

Your letter, My dearest Charlotte, arrived quite safely, and I feel truly thankful for it, tho' it has certainly given me very great pain to learn that our dearest Aunt was in so hopeless a state; how altered will Lynn be to us all, but when once death gets into a Family, it never seems to have

[1] The mortality among young girls of the well-to-do classes from "decline" (consumption) was much greater then than now.

[2] Lucretia Ffolkes.

[3] Edward West was not actually knighted until July.

an end. I shall expect to hear to-morrow that it is all over; truly shall I regret her, as when she is gone, I shall feel that I have no Parent left, and I do not want to add to the forlorn state I am in. . . . You are lucky to have fruit; for here our Dessert is only apples, and everywhere I hear of no fruit, the Birds and Squirrels have eat up all Currants and Gooseberries. I hope you received a letter from Anna yesterday. Nothing could be so civil as the Duffields, and we really spent our time very agreeably riding and driving about all day, the Country is so beautiful, the great Park, etc.

We did not leave them till 12 o'clock on Friday, and arrived at Glympton at 8; We found Mr. Way and the 2 children only at Dessert, as Fanny Lane was confined to her Bed. We chose only to have Tea, and sat with Fanny all the evening; next Morning we saw poor Mrs. Way, who we hope was out of all danger. . . . They urged our visiting Them so much that We have promised to pass some little time with Them on our return. Fanny Lane charming as ever, and the sweet Children; the Boy plain but pleasing, and the girl[1] pretty; the Boy is to go to School next Month near Oxford, a little Establishment. Edward Strickland[2] is very materially better; He and His Mother remain at Margate till October; Mr. S. and the girls are at Cokethorpe, and have given up Their Trip into Yorkshire this year; We left Glympton a ¼ before 10 and arrived here a ¼ after 5, which we are told was very good driving, the Road is so hilly. We had been all of it before, except from Gloucester here, 11 miles, which is very beautiful; narrow winding Roads, sheltered by woody hills, and the Severn running at the bottom. All yesterday it rained hard, but as the Church is in the Park close to the House, We walked there twice; the Brother, Mr. Coventry, did the duty, and He and His Wife dined here afterwards. They are two pleasing people. We only found Mrs. [illegible] here and Her little Boy, and Lady Crawley. . . . Sir Thomas is remarkably shy, but improves very much upon acquaintance; this place would suit ffolkes, it is so old, built in the Reign of Henry 1st, with Oak floors and Mahogany doors; it is an immense pile of Building, white, and appears surrounded with fine wooded

[1] Mrs. Lane's daughter, who inherited all her mother's charm and goodness, died, to her children's loss, in 1860.

[2] Owner of Cokethorpe Park, near Whitney.

Hills, but at present we have not been beyond the gravel—or rather I ought to say Cinder—Walks. We think of going from here on Friday as it is only 63 miles to Dunraven,[1] and can be easily done in a day; Anna does not seem at all the worse for Her riding and all she has done, indeed I hope she will be the better for the Tour. It strikes me that They have been very moderate in the Tithes; I rejoice at it in these depressed Times, and particularly that ffolkes has persuaded his Friends to give up the Petition to Parliament; Pray never think of a frank; expense is nothing to me to hear from those I love, and I should fear losing a letter going about so much. Were you not surprised to hear of the visit to London? It was very gallant and very flattering, but awkward and painful, but I was *firm* and only repeated what I had written to ffolkes, and regretted His useless trip. He[2] went up with Sir Thos. Hare; they were together at Harding's Hotel. We breakfast at 9, dine at 4, and go to Bed at 10; it has rained all day, We have not been able to leave the House, the Time has not flown.

This is I am sure not only not worth Postage but not worth reading, but I feel dull and am aware That it is a Complaint rapidly increasing upon Me, but as long as I breathe I shall ever feel the same affection for all the dear Inhabitants of Congham,[3] who will now I hope accept my affec^te^ remembrances, and believe me their ever attached and affec^te^ Sister L. G. B. FFOLKES.

I must write to Mrs. Bennett to announce the happy intelligence of our being there the 2nd instead of the 5th; I suppose she is at Dunraven, but We have not heard for a fortnight. We must stop and enquire at Cardiff as we pass through. She expected us for the whole Winter, our Friends are so kind.

Events now seem to have succeeded each other rapidly. Within six short weeks of the date of this letter Edward West had become engaged

[1] Glamorganshire.
[2] Son of the owner of Sandringham in 1822.
[3] The dower House, at which Sir Edward and Lady Ffolkes were living during the rebuilding of Hillington Hall.

A. E. Purdy, King's Lynn, Photo.

GATEWAY, HILLINGTON HALL.

to, and had married, Lucretia Ffolkes; had been appointed Recorder of the King's Court of Bombay; had received the customary knighthood from the King;[1] had begun and completed the hurried preparations for the journey; and had even started for India—full of hopes never to be realised.

From Sir Edward West *to* Mrs. Lane, *Glympton Park, Woodstock.*

Dunraven Castle,
August 18*th*, 1822.

My dear Fanny,—I have only time to tell you that Lucretia has consented, and that we shall be with you on Tuesday. In case you should not have room for Anna and Lucretia they will proceed to Woodstock. We shall at all events be obliged to proceed on Wednesday morning to London in order to get on with our preparations. Give my love to Mrs. Way.[2]—Your very affectionate Brother,

Edward West.

[1] On July 5.

[2] Glympton, near Woodstock, became at the beginning of the century the property of the Rev. William Way of Denham, through his wife, a daughter of Maximilian Western of Cokethorpe Park, a cousin of Mrs. Lane and Sir E. West—a gentle and good lady. The Ways died without children, and Glympton passed to a distant cousin of Mr. Way.

CHAPTER III

Departure for India—Life on an Indiaman; crew of Lascars; cockroaches; crossing the Line.

Lady West's Journal (October 1822–June 1823):—Incidents of the voyage; rain collected at sea; arrival at the Cape of Good Hope; vineyards at Constantia; Lord Charles Somerset; arrival at Point de Galle; scenery of Ceylon; Calicut sighted; landing at Bombay; official reception; entertainments; Bombay society; alarming fires in the bazaar and fort.

In contrast to all this despatch was the tediousness of the journey for which the Wests so hastily prepared.

They were married in Marylebone Church on August 26, 1822. On the morning of September 5th, farewell was taken of London friends; Canterbury was reached at night; Deal the next day. On Saturday the 7th, Lady West wrote: "We got into a boat and said adieu to the dear Land, and breathed many a prayer for the health and happiness of the dear trio" [brother, sister, and sister-in-law] "at Congham Lodge." On the 8th the ship weighed anchor, sailed towards Spithead, and was driven back to the Downs. On Thursday the 12th, Lady West says: "We anchored at Spithead, midway between the Isle of Wight and Portsmouth. Edward and I and our little secretary" [Edward Stamp West, a nephew] "went in a fishing-boat to Portsmouth, where we spent some hours very agreeably in shopping."

The newly-appointed judge hurrying from London to Bombay had taken just a week to reach Spithead!

But once on blue water, life must have been pleasant on an old East Indiaman. No groan and throb of engines in those days; no cloud of smoke to dull the ever-changing face of sea and sky; but quiet, leisurely life in clean air; the acquaintance of strange fish and bird, watched from white decks, under the shadow of innumerable sails. Passengers in those days parted from their ship as from a friend.

A letter to Mrs. Lane gives an account of the journey out, of "crossing the Line" before the days of steam, of the crew of Lascars, and of the first acquaintance with the cockroach, then comparatively unknown in English houses.

On the 1st February in the following year the ship arrived at Bombay—the "Island" of Bombay—never conquered by England; for it had been the dowry of Catherine of Braganza, and had been granted to the East India Company in 1669 by Charles the Second at a rent of £10 a year.

As early as 1662 an English fleet had been sent to Bombay to take over the island, but the resident Portuguese objected to the transfer. Delay ensued, and many of the English soldiers died while encamped on the desolate island of Aujediva. Pepys, disappointed at the dowry, considered that we had been "choused by the Portugalls," and spoke of the "inconsiderableness" of the "poor little Island of Bombaim." Hence, possibly, the good bargain with the King made by the East India Company over this long coveted port of Western India.[1]

From Sir Edward West *to his Sister,* Mrs. Lane, *Glympton Park, Woodstock, Oxon.*

(Posted at the Cape. Postmark, "India Letter. Portsmouth, 6th February 1823.")

"Milford." *At Sea.*
November 24th, 1822.

My dear Fanny,—We expect to be at the Cape of Good Hope in two or three days, and I shall take that opportunity of sending you these few lines to tell you that we are all well and comfortable, though our voyage has been, as you may observe from the date of this, rather tedious, yet the weather has been generally so delightful that we have no reason upon the whole to complain. On one or two occasions only has it been more boisterous than we could have wished, and for two or three days only has the heat been at all oppressive. Considering the sameness of a voyage for near three months, we have managed to fill up our time tolerably well, and have not found it hang very heavy. A great portion of my time has been occupied in instructing Edward,[2] a great deal in walking with Lucretia on deck; and reading books and lounging, etc. etc., has occupied the residue. It is now certain that we shall not reach Bombay in less than five

[1] By a curious coincidence Sir Edward West seems to have sailed for the East at the very time when one of the ablest and most independent of Calcutta judges, Sir Edward East, had hurriedly started on his journey West. A lost opportunity for elegiac verse!

[2] Son of Gilbert West, brother of Sir E. West, who had married the eldest daughter of Sir Martin Ffolkes.

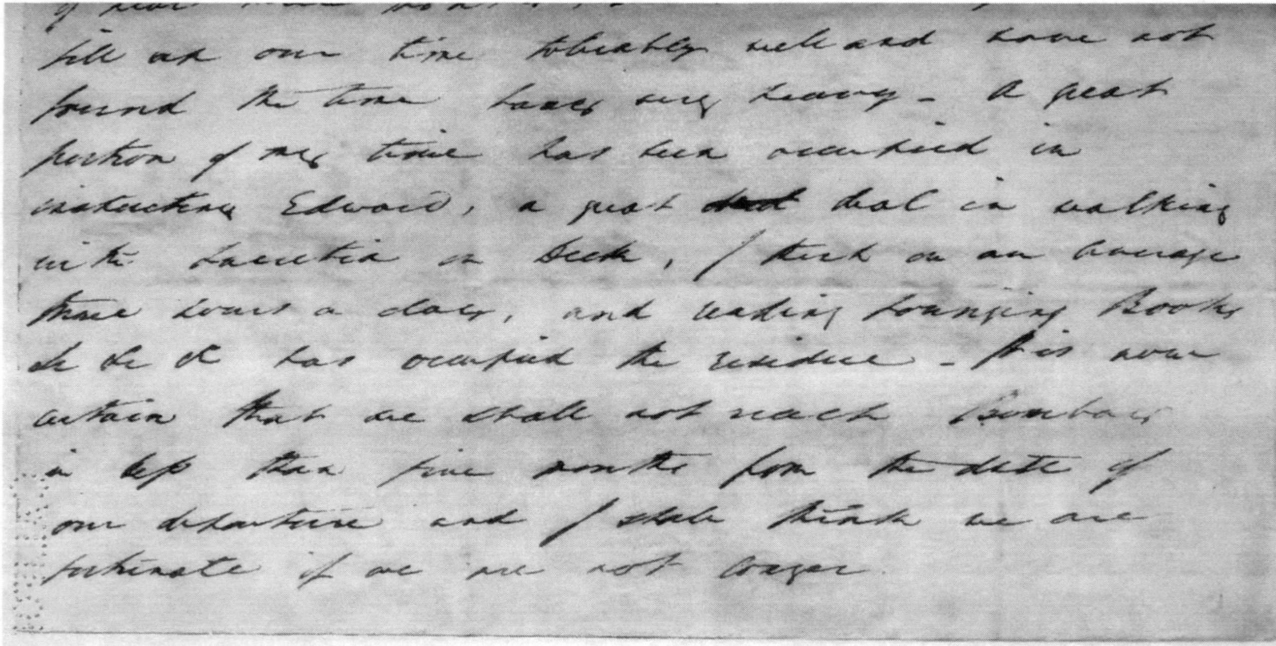

[illegible]
fill up our time tolerably well and have not
found the time hang very heavy. A great
portion of my time has been occupied in
instructing Edward, a great deal in walking
with Lucretia on deck, I think on an average
three hours a day, and reading lounging books
&c &c has occupied the residue. It is now
certain that we shall not reach Bombay
in less than five months from the date of
our departure and I shall think we are
fortunate if we are not longer

Part of a letter from Sir EDWARD WEST to his Sister.

Bedford at Sea
Lat. Long.
Novr 24th, 1822.

My dear Fanny,

We expect to be at the Cape of Good Hope in two or three days and I shall take that opportunity of sending you these few lines to tell you that we are all well & comfortable. Though our voyage has been, as you may observe from the date of this, rather tedious, yet the weather has been *generally* so delightful that we have no reason upon the whole to complain. On one or two occasions only has the weather been more boisterous than we could have wished, and for two or ~~three~~ three days only has the heat been at all oppressive. Considering the sameness of a voyage

months from the date of our departure, and I shall think we are fortunate if we are not longer.

A voyage, as you must be aware, if it be fortunate, furnishes very little incident for a letter, and my only motive for writing is to satisfy you as to our safety thus far, and as to another point upon which you will probably be more anxious, I mean our being comfortable. I can only say that no woman could be more calculated to render me happy than Lucretia; that it would be impossible to be more accommodating, more contented and cheerful than she has been among all the privations of a sea voyage, and that I was never more comfortable. The voyage has agreed with all of us, and we have all improved very much in health.

Pray give my kindest love to Mr. and Mrs. Way, and thank them for all their kindness. Remember me, too, to Ba and Edward.[1] I hope the latter is reconciled to school. I shall add a few words when we arrive at the Cape.

CAPE OF GOOD HOPE,
Nov. 30th, 1822.

We have arrived safe here. We have staid here but three days, and embark to-day.

From LADY WEST *to* MRS. LANE, *Glympton Park, near Woodstock.*

(Posted at Cape of Good Hope, Nov. 25, 1822. Received at Portsmouth, Feb. 6, 1823.)

MY DEAREST FANNY,—I have requested Edward to leave me a little space to tell you how well and happy we all are; and tho' we have now been 11 weeks on board I cannot say that we have found our time pass slowly or heavily, as the Weather has been so very delightful. We have walked about 4 hours a day and sat out under an awning to read, and, except near the Madeiras for a few days, have not found it at all hot. My dear Edward did not suffer at all from sea-sickness. I did dreadfully the first fortnight, and shrank to a skeleton; since that I have felt

[1] Frances and Edward Lane. The latter entered the Royal Engineers, and died on foreign service.

almost better than I ever did in my life, and Edward says I have not looked so well these *ten* years, and delights me by saying he *never* was happier in his life. As I foretold he has not finished his Pamphlet[1] to send Home from the Cape, but he will, I hope, do so from Bombay, as We [illegible] to live as retired as possible, and get Home at the end of seven years; should it please God to spare our Lives.

From all I hear I fear that We shall find it expensive and difficult to be quiet, as the Governor[2] is so gay, but as Judge We think it will be more *respectable;* the Governor will, I believe, receive us till our House is ready. The thing I dread most is receiving such a Host of visitors and returning their calls; and worst of all taking a *lead,* which has always been my horror. I can follow, and like it, but I hate to lead; but I doubt not that Edward will kindly assist me in all my difficulties, for he is all that is kind, attentive and affectionate, and I really have scarcely seen him irritable for one moment, nor do I believe he ever will be.

We have very few Passengers, which is very agreeable; only 3 ladies—a Mrs. Baker, a very nice young Woman going to join her Husband, Col. Baker, at Bombay; His niece, a girl of 14; Mrs. Ducat, (Her Husband is going to settle there as Physician; a sensible agreeable young Man); a Capt. Lewis of the India Service, 3 Cadets, the Surgeon, 3 Mates, and our Capt. Harwood. Nothing can exceed the civility and attention we meet with from everyone, and you will laugh when I tell you that *I* am called the *great Lady.* Our Crew has a curious appearance; only 40 English Sailors, the other 86, Malays, Arabs, Portuguese, Africans, of every Nation almost under the Sun; all looking savage, dirty and miserable, but I am told they are all that is gentle and timid. We have 3 excellent Cabins and every comfort. We have but ½ a pint of fresh water allowed for our ablutions, but I make a Salt Water bath. As to dressing, when the Ship rolls I usually sit on Batt's[3] knee to dress, and scarcely can look into a glass; we have everything tied, so that it is only oneself that runs about like a ball and is black and blue.

[1] "Price of Corn and Wages of Labour."—John Hatchard & Son, Piccadilly, 1826.

[2] Mountstuart Elphinstone.

[3] Batt, Lady West's maid, returned to England after the death of her mistress, and took charge of Lady West's child.

We have had one rather severe squall in the Bay of Biscay which [illegible] alarmed us *young Sailors*, the Masts cracking, the Sails flapping, the Officers bawling through a speaking-trumpet, our own and our neighbour's boxes and Furniture tumbling about the Cabin, Edward being called up for the Carpenter to come in to shut up the Window. His face of horror I shall never forget, and his remorse at having brought me into so much danger, and moreover his astonishment at my tranquillity and composure. We hope we shall get our Books and things there safe, but it is a constant anxiety; besides, we have a nasty insect on board called a Cockroach,[1] like a Cock-Chafer, which is sadly destructive if it creeps in amongst one's things. I hear they are at Bombay, as also White Ants and Mosquitoes, but at our excellent House in the Fort we shall, I hope, avoid them in the Sitting Rooms, as the Court is held under the same Roof, and the Ground Floor is more subject to Insects and Reptiles. On crossing the Line the European Sailors kept up the old custom of Shaving and Ducking three of their companions who had never crossed it before, and they made quite a Spectacle dressing themselves up as Neptune, Amphitrite and Mercury and an Esculapius with a smart car, etc., all to gain the grog and tobacco with which we had luckily supplied ourselves for them. It seems so singular now to look for the Sun to the North and to find the beginning of Summer at the Cape in what we call November. We mean to see everything we can in the few days we are there, and go in a Dutch Waggon to see a pretty Farm called Constantia,[2] where they make the wine of that name. Edward will add a Postscript from the Cape if he has time: I hope you will have seen dear Anna[3] at Glympton since I left her. She did right to go into Norfolk. I feel much for her, she will, I know, feel so *alone*; but I hope she will not be induced to go and live with Gilbert,[4] as I do not

[1] The common cockroach (*Blatta orientalis*). This "Black Beetle" of the kitchen was introduced into England some years before this date. Gilbert White saw them at Selborne for the first time, in 1790.

[2] In 1889 Phylloxera visited and devastated the Cape Vineyards. At the conquest of Cape Colony in 1795, Sir J. Malcolm wrote: "Their wines, of which they have a great variety, are excellent; had I been rich enough I should have purchased some Constantia."

[3] Anna Martina Ffolkes, Lady West's unmarried sister.

[4] Gilbert West, brother of Sir Edward West and Mrs. Lane.

think it would add to the happiness of either. We are going at the rate of eleven knots an hour, which will, I trust, be an apology for such very bad writing.

Of course we shall write as soon as we can from Bombay, and much hope we shall be able to give you pleasing accounts of your relations there, and that it may be in our power to serve them, as you will know that we have both the inclination; and I shall ever feel for your interest as deeply as for my own, as, believe me, my dearest Fanny, the additional tie has but strengthened my love for you, and though of late years we have been much separated, you ought to know the warmth of my heart towards you.

I shall depend upon hearing from you as often as you can write, as at the awful distance of 15,000 miles every little trifle is interesting. Pray remember me to the Stricklands,[1] and most warmly and affectionately to Mr. and Mrs. Way,[2] to whom, with you, I well know I owe my present situation, although Edward will not confess it; the whole thing strikes us as so very odd, we cannot yet believe it, or even, indeed, that we are married, and beginning quite a new life in all and every respect, and we believe that at the end of our voyage we shall find ourselves in London, or dear, dear Norfolk. My beloved Father's[3] Print hangs opposite to me—what a loss he has been to us all. I only wish that both my Parents could know how deeply I have regretted them. I suppose the House in Mansfield Street is sold. Had I remained in England everything was so painfully changed one should not have been happy: I wish I could hear that Anna was in better health and might marry, as she wants some active interest to occupy her. I shall hope to hear that your Edward[4] is happy and well, and also little Missy. . . .

P.S.—Pray do not shew my letter; it is too egotistical, and too badly and hastily written. Batt has been ill, but is now well, happy, and contented, and has been the greatest comfort to us all; I know not what we should have done without her.

[1] Of Cokethorpe Park, Oxfordshire.

[2] Of Glympton, Oxfordshire.

[3] Sir Martin Browne Ffolkes, of Hillington, late M.P. for King's Lynn. Died December 1821.

[4] Edward Lane, R.E.

From ANNA MARTINA FFOLKES (*Sister to Lady West*) *in London to* MRS. LANE, *Woodstock.*

(Postmark, Feb. 6, 1823.)

MANSFIELD STREET,
Tuesday Evening.

MY DEAR FANNY,—The beginning of a Correspondence must ever be marked with painful sensations as indicative of Separation, and after the many happy hours we have passed together, it can prove but a poor substitute, but I most anxiously have recourse to it, to lighten the heavy hour of painful Solitariness[1] which now surrounds me. You will, I am sure, be indulgent to my melancholy mood, and will receive pleasure in the account of our last sight of your dear Boy. He was in excellent time, as only half the Boys were arrived. . . . I have received many proofs of kind attention in the Duffs having pounced in upon me in three different detachments, and in the Bridports[2] having given me a general invitation to breakfast and dinner as long as I may remain in Town. I have consequently engaged myself there to dinner to-morrow. The Blaauws arrive in a day or two, which will make my Coterie complete. I have also had the pleasure of seeing Gilbert, who is most strenuous I should go to Harlesden, as he says London is quite pestilential at this time of year. I shall keep off making any removal for some days, as I have really ample occupation here, with shopping, visiting, being visited, and looking after my young Lady. . . . There has been a letter from Martin,[3] but it has gone to ffolkes, therefore I can only give you Gilbert's sketch of it. He says he seems to have suffered much from the climate in regard to his Eyes, that his destiny was in some manner left to himself in remaining at Calcutta or going up the country, and that he had been most graciously received by Lord Hastings[4] from Mr. Coke's[5] letter of introduction

[1] From death of parents, breaking up of home at Hillington, and departure of her sister to India.

[2] Lord Bridport had married a daughter of Earl Nelson's, the Admiral's brother, cousin of Lady West.

[3] Martin West, nephew of Sir E. West.

[4] Governor-General of India.

[5] Of Holkham, afterwards Lord Leicester.

and was accommodated at his Country House with a young Mitford, who also took out letters to his Lordship. Temple's destiny is still unfixed, but now talked of for a six months' breaking in, at a small school at Acton from whence he can come home every Saturday and Sunday, and then to be banished to a large school at Blackheath, where some of the Treasury Men's Sons are placed. I am gratified beyond measure in the kindness of my friends; none will allow me to dine at home. . . . I have been just blessed with a sight of a letter from dear, dear Lu. Mine are all gone to Hillington, this I have seen was to Lady Bridport—very satisfactory on the whole, as they have had a most rapid passage, and had arrived and landed at the Cape and were to stay there a few days. They seem to have had storms, and to have been in danger, but Lu writes cheerful and happy. She says she has suffered dreadfully with sea-sickness, but was quite herself again when she finished her letter. I cannot write any more. Sir Edward been well the whole time.

FROM LADY WEST'S JOURNAL

Lat. 9·44 north ; long. 24·02.

Oct. 7. Very hot indeed. We have lost the N.E. Trade Winds and have very nearly a Calm, as to-day at twelve we had sailed but 28 miles; but we have been well amused in seeing 3 small Sharks caught, ugly brown fish but with white tips to the fins, which look green in the water. They were accompanied by several Pilot-fish,[1] pretty little things which always precede them. They were striped like zebras; also there was a sucking-fish,[2] a disgusting little thing sticking on to the shark. We have also seen several pretty little fish called sea Nautilus, like a Purple Butterfly. They are on the surface of the water, and of an evening quite illumine it; some are Red. The sailors eat the sharks;

[1] The pilot-fish—a companion of sharks and ships—was considered sacred by the Greeks from its habit of disappearing when the ship was in shallow water, and so giving warning of shoals.

[2] The common remora, the sucking-fish, has suckers on its back. It attaches itself to sharks, and so is carried rapidly through the water and picks up food with little trouble to itself.

indeed many tasted of it at our table, and said it was like whiting.

Oct. 12. It has poured torrents all day, so much so that 12 Butts of water have been caught, which are very valuable. To-day the scene cannot be described, the sailors almost all nearly in buff on their knees beating, stamping on, and washing their clothes in the water which ran in torrents. At 12 we had sailed 75 miles.

Oct. 13. We have now 3 times a week hot rolls for our breakfast, and altho' sour, bitter, and heavy, I really enjoy them.

Oct. 27. We have this day passed the Sun, and we shall have to look in the North for it. It is now perpendicular over our heads, also the moon. They are certainly more brilliant, and the clouds more beautiful than I ever saw them before.

Nov. 19. Last evening two very large Whales came close under the Poop; to me they appeared quite enormous, but I was disappointed in the little length they threw the water.[1] They were supposed to be about sixty feet long. A large porpoise was harpooned last evening; an ugly thing, a Bird's beak and animal's carcase—the English sailors eat it.

Nov. 27. At eight o'clock Table Mountain was in view, but at the height of 3000 feet it only looked like a cloud. At one o'clock we were within four miles of the shore, which presented a beautiful range of fine mountains; the sea a deep bottle-green colour. The sight of land, and the appearance of a pretty bay and an active scene, has inspired me with an indescribable feeling of melancholy which is unaccountable.

Nov. 28. Cape of Good Hope. We had rather an unpleasant landing at the jetty last evening, there was so much surf. . . . I saw many waggons with eighteen Bullocks paired and driven by one man. The streets are pretty, clean white Houses with a canal in the centre of each street, and a row of trees on each side. I walked along a shady avenue of good oaks with a Myrtle Hedge, past the Governor's house, to see the Wild Beasts and the Secretary Birds, curious long-legged things from the Interior. The Hottentot men and women are hideous; the men wear Hats like Bee Hives. We are at Morrison's Boarding House, which looks clean and

[1] Pictures are apt to exaggerate the height of the column of moist air exhaled by a whale on coming to the surface.

comfortable. Most of the inhabitants are Dutch; everything appears abominably dear; we have enjoyed good bread, butter, French beans, vegetables, and oranges extremely.

Nov. 29. The streets, or rather roads, are over one's shoes in dust. At 12 we drove 10 miles to Great Constantia; a very pretty drive, the fine mountains on one side, sometimes the sea on the other, now getting shady lanes, but usually a sort of wild Heath and wild flowers of every description. It was dreadfully hot, but we explored and gathered many pretty specimens: my only wish was to fly with them to dear Hillington. The Silver Tree is there as large as a fir, and quite beautiful in rows. In England it is a Green House Plant. We found Mr. Grooty,[1] the owner of the vineyards and grounds at Constantia, very obliging. We walked about his vineyard and garden, and found everything very luxuriant and fine. We tasted of 5 different sorts of Constantia. I recollected that there was a good deal at Hillington, or I should have sent some home. Our carriage was a sort of Barrouche and four-in-hand of nice, gay, small Cape Horses, and our Coachman in the Bee Hive Hat. On our return We found Lord and Lady Charles, and Miss Somerset's cards on the table, and in a few minutes they called again, leaving a note to ask us to dine to-morrow, and that hearing we were to embark, they had called on Capt. Harwood, and asked him to stay. I think I saw some slaves selling to-day in the market, but I turned away my head, it was too degrading to look at.

Nov. 30. Lord Charles and Miss Somerset called and sat some time with us—their society is so small that it is a great treat to see any one just arrived from England. The last two years they have had dreadful harvests—the wheat mildewed.

Dec. 1 (*Sunday*). I must say I rejoiced extremely to get on board again, and found the walk on the deck cool and pleasant; little did I think I should be so reconciled to the walk on the deck of a ship as to like it. I have sat on the poop of the ship all to-day to watch the retreating of the mountains and the Town. Every one almost has a fishing line, and an immense quantity of cod, young sharks, Cape salmon (Redfish) have been caught. We have sailed only 17 miles to-day.

[1] Probably Mr. Cloëte; although the farm was called "Groot Constantia."

Dec. 3. I was quite shocked when I got up this morning to see Table Mountain quite close, and that we were just off the shore; the fact was the current was so great yesterday it sent us back again into the Bay.

Dec. 4. A fine bright day; we are sailing well. The first view of the Cape I shall never forget—its high, rude barren rocks; and on our first arrival hearing of the loss of the *Sarack* in June at anchor in the Bay; and of 9 vessels being stranded, wrecked, and lost in one night; such a winter had not been known for years; seeing the hulls of the ships on the sands did not make the approach more cheerful.

Dec. 11. The melancholy anniversary of the death of our best and most beloved father, a day never to be forgotten or the loss [illegible] to His children, Domestics, Tenants, and friends, but I hope and pray that he is happier than We could make him here.

Jan. 1, 1823. A New Year; God grant that it may be prosperous to all those I love. . . . It is tremendously hot. We luckily keep our S.E. Trade Winds and those very fresh. We have sailed 192 miles. We had last evening quite an entertainment to bury the old year and welcome the New. Almost all the gentlemen dressed in masquerade, and very good characters. Batt was the Dress fancier, Maker, and dresser to them all; we had Singing and a Band, but the ship rolled too much for any Dancing.

Jan. 4. We retain our S.E. Trade Wind longer than was expected. Lat. 8·46 South; Long. 78·46 East. A large whale was close to the stern of the ship to-day.

Jan. 18. At two o'clock We had a distant view of Ceylon; when within 20 miles a delightful fresh smell of vegetation was very perceptible, of leaves, flowers, etc., which was very enjoyable.

Jan. 19. At six o'clock this morning We cast anchor in the harbour at Point de Galle.[1] Mr. Stark, the Collector of the district, came at 12 o'clock, in a Boat with a nice awning, to request us to go on shore to visit him, which we agreed to do at 3 o'clock; soon after we had a note from Mr. Gibson to say he had had Palanqueens waiting for us at the Quay since the morning, and to beg us to fix our own hour for dining. We regretted our pre-

[1] Ceylon, a Crown Colony, won from the Dutch in the general war succeeding the French Revolution.

engagement, went on Shore at ½ past 3, and were welcomed by the Commandant Capt. Macdonald, and all the principal Inhabitants, who received us with a Salute of 21 guns—I believe I did not see half I ought, the novelty of getting into a Palanqueen rather distracted my thoughts; the Harbour is very picturesque and beautiful; Banks of Hills covered with Cocoa Nuts and Bread Fruit feathering down to the Sea, with a few natural rocks which form the Harbour; the ride from the Quay to Mr. Stark's was beautiful, like fairyland, the sea on one side, woods of cocoa-nuts on the other, with the huts of the natives amongst them; Mr. Stark has an excellent House, large lofty and airy rooms, nicely but little furnished. I enjoyed my ride extremely in the Palanqueens. I only felt for the heat and fatigue the Bearers must have experienced, but I am assured that one shall soon lose that proper feeling of humanity. I had 4 Bearers, Edward followed in one with 6, and Batt and little Edward came together with 4. In the evening we were to call for a few minutes upon Mr. Gibson, instead of which we were carried to a Capt. Dickson. We were all aware of our mistake but no one seemed to like to explain it; it was attended with some advantage, as he offered us his Boat to return to the ship, which we gladly accepted as the rocks are rather dangerous to strangers, and I have not much faith in our Lascars; it was too late for us to rectify our mistake and to call upon Mr. Gibson, but Mr. Stark promised to explain it all, as it was a complete Comedy of Errors. The Fire Flies, of which I saw an abundance, are quite beautiful, like little Diamonds glittering in the Grass and in the Air; Upon the whole I was so much pleased with this first view of India that I should have liked to have passed another day there, and I am more than ever convinced that I shall like Bombay, if what they say of the Climate is correct. Everyone seemed to try to outdo the other in civility towards us. With all our delays We did not get back to the Boat till 9; it was fine, and moonlight, so that We enjoyed the row in the boat extremely.

Jan. 20. We weighed anchor last night at 11; setting the sails by moonlight was very pretty. We tacked twice before morning and were soon out of sight of Land.

Jan. 25. A fine land breeze this morning brought us within 10 miles of the Shore off Calicut, it looks pretty low,

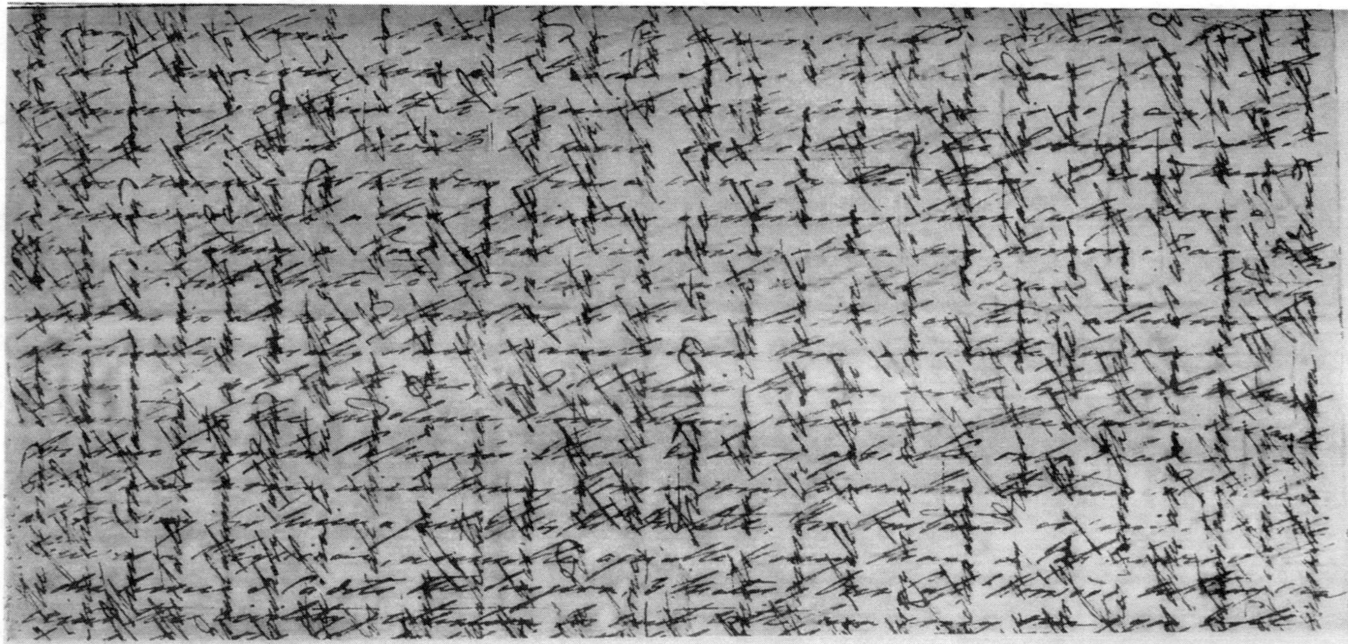

Page of a "single sheet" letter of 1822,
Written by LADY WEST.

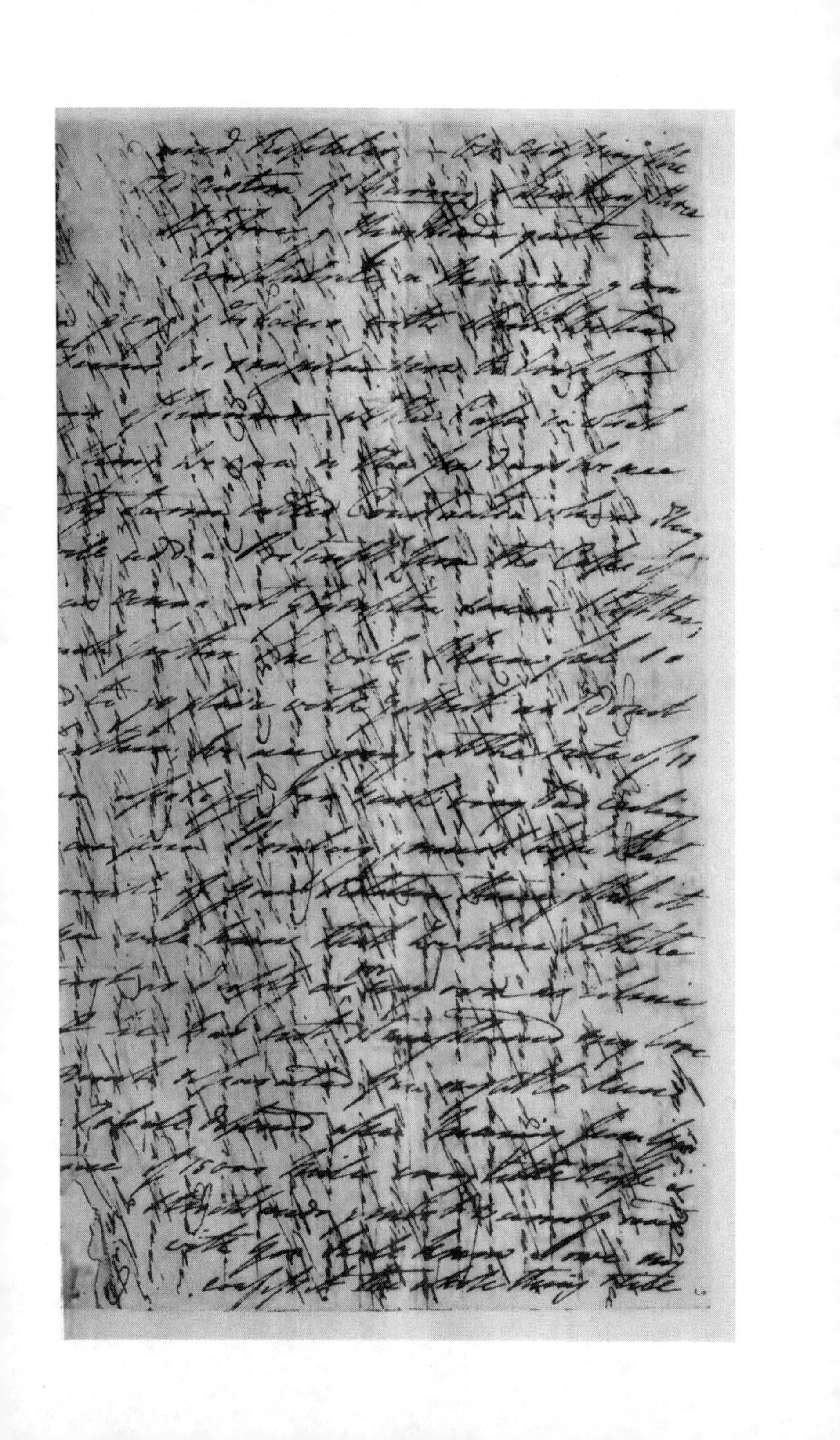

and covered with Trees to the Water; but enormous high Ghauts or mountains in the Interior covered with white cloud. Boats came off to us with Fruit, Parrots, Miners,[1] Monkeys, Poultry, Eggs, etc., all cheap as dirt. The people were dressed, or rather undressed, much like those from Point de Galle, some rather more picturesque, with Hats made of Palm leaves as large as Parasols, fastened on their Heads, and from eating Beetle Nut the inside of their mouths and Lips crimson, which made them look rather more savage.

We have now regular sea and Land breezes, but between the two it is very hot. Therm.: 85°.

Jan. 26 (*Sunday*). We had Service to-day, probably the last time; the idea was rather melancholy, after passing 21 weeks so comfortably.

Feb. 2, 1823. At ¼ past 8 this morning the Bombay Light-House was seen from the Masthead, a good breeze against us. I shall doubt our anchoring in the Harbour to-night; it's odd, but I am not at all anxious to arrive. I have been so comfortable, and must expect trouble and annoyance. At 4 o'clock we began to see the Harbour, Salsette, and the Houses near the Light-House, which looked very pretty. At 7 the Pilot boat came to us. At 7.30 we anchored. I have been a great deal annoyed at hearing that Lady Colville, Mrs. Barnes, Lady Buller—all nice women—are gone home through ill-health. I fear that My society will be very small; Mr. George Forbes has been introduced to us.

Feb. 3. We anchored last evening. At 9 this morning Sir Anthony Buller[2] and Mr. Stewart[3] arrived to fetch us. We left the Ship with regret; received 3 cheers from the English Sailors; guns were fired upon our arrival; Palankeens and Carriages were waiting to take us to Mr. Stewart's, where we found Mrs. Stewart waiting breakfast; at 12 o'clock the Mayor and Aldermen assembled at the Court-House for Edward to take the oaths, when more guns were fired. He lost no time, as he had some business to do. I went to see our House, with which I was much disappointed, not as to its size, for it is immense, more like

[1] Mynah—a favourite cage-bird in India.
[2] A King's Judge from Calcutta acting as Recorder *pro tem*.
[3] Brother-in-law of Sir Charles Forbes.

a Barn; in fact it looked unfurnished and wretched, but I hope I shall be able to make it more comfortable. We had a party of 24 to Dinner, and in the evening was the Race Ball, where Edward and I went for ½ an hour. I was introduced to so many I never can recollect them. Mrs. Stewart appears a very domestic pleasing woman, and I doubt not will be my directress in all family matters.

Feb. 4 (*Wedn.*). We have had an inundation of Visitors all the morning—it is very annoying to be so looked at—returning them will be worse. The Governor sent us an invitation to His country house. We should have liked to have accepted it, but, as Edward has daily business at the Court, it would not have been convenient. Besides, We hear they keep such terrible late hours. I have written to Lady Bridport, and Martin at Calcutta. We have been looking over our house, and Sir Anthony Buller's furniture. I do not know what I should have done without Mrs. Stewart. She orders everything, hires Servants, arranges everything for me. I could almost liken her to dear Anna[1] in kindness and activity.

Feb. 8. We dined at Parell[2] at the Governor's to-day. We were invited at a quarter to seven. It is a magnificent Place, with an abundance of beautiful Chandeliers, 9 servants waiting in different Costumes. It reminded me of the Arabian Nights' Tales. The Governor took me down to Dinner. I found him very pleasant and liked it well. The Dancing was very languid.

Feb. 9. Attended Church, which has a nice organ and really looked very English, except that it was so deserted. Weather very hot for winter. Musquitos very troublesome.

Feb. 13. More Morning Visitors. They appear to be quite endless. Getting up by candlelight is very disagreeable. Several officers of the 24th dined here. Edward much engaged with petitions. The Court is in sad order, but He will soon make it better.

Feb. 19. We went to the marriage of Hormagee Bomangee's[3] son and daughter to their first cousins. The Brides were 6 and the Bridegrooms 11. They were all loaded with magnificent Pearls and Precious stones, each

[1] Lady West's sister.

[2] Five miles from the fort at Bombay. The Governor's country residence.

[3] A philanthropic Parsee.

Pair seated on a Couch with a cloth between them which was held up till some Prayers were said and some Cotton wound round them, and some herb tied round their wrists, then the Curtain was withdrawn and the little creatures saw each other. The mothers were there all splendidly attired within a railing. The Priests mumbled some Prayers, and strewed them with Rice, and burnt Incense. Afterwards they were *carried* and put upon Horses magnificently caparisoned, and led all round the Town with thousands of lamps and multitudes of People. We afterwards ascended to be showered with otto of Roses, eat cake and drink wine.

Feb. 21. Edward had a letter from Martin West to announce the death of poor Sir Henry Blosset on the 1st. He had left England only three months before us.[1] We continue to dine early, find our evening drives very pleasant, but the returning Visits is a great bore, as all the people I have yet seen are unpleasing and vulgar, and wishing to be Fine ladies; I foretell that I shall not be intimate with any, and we shall live happily to Ourselves. I am almost in a fever with the venomous bites of the Musquitos.

Feb. 25. We dined at the Prendergasts, a large party of 26. I had heard so much of her finery and his stiffness that I was quite agreeably surprised, for they were both markedly polite, civil and attentive to us. He had heard much of Sir Edward's abilities, through his brother at Madras, from Sir Charles Grey. We had music, and I rather liked my day. I have sent long letters to dear ffolkes, Anna and Mrs. Blaauw. Edward has also written to Mr. Wynn and the Duke of Buckingham.

Feb. 28. We dined at Parell, a party 130; the Governor gave the Dinner to us, and handed me to Table. I passed a very tolerably pleasant day, but amongst strangers, and those not very elegant, it cannot be very agreeable; there was a Ball in the evening. We did not get home till 12 o'clock.

[1] Sir Henry Blosset, Chief Justice of Calcutta—an excellent King's Judge, universally respected—arrived Dec. 1822 and died Feb. 1823. A native newspaper of the time says: "Among the millions whom God has created there can be but few persons possessed of such excellencies, so wise, so merciful, so condescending, so zealous in repressing the wicked, so kind a protector of the poor and upright." He died suddenly after his first Quarter Sessions.

March 1. Gen. Smith[1] and Miss Pottinger came here to spend a few days; very low at Mrs. Smith's departure for England. He is always sensible and polite.

March 6. Another nice 4 o'clock dinner; Mr. Clark of the *Milford* dined here. Wrote to Lord Nelson, dear Anna and Charlotte.

March 9. We dined yesterday at Mr. Warden's;[2] the Dinner was given to us, an enormous party of 45; I had the Post of Honor, and found it pleasant, as one usually does.

March 12. Capt. Alexander, the Capt. of the *Alligator*, and Lord Henry Thynne dined here yesterday. They will live here the week they will be at Bombay. They bring no news except that Mr. Canning stays at home. They are both pleasing Men. The *Almorah* has started to-day and taken our Letters to dear England.

March 18. The weather is getting hotter every day, the Musquitoes very tiresome indeed at every hour of the day; they pursue me till they sting me.

March 20. We passed a very pleasant day, a party of 15; the Ashburners, Nicols, Lord H. Thynne, Capt. Alexander, and our own party. We went to see the Caves of Elephanta. We had a pleasant sail there and back again, a nice cool Dinner in the Caves, with which I was very much pleased. They were much more extensive and in less state of decay than I expected, and the Figures more perfect.

March 24. We have just taken leave of Capt. Alexander, Lord Henry Thynne, Mr. Blankley, and Mr. Michel, and feel quite low at their departure. Agreeable men from England, two of them connections of ours; very interesting at this remote spot. Edward has given Capt. Alexander a letter of introduction to Sir Charles Grey.[3]

April 1. A sad hot restless Night. We were awoke at 2 by the roll of Drums to announce a fire, and we all met *en robe de chambre*, fearing from the look that it was in the Fort. Thank God, it was not. I have been to see it this Morning; it was in the Bazaar, and has destroyed 100 huts.

[1] Sir Lionel Smith, Commander of the 4th division of the army of the Deccan in the last Mahratta War. An excellent and humane soldier, who had seen much service. His military career began at a school which has sent many a good soldier to India. He was expelled from Winchester for leading the "great rebellion." Miss Pottinger was his niece.

[2] A member of the Bombay Government, adviser of Elphinstone.

[3] King's Judge at Madras.

April 9. Dr. Ducat, I am sorry to say, leaves Bombay, as he has got an appointment 30 miles off. Therm. 91°. We shall sleep to-night on the Esplanade in the Stewarts' Bungalow.

April 10. The Bungalow was hot. Musk rats[1] running about our room perfumed the air very disagreeably, and a troop of ants lodged themselves in our bed. Nothing is ever shut in this country, so that one seems to dress to amuse others.

April 14, 1823. The Sessions commenced to-day. Edward made a charge to the Grand Jury, which has, I understand, given universal satisfaction, it was so clear and good ; His conduct is such that he must be respected. The Court already wears quite a different appearance. Sleeping on the Esplanade is the greatest delight, and drinking tea on the Beach.

April 19. Edward finished the Sessions yesterday, to the astonishment of most people. I have written to-day to Fanny Lane[2] and sent newspapers to ffolkes.[3]

May 1. Edward decided on a most interesting case[4] yesterday about Money and Interest, with which he felt quite at home. It had been pending twenty years, and had excited great anxiety. He ought to be popular with all People. He is so active and kind to their interests. I believe the natives feel it already. So says Hormajee.[5] We are living the quietest, or most People would say the most humdrum life possible, going to bed at 9, getting up at ¼ to 5.

May 9. We have been removing our things from the Stewarts. Edward very unwell with a violent attack of sneezing brought on by going in the sun to see the jail. We have declined invitations during the hot season.

May 18 (*Whitsunday*). A sad, long prosy sermon from the Archdeacon ; it put me to sleep for the most part of it. I really felt quite ashamed.

May 19. Last evening at 9 o'clock a fire broke out in

[1] The Musk Shrew, "Musk Rat" of Anglo-Indians, an insectivorous animal, compensates for its unpleasant odour by living on cockroaches and other insects.

[2] Sister of Sir E. West.

[3] Sir W. Ffolkes, Lady West's brother.

[4] The "Rice" Case.

[5] Hormajee Bomanjee. A Parsee distinguished for his talents, integrity, and personal influence in Bombay. He died February, 1826. See page 253.

the Fort amongst the bales of cotton near the Church and Mr. Stewart's office; and want of water made the People very apprehensive it might extend to the Castle where the Gunpowder is kept. If so the whole Island might have been blown up; it was fortunately a calm night, and the loss of about 3 lacks of Rupees is all the damage that has been done. Mr. Stewart and Edward were actively moving away all the books and papers from Mr. Stewart's office; it was an awful sight, and I was thankful to see them return in safety at ½ past 2 o'clock.

May 23. Again morning visitors; but alone at dinner: quite a relief to Edward after being in Court all day, as he has so much to do. Everything has been in such a disordered state. But already it wears quite a different aspect. I am told that the natives say that God has sent an Angel to protect them.

May 25. Two ships arrived from England, the *Pigot* and the *Farquharson;* the latter brought us an abundance of Newspapers and two letters, one from my beloved Anna from Glympton, Dec. 15. Thank God they were then all well at home. No one who has not been absent can tell the real happiness of hearing from home, and how they are going on.

CHAPTER IV

Sir Edward West labours to reform the administration of Justice —Misrepresentations in "Glimpses of Old Bombay"—Sir E. West's first Charge to the Grand Jury—Condition of the Jails —Case of Parsee rice merchant—Dismissal of William Erskine —Elphinstone's testimonial to Erskine—Libellous "Memorial" from the Bar: Barristers suspended: Attorneys as Advocates— Sir Charles Forbes—Newspaper war on the Erskine case.

Lady West's Journal (June-August 1823):—Sir E. West's judicial labours; sudden death frequent; flogging of untried natives; cocoa-nut day.

FROM the date of his arrival in Bombay until his death, which occurred in 1828, almost simultaneously with that of Lady West and Sir Charles Chambers, Sir Edward West laboured incessantly for a purer administration of justice, for more equal laws.

As a King's Judge he had to contend, single-handed for a time, with the irregularities of the Recorder's Court, and enforce, without favour, the English justice he had been sent to administer—and that in a community which had ostracised Sir James Mackintosh for such an attempt.

Though opposed by two able and popular Governors of the old school in succession, he accomplished much of his task before his death. His unselfishness and courage were acknowledged at last by a hostile press, and after his death the natives of Bombay founded a scholarship[1] in his honour; a spontaneous act, altogether without precedent in India. But he was never forgiven by those whom he was obliged to oppose. His keen sense of even-handed justice exposed him to slight and insult. Attempts were made, as will be seen, to drag him into duels, and after his death his memory, as was to be expected, has been severely handled by the admiring biographers of his opponents. Within the last few years, however, an attack so absurdly and grossly unfair has been made upon him that it has become necessary to inquire carefully into the little known history of the time, and to give an account of it, supported by references to contemporary authorities.

In "Glimpses of Old Bombay," a large quarto volume published in London in 1894, is the following paragraph, obviously intended to be a serious statement of fact; and one, too, to which reference is made in the "Dictionary of National Biography."[2]

"It was a great day for Bombay when the Supreme Court of Judicature was substituted for the Recorder's Court. On the 8th day of May 1823, at a few minutes past 10 A.M., the new Charter of Justice was read and proclaimed, after which Sir Edward West took his seat as Chief Justice. On the publication of the Charter, a

[1] Stocqueler in his "Handbook of India, 1844," p. 529, speaks of the Scholarships founded by Sir Edward West. It will be seen (p. 316) that they were founded by the natives in his memory.

[2] "William Erskine." Supplement "Dict. Nat. Biography."

royal salute of twenty-one guns was fired, and upon the Chief Justice being sworn in, seventeen guns. The echoes had hardly died away when an event came upon Bombay like a thunder-clap. The Chief Justice dismissed William Erskine from his office of Master in Equity, and Clerk of the Small Cause Court. He next suspended five barristers; and thirdly, but not last, he deported Fair, the editor of the *Gazette*. . . . I cannot imagine a case that is calculated to awaken a deeper sympathy than that of Erskine. Any man wounded in the tenderest part, and the object of unfounded suspicion, may be as true a martyr as ever died by stake. Erskine's case was that of a sick man whose subordinates allowed his affairs to drift into confusion and startle the auditor with a balance on the wrong side. Erskine's probity was undoubted. It was in vain that he was an elder of the Kirk . . . the Judge was inexorable . . . Erskine was like his native heather, which when burned to the ground one season springs up the next. . . . Here is the sequence. Sir E. West bestowed the office of Master in Equity on his Nephew."

Now it is perfectly easy for any one who refers to contemporary history to learn that there was no Supreme Court, and consequently no Chief Justice in Bombay in 1823—that the new Charter appointing a Supreme Court, and credited with causing undue elation in its Chief Justice, was not read until a year after that date; that Erskine was dismissed on the 18th June 1823 from the Recorder's Court; that the Supreme Court was established on March 8, 1824; that the barristers who sent a libellous memorial to Sir Edward West on the limitation of their practice, and of their exorbitant fees, and on the dismissal of Erskine, had been suspended for six months and readmitted before the establishment of a Supreme Court at Bombay.

Again, it is equally easy to ascertain that Erskine was not a martyr, and that his dismissal was not unjust; that there was no question of accounts with a "balance on the wrong side."

Further, it will be seen by any one who cares to follow this narrative that Sir Edward West did not deport Fair, or any other newspaper editor.

And again, that the important office of Master in Equity, held by Erskine, was given to an able and trustworthy lawyer, a Mr. Fenwick, who was no relation, not even an acquaintance, of Sir E. West before they met in India.[1]

The whole paragraph is an example of the deliberate manufacture of history.

Sir Edward West landed in Bombay on February 3, 1823, and on February 12 took his seat as Recorder. On April 19, 1823, he delivered

[1] One of the posts in the new Supreme Court of 1824 fell to a nephew of Sir E. West. That was probably the foundation for the last statement in this extraordinary paragraph.

his first address to the Grand Jury. The address shows the Recorder's love of fair play, and his disregard of popularity among influential residents, who, naturally enough in such a climate, wished to escape the Jury list. It also gives an insight into the irregularities of the Recorder's Court, and of the jail. Sir E. West in his address says:[1] —

"I have had many applications for exemption from service on Grand and Petit Juries. These applications it has been my painful duty in every instance to refuse, a duty particularly unpleasant of performance in a small society like this, where I expect soon to have the honour of being personally known to every individual gentleman. I have, however, proceeded upon this principle, that exemption granted to one would be an injustice to all the rest. The burden of attendance, if borne regularly by all, will press heavily upon no one, whereas were many exemptions granted, the duty would be almost intolerable to those who are obliged to bear it.

"Gentlemen, I cannot but think that the disinclination which I have observed in several members of this Society to attend on juries has originated in what it would be vain to conceal, I mean the very great irregularity and disorder of the Court, which render the best planned institutions inefficient, and double the labours of

[1] The address is printed in the *Bombay Courier* of April 9, 1823, from which these extracts are made.

all those connected with them. . . . For those irregularities I should not presume to blame any one: they have been caused chiefly by unfortunate circumstances, over which no human being could have any control: I mean the frequent vacancies[1] of this seat which I have the honour to occupy. Gentlemen, during the short time I have been here, I have done my utmost to remedy and correct that disorder and those irregularities; and whilst I continue to occupy this place, it shall be my utmost endeavour to restore this Court to that station in public opinion which it was intended by the Legislature to fill, and which it has generally filled. . . . To this object there is no sacrifice of time, recreation, or any other pursuits of my own that I would not readily make. . . . There is one topic on which it is necessary to say a few words—I mean the state of the jail; you will have the goodness to visit it before you are discharged. It is unnecessary for me to point out the particular point to which your attention should be directed. I will only say that you should take care that those prisoners who are confined there for punishment should not be treated with any harshness or severity beyond the law; and that those who are confined there

[1] The frequent deaths of the Bombay judges, and consequent temporary filling of their seats by judges from Calcutta and Madras. Sir Alexander Anstruther died in 1819. Sir George Cooper (from Madras), temporary Recorder of Bombay in 1820, died the following year. Sir William Evans arrived in 1820, and died in 1821. Sir A. Buller (from Calcutta) arrived as temporary Recorder in 1822, and left on the coming of Sir E. West in 1823.

merely on suspicion should have every indulgence consistent with their safe custody. . . ."

These were old grievances. A memorandum had been presented by members of the jury to Sir A. Buller, Acting Recorder, regretting—first, that none of the improvements in the jail suggested by former Grand Juries, not even those regarding cleanliness, had been carried out by the governor (Elphinstone); secondly, that many names were omitted from the list of those liable to serve on juries.

Sir Edward West, with the members of the Grand Jury, visited the jail, and their recommendations to the Bombay Government were adopted, and much later on partly carried out. The King's Court, in the meantime, which had drifted into, more or less, unavoidable disorder, began to fulfil its intended functions. Cases in arrear were tried, statements sifted, verdicts given; and natives and Europeans alike—those, at least, who were on the side of order and justice—welcomed the energy and the impartiality of the Recorder. "The court already wears quite a different appearance"; "Such despatch has not been known since the days of Sir William Syer," are notes in Lady West's diary.

Among causes tried during the spring sessions was an old-standing dispute between a rice merchant and the Bombay Government. A Parsee[1]

[1] Cursetjee Monackjee.

of known respectability signed a contract with the local Government in 1802 to supply the military department with rice. The price to be paid was below the market value, but it was agreed to by the merchant on the condition that for one year all rice required for military purposes should be bought from him alone. The merchant consequently made extensive purchases, and fulfilled his part of the contract. The value of rice then fell; and at the same time a large quantity of it was required both for Sir Arthur Wellesley's troops and for those of Bombay. The local Government therefore deputed Major Moor to buy rice privately from other sources, and afterwards from the Bombay merchant himself, at the reduced price. On discovering the destination of the rice, the merchant claimed from the Bombay Government the amount of his loss due to the breach of contract. Major Moor and the Military Board considered the claim justified; but the case dragged on—small compensations were offered by the Government and refused by the merchant, who, according to Sir Charles Forbes,[1] was threatened with banishment if he persisted. At last, in 1818, his case was to come before the King's Court; but in the three following years the three successive Recorders of the King's Court died,[2]

[1] House of Commons, May 25, 1824.

[2] Sir A. Anstruther in 1819; Sir G. Cooper (Acting Recorder) in 1821; Sir William Evans in 1821.

and the merchant's counsel fell ill, and left Bombay; and it was not until 1822, when Sir A. Buller was Acting Recorder, that the trial took place. The judge gave the Parsee a verdict for a part only of his claim, but granted a new trial, which came before Sir E. West in April 1823.

Sir E. West heard patiently all the circumstances of the case, and, with the full consent of the aldermen on the bench, awarded the merchant the original sum lost, together with fifteen years' interest, omitting that on the five years during which the suit had not been pressed.

In summing up the Recorder said: "Those who composed the Government during these transactions are passed away, and I am confident that no one would meet with such treatment from the present Government. . . . The plaintiff has been treated most shamefully. It is acknowledged by Major Moor, and admitted by all, that he was a most faithful and zealous servant."

Yet in spite of a piteous appeal from the old merchant, worn out with anxiety and hard pressed by creditors, begging the Government for the sake of his children not to defer his claims for another term of years, Mountstuart Elphinstone decided to refer the case to the Privy Council. Three years later the Directors in England, after taking the advice of all their law officers, decided to withdraw the appeal, and abide by Sir E.

West's judgment; and justice was done to the now embittered old man.[1]

Sir E. West's judgment could not have been agreeable to the local Government, and no mention of the trial appeared in the local newspapers.

But on June 18, 1823, an event occurred which excited fiercer passions, and divided Bombay society for years. William Erskine, an old resident of Bombay, who had left a lawyer's office in Edinburgh fifteen years before to become Clerk of the Court for Small Causes, and who had lately been made Master in Equity and a magistrate; amiable, given to literary pursuits, an elder of the Kirk, son-in-law of Mackintosh, friend of the Governor, was dismissed from his office by the Recorder's Court, with Sir Edward West at its head.

Mountstuart Elphinstone, a servant of the Company, now Governor of Bombay, popular and enjoying his popularity, and never disloyal to friends, sided with the crowd against the King's Judge. At a meeting of the Bombay Literary Society[2] Mr. Elphinstone proposed that a letter should be addressed to Mr. Erskine, couched in the warmest terms, to say that his "unexpected return to his native country" had prevented the Society from expressing its regret at his departure, and the high sense it entertained of the "im-

[1] *Oriental Herald.*
[2] Founded by Sir James Mackintosh and Sir Charles Forbes.

portant benefits that he had conferred upon it," that he would always be remembered with "sentiments of truest respect and esteem."

Mr. Erskine was also requested to sit for his portrait, for the purpose of having it placed in the rooms of the Society.

It was a covert attack on the King's Judge; and as the Bombay newspapers, more or less under the control of the local Government, published the Governor's warm farewell to Erskine in large type, and omitted all mention of the proceedings of the Court, the first impression on looking over the records of the time must be that a serious miscarriage of justice had taken place.

Erskine, however, retired to Calcutta, and there fortunately was printed and distributed an anonymous pamphlet of fifty-eight pages, besides some sixteen columns in a Calcutta newspaper,[1] defending Erskine, and attacking the Recorder and the Court.[2] From these we learn that on the 18th of June 1823, at a special court, consisting of the Recorder, the Mayor (John Leckie), and three aldermen, Sir Edward West stated that, owing to the complaint of some natives, investigations had been made by the Court regarding the conduct of the Clerk of the Small Cause Court (Mr. Erskine), and that the decision of the Court

[1] *Bengal Hurkaru.*

[2] It is only fair to Erskine to say that, according to Silk Buckingham, Erskine "disclaimed all participation in the pamphlet, and never questioned the correctness of the Court's judgment."

would be made public in order to convince the native community that the Court would protect them.

The first case brought forward seems to have been one in which a Parsee widow, with seven children and an income of only 17 rupees a month, had been for some time unable to obtain a sum of 459 rupees which had been paid into Court for her. Finally, the money had been paid, but a fee of ten rupees had been deducted by Erskine, for taking the money to the widow's house. The woman had some difficulty in getting a receipt for the fee. Erskine seems to have admitted the charge, and to have acknowledged that the fee was not allowed in the official table.

Another charge was that for a long time one rupee had been demanded by Erskine for each seal, instead of half a rupee, the proper sealer's fee. This had been pointed out to Erskine by Sir Edward West, who had requested that the legal fee only should be charged; Erskine had, however, continued to claim and receive one rupee. Again, suitors had been charged fees for subpœnas when no subpœnas had been issued.

Erskine seems to have admitted the irregularities, but to have stated in defence that, owing to ill-health, and various causes, the business of the office had been left very much to his native clerk. Due consideration having been given to Erskine's defence, the Recorder announced the findings of the Court. They were—that a fraud of considerable extent had been committed for Mr. Erskine's benefit; that, in addition, there had been contradiction in his account of the transactions; that the Court might punish him summarily as their officer; that the issuing of subpœna tickets without subpœnas was alone a contempt of Court; that there was more than sufficient evidence for his dismissal from his office; that in this decision the Court was unanimous.

The charges were not very serious ones for a Bombay official in 1823, and it is impossible not to feel some sympathy for Erskine. Interested chiefly in literary pursuits, he had merely conformed to the habits of many respectable persons around him. The unauthorised gains had come to him chiefly through his clerk; and had been taken not from his fellow-countrymen, but from those for whom Europeans had, as a rule, little or no sympathy. If Erskine had not held office in the Recorder's Court, and had not taken an oath to receive legitimate fees, and no others, the disaster would not have befallen him. Disasters of that kind were nevertheless inevitable. They were the result of the clashing of stricter justice and morality in a new generation with older standards of conduct.

Probably, too, students of history would agree that in the early days of the last century a higher code of ethics existed among Europeans living at home, surrounded by their children and other relations, and under the eyes of friends and acquaintances, than among persons of the same class abroad, surrounded by strangers and alien races. The difference was undoubtedly to be seen in Bombay at this time. Lady West's letters and journal show continual regret at the absence of simple, kindly, honest life—the life of "nice" people, to be found then, as now, in English homes. As late as 1840, W. Delafield Arnold,[1] describing the arrival of a newcomer from England, says: "The first experiences of Indian society are to most disappointing, and even shocking, and lead for a time to complete seclusion."

Some years later Philip Anderson, Chaplain to the Company at Bombay, probably stated the case very fairly.[2] The Company, he said, were "not much worse than the age in which they lived." "Be it remembered that the Company began to trade in a reign during which the Lord Chancellor was accessible to bribes. They struggled for existence at a time when Charles the Second supported himself by receiving secret service money from France, and they purchased the goodwill of William the Third for ten thousand pounds, and of the Duke of Leeds for five thousand pounds; so that the immorality of the age may be urged

[1] "Oakfield," p. 48.
[2] "The English in Western India." Bombay, 1854.

as an excuse for many charges brought against them. . . . Anglo-Indian society was, as it ever has been, one degree worse than English. . . . Now that the world bears itself more morally, there is still rather a lower standard of principle in Bombay than in England."

It could not have been difficult thirty years before this was written for an old inhabitant of Bombay, without loss of much self-respect, to find himself doing at Bombay as Bombay "society" did.

So Erskine was dismissed, a Mr. Fenwick was appointed in his place, and notice appeared in the papers,[1] signed by the new Master in Equity (Fenwick), stating that any one who had been a suitor in the Small Cause Court during the previous two years, could have his bill of costs "made out, taxed and delivered" to him, and any overcharge refunded.

Anxiety among some members of Bombay "society," caused by Erskine's dismissal and the coming taxation of his costs, was soon to be increased. Mr. Norton, the newly arrived Advocate-General to the Government of Bombay, had introduced a scale of fees higher than those sanctioned by the Master in Equity, and "on an average seven times as great as those usually received in England."[2] Together with two other

[1] See advertisement column of *Bombay Gazette*, November 12, 1823.
[2] *Oriental Herald*, vol. ii. p. 488.

barristers, Mr. Norton was making at this time such extravagant demands for fees, that a lawsuit on which they were engaged could not be proceeded with, and the solicitor, Mr. Ayrton, appealed to the Judge for redress against what he considered extortion. One barrister had even refused a "fee of £12 for a single bill, for which £1 would have been charged in England."[1]

Sir Edward West decided against the barristers, and directed that any fees beyond those usual in England must be left to the discretion of the Master in Equity and of the attorney, the only persons capable of judging of the importance of the case and of the client's circumstances.

This decision led to the writing of a round robin to the Recorder. At a meeting of the Court, on October 10, 1823, a long-winded memorial, signed by the barristers, was presented to the judge, asserting that new and illegal practices had been introduced, that the Recorder had been guilty of "irregularity" in the administration of justice, whereby the professional rights and privileges of the Bombay barristers had been prejudiced; that the Small Cause Court itself was illegal; for, although, in order to give cheap justice to natives, a Court for Small Causes to which barristers were not admitted had been established in Calcutta and Madras, the power to establish such a Court had not been extended

[1] *Oriental Herald.*

to Bombay; that the introduction of attorneys to practice as advocates was another innovation of an injurious tendency;[1] that the Court had been illegally held in private for the punishment of alleged offences (in the case of Erskine), and that the rules of the Small Cause Court were not warranted by the King's Charter.

Two days later, at a meeting of the Court, the Recorder stated that he was bound to take notice of this "libellous memorial," handed up to him by gentlemen of the Bar, who ought to respect the Court and know that their own characters rose and fell with that of the Court . . . that their accusations were unfounded — that Mr. Norton, the Advocate-General, after only twenty-five days' practice, and limited knowledge and experience acquired in that time, was ready to announce that rules made by Sir William Syer in 1799, adopted by succeeding Recorders, accepted by the barristers, and sanctioned by His Majesty, are not warranted by law nor charter and tend to subvert justice; that still more offensive was the unfounded assertion that the practice of the Small Cause Court was not in conformity with the rules. The examinations

[1] The following pencil note in Sir E. West's handwriting is on the margin of the MS. copy of the "Memorial":—"This is no innovation; it is permitted by the Charter, by which the characters of Advocate and Attorney are not disjoined." And on another page in pencil:—"This has been the usual course pursued by the Bar, to insert in the papers and elsewhere the most untrue account of what has passed."

of Erskine, the Recorder stated, had not been held in private; the whole Court had sat in chambers, as it had a right to do, and as necessary for justice, and that both plaintiff and defendant had been examined by a rule of the Court. He would ask the gentlemen of the Bar what excuse they had to offer for the libellous memorial.

Each barrister was then heard in turn, and the Recorder, after conferring with the other members of the Court, stated that they had considered the memorial, and that nothing put forward on the part of the Bar had mitigated the impropriety of their conduct; that on account of the insult offered to the Court the sentence was that the barristers be suspended for six months, and that in the meantime attorneys be allowed to practise as advocates.

A note in Lady West's handwriting says:—

January 24, 1824. Everything went off well in Court yesterday with only one Barrister, and we hear that there is more business than ever there was. We learn that at Madras every one thinks that Edward has acted right in everything; at Calcutta of course there are two opinions,[1] but conscience tells him that he has only done his duty.

The following appears in the *Oriental Herald*:[2]—

"The suspended Barristers were to be restored to the exercise of their functions on the 7th of April; the six months' idleness, to which they were originally doomed, being then to expire. The greatest evil to them of such a

[1] Erskine had retired to Calcutta.

[2] Published in London, December 1824, vol. iii. p. 134.

suspension was no doubt the loss of fees, of which all appeared to be so inordinately fond; but we sincerely hope that Sir Edward West will persevere in the good work he has begun, of reducing the enormous charges on the unhappy natives, to many of whom such exactions would have the effect of forbidding their approach to a court of law, and thereby subject them to wrongs innumerable, without a hope of redress."

On the 21st of June, in the House of Commons, Sir Charles Forbes moved for papers relating to the suspension of the barristers and the proceedings in the Small Cause Court.

Few Anglo-Indians of those days stand out in brighter relief than Sir Charles Forbes. Born in Aberdeenshire, and in later life Lord Rector of its University, he was now head of the chief banking firm at Bombay; a man possessed of instinctive love of justice, kindliness of heart, and honesty. So trusted by the natives, that he was probably the only person in all India who, during the crisis of 1803, was able to raise money from the native bankers, and so enable the campaign which ended in Assaye to be carried on. "A 'Tory of the Tories,' he never allowed his political creed to cloud his fine judgment and keen sense of right and wrong." He knew the people intimately, spending a large portion of his fortune among them, and "one of his last acts was the appropriation of a very large sum of money to procure for the inhabitants of Bombay pure water in all seasons."[1] His fame spread through the whole

[1] "Dictionary of National Biography."

country, and twenty-seven years after he left Bombay the natives of India subscribed £9000 for the erection of a statue in his honour.

The support of Sir Charles Forbes in the House of Commons, and the warm friendship of Sir Charles's relations in Bombay, must have greatly helped Sir E. West in his difficult task.

Sir Charles Forbes considered the conduct of Sir E. West perfectly justified. Mr. Brougham, Sir J. Mackintosh, and others joined in an animated debate, which lasted two hours. No account of the discussion was allowed to be published.[1]

Mr. Elphinstone, too, refused to allow any public discussion of the differences between the Bombay Government and the Recorder, and the Bombay newspapers made no mention of the examination and dismissal of Erskine until four years afterwards, when Mr. Elphinstone was about to retire. Then the storm suddenly broke, and a fierce and unseemly conflict of words between Erskinites and anti-Erskinites raged for some months. Erskine, who was living contentedly at home, must have longed for deliverance from his friends.[2] The attack was begun

[1] *Oriental Herald*, vol. ii. p. 460; *Bombay Courier*, Nov. 20, 1824.

[2] Erskine suffered from his advocates. He himself seems to have accepted the inevitable with dignity and moderation. There is a pleasant entry relating to him in after life in the Diaries of Sir Charles Bunbury by Mrs. Henry Lyell: "April 25, 1847.—I was introduced to Mr. Erskine, a very clever and highly accomplished man, and in particular a distinguished Oriental scholar. He is very pleasing and of great modesty. . . . Mrs. Erskine, a daughter of Sir James Mackintosh, is a very agreeable person."

by a letter from an Erskinite signed "Vindex." The charges against the Recorder made by this writer, and by other friends of Erskine, were that Erskine had been suddenly dismissed, without trial, from a lucrative appointment of 23,000 rupees a year; that Sir E. West had conducted the examination in secret; that Erskine had been taken by surprise, and had been unable to make his defence with vigour; that he had been refused a trial; that he had been ill at the time of the Parsee widow case; that all extortion had been the work of his native clerk; that it was illegal to tax costs; that there was no precedent for so doing, and therefore it was impossible to tax Erskine's bills fairly; that only fifty suitors had applied to the Court to have their bills examined, and that as yet only twenty of them had obtained repayment of overcharges; that the taxation of costs took place during the suspension of the Bar, and that, therefore, the attorneys could not apply to the Court to review the taxation.

In answer, the writer of a letter signed "Giovanni" pointed out that attorneys were permitted to act as advocates during the suspension of the Bar, and that the suspension was over in April, while the "clamour for justice" by Erskine's lawyers went on till November; that he knew Erskine well, that "his case was desperate"; that Erskine had not been "taken by surprise," that he had been continually warned; that the examination had not been conducted secretly, but before mayor, aldermen, and the registrar, who took down the answers, as can be seen by Erskine's own pamphlet; that this pamphlet, published to "libel the Court," by the "especial care of Providence" vindicated the judge, so that "every copy which could be laid hold of had been taken up by the Erskinite faction";[1] that a trial had been offered, but had been refused by Erskine, who threw himself upon the mercy of the Court;[2] that the Court had the "exclusive patronage within itself of all offices belonging to it," and had full power to dismiss without trial, which in this case was "the most lenient proceeding";[3] that at the taxation of costs Erskine's interests had not been neglected; that he had been represented by able men; that Mr. Morgan, his solicitor, Mr. Wedderburn and Mr. Crawford, his attorneys, and Erskine's native clerk, had all been present at the taxation of his bills;[4] that the taxation had been conducted according to a table of rates acknowledged to be just by both Erskine and his clerk; that Erskine's solicitor had admitted that the taxation had been "most liberal"; and that the two attorneys and the Advocate-General (Norton), "who would have been ready to make a noise in Court if such taxation had been irregular," made no objection to

[1] *Bombay Gazette*, November 28, 1827.
[2] Idem., October 17, 1827.
[3] Idem.
[4] Idem., December 5, 1827.

it; that the taxation had been conducted not upon precedent, but upon principles of common honesty between man and man; that in Erskine's bills charges had been made for "money alleged to have been paid, when no money had been paid; for business alleged to have been done, and folios furnished, when no such business had been done, and no such folios furnished"; for sham subpœnas[1] and seals; extortions all of them from the poorest class, the suitors of the Small Cause Court. That there were "bills drawn up in a most careful manner in Erskine's own handwriting, one 33 per cent. and the other 100 per cent. above legal charges."[2]

Then follows a list of overcharges refunded.

The writer also stated that even if Erskine was ill during the Parsee widow case, he might have allowed the widow's son—the widow could not attend without loss of caste—to have the paltry sum owing to her; but that instead of this he got out of bed and took the widow's money to her himself in order that he might charge an illegal fee of ten rupees for so doing; that Erskine continued to be a magistrate (under the Company) after dismissal from the Recorder's Court; that his native clerk had in Court threatened to banish people from the "island" if these extortionate demands were not complied with. And that

[1] *Bombay Gazette*, December 26, 1827.
[2] Idem., December 5, 1827.

"yet 'Vindex' wonders why these poor wood-cutters and rice-sellers did not boldly claim taxation of their costs" in greater numbers![1]

The editor of the *Bombay Gazette* says: "We abstained from publishing 'Giovanni's' letter until perfectly satisfied as to the truth of its premises."[2] "We have every reason to believe that the taxation of Erskine's bills of costs was conducted on just and equitable principles."[3] "As to the justice of his (Erskine's) dismissal from the Recorder's Court, we think that there cannot exist a doubt about it. It is sufficiently obvious that the aim of 'Vindex' is not to defend Mr. Erskine, but to attack the Recorder."[4] The writer of a letter signed "Verax" states[5]: "Unless you have been constantly in Bombay since the dismissal of Mr. Erskine . . . you would be astonished at the recital of all the acts of blind prejudice which have been committed by a knot of persons who have felt angry with that decision. . . . They will now know that their actions can be traced to their true source; and they may dread if they continue in the same course that a history may be opened up that will load them with disgrace."

It has been difficult to condense the correspondence. The letters are of great length, and not always in good taste. Enough has been

[1] *Bombay Gazette*, December 26, 1827.
[2] Idem., October 17, 1827. [3] Idem., November 14, 1827.
[4] Idem., January 9, 1828. [5] Idem., November 14, 1827.

quoted to show the assertion that Erskine suffered martyrdom at the hands of Sir Edward West to be as unjust as the statement that Sir E. West was at the time Chief Justice of the Supreme Court is inaccurate.

It may have been true that Erskine flourished "like his native heather" at a time when Sir Edward West was dying in India, but it is quite impossible for any reasonable person to follow the author of "Glimpses of Old Bombay," and consider Erskine to be "as true a martyr as ever died by stake."

FROM LADY WEST'S JOURNAL

June 12, 1823. Edward has been much engaged in Court detecting frauds. . . . These are unpleasant things, but he came to administer justice and correct abuses, and he will do it . . . but it will make him unpopular. . . .

June 18. This has been to me a nervous day, as Edward summoned a Special Court for the purpose of dismissing Mr. E. from the situations he held under the Court for extortion and negligence. It must be an unpopular measure and an unpleasant one, though the cases were so clear that I should think that even his friends had best hold their tongue on the subject. Edward will send home the proceedings to Mr. Wynn.

June 19. We have violent rains, but intermissions which I did not expect. We drove to the jail early this morning. I sat in the carriage while Edward looked it over. Every one must be astonished at his activity, as people in general seem asleep.

June 24. The Monsoon is come in earnest; it rains so violently it is almost dark.

July 6. Edward is a good deal worried by this business

of Mr. Erskine's. I shall be glad when he is gone, leaving money to pay all demands upon him. A lucky day, so many ships have come in from England. The *Charles Forbes* has brought me a letter from dear Anna as late as April 1st, and one from Lord Nelson.[1]

July 14. To-day Sessions commenced. I have been sending out Invitations for a grand dinner for 24 people, the number our table will hold. I do hate and dread the thoughts of it.

July 15. Edward sat in Court from ½ past 10 till ½ past 5, and tried six Cases out of ten. I fancy such despatch has not been seen since the time of the first Recorder, Sir William Syer. In fact every one says the Court was never before in such good order.

July 16. Edward was in Court again from ½ past 10 till ½ past 5, but he does not mind the fatigue; he is so interested in all he does.

July 28. Edward to-day, upon a renewal of Mr. Norton's improper conduct, made a most eloquent speech to him and the other barristers, and adjourned the Court.

July 30. I know not when I have been so shocked as I was last evening to have Mrs. Newnham's death announced to me. She took Tiffin here last Thursday, had an attack of fever that night, expired last evening. Here people die one day, and are buried the next. Their furniture sold the third, and they are forgotten the fourth. . . . Oh Lord! preserve my husband to me.

Aug. 5. Mrs. Newnham's English maid died last evening.

Aug. 8. We dined yesterday at Col. Barker's, the first time we have been out for 3 months, a cheerful pleasant dinner; for India the Party was very diminutive, only 19; the Archdeacon was there and must have had a dull day, as People did not seem to talk much to him.

Aug. 10. To my English ideas it appeared very unfeeling and indelicate, that yesterday poor Mrs. Newnham's Pianoforte, Drawing-room Furniture, Chandeliers, and her little things were sold by auction. I did not go to see them even. Edward is very unwell with a violent attack of sneezings.

Aug. 11. We had an Invitation to dine with Mr. Elphinstone on the 27th, which we have refused, after his

[1] The admiral's eldest brother; Lady West's cousin.

shabby conduct in voting an address and complimenting Mr. E., a man who was dismissed from the Court for improper conduct. What would Mr. Elphinstone say if Edward did the same by him?

Aug. 21. To-day is what is called Cocoa-Nut day, when it seems almost all the population go and throw Cocoa-Nuts into the Sea, to appease Neptune. After that they begin to go down the Coast with their Boats, thinking that the violence of the Monsoon is over; it was a curious scene, the whole Esplanade covered with People of all Nations, and Children, and a sort of Fair with swings and odd savage-looking amusements.

Aug. 24. Mr. Elphinstone was at the Scotch Church. He is not over-burdened with religion; for popularity he goes sometimes to one, sometimes to the other. Edward's life will not be a bed of roses. From hearing Petitions such extraordinary things came out. Mr. G. has the Natives flogged without any examination, trial, or usual formality. A Friend sends a note to him and says, "Pray flog the Bearer," and it is done. If they were not a timid, gentle race there must be an open rebellion. Edward will have it all corrected, notwithstanding what has occurred since the dismissal of Mr. Erskine.

Aug. 30. My beloved brother's birthday.[1] The last we spent together. I hope we may again some few years hence when we shall be much altered, except in our affection to each other, which I hope is unalterable.

Aug. 31 (*Sunday*). We have had an extraordinary sermon from the Senior Chaplain, Mr. Davis, occasioned by the early death of a young man in the civil service at the early age of 21. He gave us the whole account of his religious feelings and sentiments . . . that with his instructions he had died the death of the righteous; and compared it to a most awful death of a most hardened sinner, the Hon. Mr. N. Dreadful I think to introduce individuals and to quote their expressions at such a moment; indeed, should it please God to take me whilst I am here, I have begged that Mr. Davis shall not be asked, as of course in my situation I should be a most happy subject for a Discourse. I should wish to die as I have lived, quietly, and little talked of.

[1] Sir William Ffolkes.

CHAPTER V

Treatment of untried prisoners and debtors—Sir Edward West's address to the Grand Jury—State of Bombay jail—Transportation to New South Wales desired by European soldiers—Insolvent Laws—Board of Control—Letter from Lady West on expedition to the Deccan, and visit to Sir Lionel Smith.

Lady West's Journal (September 1823–April 1824):—Life in Bombay; visit to Poona, Siroor, Karlee; horse races; social slights to Sir Edward West; suspended Barristers return to Court.

SIR E. WEST's next step was an endeavour to separate prisoners who had not been tried, many of whom were innocent, from convicted criminals, and to improve the position of debtors. In an address to the Grand Jury on July 14, 1823, he says:—

"Those who are committed to gaol merely for safe custody till trial, and whom therefore the law considers innocent, are confined with those who have been found guilty. . . . Any one committed for a paltry offence is associated with those who have been convicted of the most heinous crimes, even murder. This is most improper, but it was not easy to find a remedy. The Foreman of the Jury and I paid this subject considerable attention. We examined the gaol, and a plan of it, but could not devise any possible plan for remedying this abuse. . . . However, a remedy is now in course of being applied, as the Court has received a communication from the Government, stating that the Honourable the Governor in Council has given directions for the erection of a penitentiary capable of containing 175 persons. This certainly is a measure of the greatest utility, for you must be perfectly aware that in many cases of the most heinous offence imprisonment is the only punishment short of death which the Court can inflict. I allude principally to offences committed by European soldiery. Their transportation to New South Wales is no punishment. On the contrary, the expectation of such a sentence has frequently been a motive for crime. It is notorious that the hope of being sent to a better climate than this has actually in many cases prompted European soldiers to commit the most dreadful crimes, and in other instances to confess crimes which they had never perpetrated. . . . Since my arrival I have paid considerable attention to the subject of debtors, in the hopes of being able to effect a diminution in the number of prisoners confined for debt, without any injury to the public. . . . Prisoners confined for debt may apply to be discharged; but on the creditor undertaking to make the debtors a certain weekly allowance, such application may be refused, and the debtor may be confined in jail for life. I cannot but think it would be desirable to have an Insolvent Act, which would in some degree limit the period of imprisonment, extended to this country."

In such a matter as the relief of native debtors not much help was to be expected from the Council at Bombay. Sir Edward West, however, wrote to Mr. Wynn, and urged upon him the importance of extending the Insolvent Laws to India; but it was not until March 1829 that they were introduced, and then into the three Presidency towns only.

It was to Mr. Wynn, as President of the Board of Control, not to the Governor and Council of Bombay, that Sir Edward West, as a King's Judge, was responsible; and to Mr. Wynn, as we learn from a letter to Mrs. Lane,[1] and from notes in the diary, Sir Edward West wrote a full account of every transaction of the Court. Some years previously, when Fox and Burke had advocated the transfer of India to the Crown, the Company had resisted desperately, helped by Pitt, and to escape a Board of Commissioners had accepted Pitt's Board of Control. Like an Indian prince who had called in a powerful European ally, they soon realised that under the Board of Control they had lost for ever absolute independence.[2]

[1] Page 86.

[2] Mr. Wynn was removed from the Board of Control during the short and unfortunate Ministry of the Duke of Wellington.

From LADY WEST *to* MRS. LANE, *Glympton Park, Woodstock.*

(Post-mark, "India Letter, Plymouth.")

BOMBAY, *March 6th,* 1824.

The sight of your handwriting, my dear Fanny, I need not I hope say, gave me great pleasure. The letter was dated the 30th August and reached this place on the 19th Feby. It was the first I had received. I wrote to you a second time on the 31st May, and the letter has, I hope, reached you. I am sorry to say that Edward, with a long continuance of sittings, and great anxiety for the Court, was very unwell in the month of Nov.; so debilitated by the damp weather. We took an excursion for two months, from the 12th of Nov. to the 12th of Jan., to see Poona,[1] and to visit Sir Lionel Smith, 40 miles further at Siroor, as he had the Command of the Deccan. As soon as you ascend the Ghauts Mountains the Climate is like England; one can bear a shawl and a blanket at night; it seems to give one new life and vigor. The scenery of the Ghauts is beautiful, the City of Poona much in decay since we have had it, and the Peshwa's[2] Palaces miserable Places. We saw his Pagodas and were allowed a peep at his Gods Vishnu, etc. by Torchlight; to Christians a most disgusting spectacle; on Our way we saw the Caves at Karlee which were worth the trouble of scrambling up a very dangerous path to them. We passed three weeks at Poona with a charming bachelor, Capt. James, and journeyed on to Siroor with Sir Lionel Smith and his Aides-de-Camp who met us there, where We passed three weeks, and meant to have kept House, as we took Servants, Furniture, and everything to put into one of Sir Lionel's empty Bungalows (a detached low suit of rooms) but he would not allow us, and we joined the Mess (he and his Aides-de-Camps) every day, and were *Camp fashion*, each taking their own Chair, Plate, Knife and Fork, Spoon, Cup and Saucer, Glass, Napkin, etc. etc. It was very sociable

[1] Poona, the Capital of the Mahrattas, had been taken by Sir Lionel Smith in 1817. See pages 50 and 116.

[2] The Peshwa was the recognised head of the Mahratta Confederacy; originally the chief minister to the Mahratta King. Peshwa literally means "He who precedes." See "Letters and Papers of Bombay Secretariat," by G. W. Forrest, C.I.E.

and pleasant, and my being usually the Only Lady I learnt to play short Whist with Edward, who says I play very well; but I must tell you he usually thinks all I do is well, I believe I may say there never were two People happier in each other. After this little remark I must say Sir Lionel is a very gentlemanlike, agreeable Man.

Siroor was once the largest Cantonment this side of India, but the Troops are now removed to Poona. The two Edwards[1] rode on horseback, I and Batt went in Palankeens, and took a third in case Edward should be tired: We had Camels and Poniės for our Luggage, Porters innumerable, 36 Palankeen Bearers, 21 rank and file, I believe more for State than use, that we appeared like an Army in motion. We usually took one Stage about 14 miles a day, either very early or in the evening, resting during the heat of the day: We took double-poled tents with us, but Government have built what they call Rest Houses, not better than English Cow Houses, at about 14 miles from each other for the accommodation of Travellers. Once we took 3 stages at once, sending on relays of Hamauls, and made our Beds regularly in the Palankeens, but I could not sleep, from the fact of being carried by Men, though they certainly look little better than savages: Use reconciles one, or I should never like the appearance of the nearly naked People. I am obliged to think the Brown skin *a dress.* We saw very few odd animals, reptiles, Birds or Insects; I think as little to interest one as is possible; I hope our next excursion may be by Sea. I shall hope to visit the different Presidencies to see Edward's different friends—Sir Christopher Pullar[2] at Calcutta, Sir Charles Grey[3] and Sir Willingham Franklin[4] at Madras, and the new Recorder at Penang, Sir Francis Bayley.[5]

We are hoping every day for the arrival here of the two

[1] Sir Edward and his nephew, son of Gilbert West.

[2] A lawyer of great promise. Had won the University prize for Latin verse when at Christ Church, Oxford; afterwards Fellow of Queen's. Appointed Chief Justice of Bengal in 1824. Died six weeks after his arrival in India.

[3] Sir Charles Edward Grey of Backworth, Northumberland. Fellow of Oriel. Chief Justice of Bengal 1825. Afterwards Governor of Jamaica.

[4] Fellow of Oriel, Oxford. Died May 31, 1824. See page 156.

[5] Sir Francis Bayley had been appointed Recorder of Penang. He arrived August 24, and died about five weeks afterwards.

Puisnes, Sir Ralph Rice [1] from Penang and Sir Harcourt Chambers from England, and wonder that we have not heard from either, as I hope they will both come and live with us until they can get Houses of their own. I rather hope that Sir H. Chambers is married; should she be a nice person it will be a great comfort, as I sincerely regret to say that our kind friends the Stewarts [2] leave this Place by the Ship that takes this, on account of both their healths; they talk of going only to the Cape or St. Helena and returning, but once so far, I think they will go home, as she has a son who is to be carried on board a Ship, I fear in the last stage of decline.

In this Country where there is so little heart, sociability, and I may almost say amiability, I cannot describe what their loss will be. The Society here is very formal, and the Ladies very self-sufficient and consequential, thinking of little but their fine Pearls and *local* rank. We of course dine out a good deal, and give a Dinner of twenty-two about once a fortnight. From my being the first lady, Edward the 2nd gentleman, we are terribly observed, and of course I doubt not pulled to pieces, but thank God we are still quite English, and domestic, taking our walk together every evening, our tea and our bath afterwards, and I am as active and lively as ever; none of the indolence and finery of an Indian lady; the Military men are by far superior to the Civilians. In a year there will be a great change, the Commander-in-Chief is going home, and I believe the Governor, and I suppose the Archdeacon will not stay above another year. Our residence has been certainly made very unpleasant from the improper conduct of the Governor trying to whitewash Mr. Erskine (son-in-law of Sir J. Mackintosh) who held two offices under the Court, and whom it was necessary to dismiss. He was going to England, and Mr. Elphinstone handed a laudatory address to him which hoisted the flag of opposition against the Court, and emboldened its Barristers openly to libel and insult it. Edward has kept up a regular correspondence with Mr. Wynn,[3] and

[1] Arrived in Bombay, October 27, 1824, and left India ill October 1826, and died shortly afterwards.

[2] Brother-in-law and sister of Sir Charles Forbes.

[3] Right Hon. Charles Watkin Williams Wynn. President of Board of Control, 1822-1828. Secretary at War, 1830. Was said to have thrice refused the Governor-Generalship of India.

sent him every paper and document that he must be satisfied with what Edward has done; but he is of an anxious temper, and he will not feel quite comfortable until he hears from Mr. Wynn. The Governor is now aware of how improperly he has acted, and courts Edward in every way.

I am surprised at the Pullers going to Calcutta, at their age, with only one Child and money enough; besides, much too gay a Place for their feelings, I should think. Surely your Brother Martin never could apply for it, a Puisne is all he could expect at present. Martin[1] is not yet arrived from Calcutta. I hope for the best, but I fear that he is a dawdle; if he is active he might do great things here. Edward has so much patronage, but he will never give it to inefficient people. Batt has been the greatest of all comforts to me, she is very happy and does not think of marrying at present. Mr. Way is acquainted with Mr. Charles Forbes, M.P.,[2] brother-in-law to Mr. Stewart here, who has *every* Paper about the Court, should Mr. Way feel an interest about it, he could see them there to shew how ill Edward has been treated. Edward writes by every Ship to Mr. Wynn.

March 7. Poor John Campbell [Stewart?] is just put on board, and they sail to-morrow. We shall go and take leave of them before they go, I feel so sorry, hurried and bewildered at their departure, that I hardly know what I have said and cannot read it over. Remember Edward most affectionately to the Ways,[3] the Stricklands,[4] McBrides.[5]

P.S.—Although the Archdeacon's term of residence is much shortened here, he talks of staying a year or two longer.

[1] Martin West, nephew of Sir Edward West.

[2] Afterwards Sir Charles Forbes.

[3] Of Glympton.

[4] Of Cokethorpe.

[5] J. D. Macbride, Principal of Magd. Hall, Oxford, from 1813 to 1868; son of Admiral Macbride, uncle of Lady West. Magd. Hall was moved from the neighbourhood of Magdalen College in 1815. It is now Hertford College. Dr. Macbride "was well-off and extremely liberal, especially in helping poor members of his college" ("Dict. of Nat. Biog."). "The excellent principal" (of Magdalen Hall).—Dean Burgon, "Lives of Twelve Good Men." At the jubilee of his headship in 1862 at a gathering of members of the college the scholarship which bears his name was founded.

From Miss Maria West (*Sir Edward West's sister*) *to her sister*, Mrs. Lane.

(Franked by Geo. Harrison.)

Harlesden Green, *Sept.* 28*th*, 1824.

My dear Fanny,—As when I leave this part of the world I hear but little of the proceedings of the family, and likewise am not in the way of procuring a frank, which your present distance from London makes almost necessary, and as a common chit-chat letter is not worth the postage, I wish to send you a few lines before I take my departure for Malvern. . . .

I do not know whether you keep up any correspondence with India, or if you have lately heard from Anna-Martina,[1] who is the greatest dispenser of the family news, which makes her letters very interesting. If you have heard from either of these quarters perhaps I shall be telling you old news. However, I must take my chance. Anna-Martina has been travelling about a great deal; after going to Ramsgate the beginning of the Summer, she selected to make an excursion to Edinburgh. Accordingly they set off, a party of five, and went in one of the steam-packets, which have now become a very general mode of conveyance. They were three nights on board, and she and many of the party were very sea-sick, and not much pleased with their accommodation; however their tour, after their arrival in Edinburgh, was very agreeable, as they visited Loch Lomond and several other lakes and places extremely well worth seeing. They were absent about three weeks, and she is now on her way into Norfolk, where she proposes staying two or three months, and afterwards going to Northerwood to spend about the same time with Mrs. Michel.

The accounts from India appear, upon the whole, to be satisfactory. All this anxious and unpleasant business respecting the Court, we hope, is at an end, and though it has made a great many parties, which makes the society at Bombay unpleasant, yet Edward's promotion,[2] and his having Judges to act with him, will give him more power,

[1] Anna Martina Ffolkes, Lady West's sister.

[2] To Chief Justiceship of Bombay.

and not quite so much responsibility, and he will probably be able to get away for five or six months, which Lucretia is anxious he should do on account of his health and spirits, the latter having been a good deal depressed by what he had had to contend with. Mr. Wynne has offered him the Chief Justiceship of Madras, which is considered a better thing than Bombay, but their friends (the Stewarts) appeared to think that he would not wish to make the exchange. I have but little to tell you with regard to the family here; we are all well, and going on much the same as when I last wrote. Gilbert proposes going into Norfolk in November for about a fortnight or three weeks, when the three girls will accompany him . . . Martin [1] is gone into the Country for two months during his vacation, and Lady Maria [2] and the children have accompanied him.

FROM LADY WEST'S JOURNAL

Sept. 1, 1823. Altho' so far removed from dear Norfolk, I did not forget the commencement of the shooting Season, but here one knows nothing about seasons, or how the year goes. Edward has been engaged in examining Mr. G., one of the Police Magistrates, for tying a Hamaul to a tree and flogging him without any warrant.

Sept. 5. This day year we took our departure from Mansfield Street for Deal, and tho' the time has passed happily, still I wish that more of our transportation had gone, and that the time of seeing my beloved Brother and Sister was nearer at hand.

Sept. 12. We dined yesterday at Col. Baker's, a party of 32, and a few more in the eveng for Quadrilles. I sat next to the Governor at dinner and found him, as I always do, civil and attentive; indeed, on the whole I passed a pleasant day. I did not dance, nor do I think I ever shall here, or possibly anywhere again. Edward also liked the party.

Sept. 13. No ship from England. We have been expecting one the last month, and begin to get quite impatient. Oh for steam vessels!

[1] Martin West, brother of Sir Edward West and Mrs. Lane.

[2] Lady Maria West, sister-in-law of Sir Edward West, and daughter of Lord Orford.

Sept. 29 (*Michaelmas day*).—The ffolkes's going to Lynn [1] to the Entertainment there; it makes me look back with deep regret to the loss we have sustained in our beloved father, and of past happy times never to return. God give us health that we may return to England again.

Oct. 1. Edward has been obliged to adjourn the Court on account of the Barristers charging such exorbitant Fees that business cannot go on, and on Friday he will lecture and perhaps be obliged to suspend some. The beginning of the season for Pheasant Shooting, and here the therm. 84°.

Oct. 3. Edward read the Affidavit of the Attorney against the Advocate-Genl.[2] and the Barristers, with many improper letters from them, and then called upon them for their defence, which is fixed for next Tuesday. Glad shall I be when it is over, as all these things, tho' absolutely necessary if the Court is to maintain its dignity, make me very nervous and uncomfortable.

Oct. 7. This has indeed been an eventful day in the Court, for all the 5 Barristers have been suspended for six months, and the Attorneys are to act in their places, from the libellous and improper memorial they presented to the Court. Mr. Norton's conduct was so insolent, he ought to have had a little more punishment, but the 3 Aldermen and Edward thought it would be sufficient if he can be made to act and feel as a gentleman. I fear that he will be a constant annoyance during our whole residence here.

Oct. 8. After the anxiety of yesterday one feels quite low and annoyed that such strong steps have been necessary, but it seems unanimously the opinion that it was the only thing to do, and now I wish that the Barristers may have the sense to withdraw the Memorial, and I doubt not but that the Bench would readmit them, which would be an end to all further irritation.

Oct. 13. Edward did very well without the Barristers, as some of the Attorneys are much superior; in particular Mr. Ayrton, who was recommended to Edward by the Duke of Buckingham.

Oct. 15. Edward has been the whole day engaged in the trial of 6 English Soldiers for shooting a Black Man, and I am sorry to say that it has been clearly proved against one.

[1] Their country town. [2] Mr. Norton.

Oct. 18. Edward has passed the awful sentence of death on the poor Man, who will be executed on Tuesday. Edward felt the [illegible] necessity, as had he escaped no native would have been safe, but suffered very much before the judgment and after it; he has so much feeling.

Oct. 20. Term begins to-day, and 3 different Aldermen. Mr. Stewart[1] is one, which is a great pleasure to Edward, also that there are more cases on the Board than usual, and that business pours in from all Quarters since the suspension of the Barristers, which proves the necessity of the step which has been taken.

The poor man being hung to-day, has never been out of my thoughts.

Oct. 27. The long wished for *Katherine Stewart Forbes* is arrived, and has brought Edward a most gratifying letter from Mr. Wynn, of the 30th of May, telling him that this Court was to be made Supreme, and that he should appoint him Chief Justice from the high respect he had for his character, and that he would have the choice to go home at the end of 7 years on His Pension, or 10; we now only wish for the arrival of the other Judges.

Nov. 9. We dined yesterday, a party of 22, to meet Sir Charles Colville. It is astonishing how polite People are since they heard of Edward being Chief Justice.

Nov. 13. Mr. Adam[2] arrived from Calcutta last evening, and has just called here.

Nov. 14. Edward has been very unwell the last Month; we shall go on Monday to Siroor to visit Sir Lionel Smith[3] and stay in the Deccan till the Judges arrive.

Nov. 27. We have accepted Capt. James's hospitable and agreeable invitation of remaining with him (at Poonah). He is civility and attention itself; he has a very pretty English House with a nice Garden, and everything that is comfortable. On the way we met several men on horseback preceded by their Pages, carrying shields and spears.

Dec. 1. Sir Lionel Smith arrived yesterday, and spent the day here. He is always cheerful and agreeable. We are made so much of, I should not wonder if we were to buy a House here next year; it seems so much more cheerful and sociable than Bombay.

[1] Brother-in-law of Sir Charles Forbes.

[2] Cousin of Mr. Elphinstone. Temporary Governor-General.

[3] See page 83.

Dec. 3. Edward dined yesterday with Colonel Warren at the Mess of the 47th, which he seemed to enjoy. He met all the agreeables and grandees; every one speaks most highly of Mr. Lane.

Dec. 4. Yesterday we went into the City of Poonah, which contains 80,000 Inhabitants; melancholy to see how ruinous it is becoming. Our object was the Peishwa's Palace, an immense Pile of Building; fine gateway, and the ceilings like mosaic work, some in coloured glass, which must have had a brilliant effect when the Walls were covered with Mirrors. The wooden carved work is fine, but the rooms small, tho' numerous; the Peishwa is living at Calcutta.[1] A jail is building here, but at present this Building contains the Prisoners, the Mad, and the Hospital—which made the visit a melancholy one.

Dec. 6. Loonee [Loni?]. We left Poonah at 6 o'clock this morning, a large Party, Sir Lionel Smith and his two Aides-de-Camp. We have now a retinue of Camels, a long march over a very bleak barren country without a Hedge, a tree, or the smallest appearance of vegetation. A little reminded me of dear Norfolk, it is really so cold and bleak; we eat a most excellent breakfast. We are all now writing letters for England, at the Rest House.

Dec. 7. Kundapoor. Another 14 miles we journeyed, this morning before breakfast, as Sir Lionel likes to start at daylight. This is a pretty, wild spot, with several handsome Pagodas casually built close to a River, and sometimes *in* it, with flights of steps, I suppose for the convenience of their ablutions.

Dec. 8. Siroor. Here we are at Sir Lionel Smith's; another 14 miles trajet over the most bleak and dreary country; I believe unusually so from the scarcity of rain, as there is not a vestige of grain except on Sir Lionel's Farm, which looks quite English. Fine Clover and Lucern, and his Kitchen Garden full of nice Vegetables. It seems at the World's end now, so deserted; as all the Cantonment is removed to Poonah. He has four different Bungalows. We have one and meant to keep House, but he insists on our living with him.

Dec. 12. Little Edward's[2] birthday. He has regained

[1] The Peishwa was afterwards given a residence for himself and his immediate following near Cawnpore.

[2] Nephew. Son of Gilbert West.

the roses since we have breathed the fine Deccan air, and led such a healthy life.

Dec. 14. No church and no service, which always strikes me as so melancholy. We however read it ourselves. We pass most of our time in reading. India has very few attractions, though I have the kindest and best of Husbands.

Dec. 22. Mr. Adam has just arrived on his way back to Calcutta by land. He has been the Governor there a short time, and seems a mild pleasing man. He is a cousin of Mr. Elphinstone's. I saw him at Bombay. He is now only one of the members in Council. He was accompanied by Captain Riddell. We all dined with Captain Griffith, who lives here. He was at Harrow, and recollects dear ffolkes at Mr. Evans's.

Dec. 30. It's quite a comfort to see Edward looking and feeling so much better, but still he is not what he was when he first arrived. The Rains made a sad change in him; so debilitated.

Dec. 31. The last day of the year, which always brings with it a train of thoughtful and melancholy ideas. I hope we are all better than we were last year, and that if it pleases God to allow us to live, we may improve. To-morrow, we say good-bye to our kind and hospitable friends at Siroor, having passed more than three weeks most comfortably and quietly amongst them.

Jan. 1. 1824. We dined early yesterday with Sir Lionel, and came 14 miles to tea. Sir Lionel, Captain Keith, Capt. Cooke, Dr. Hewitson rode half-way with us. We regretted so much saying adieu, that our parting was quite affecting, but hoping soon to meet again.

Jan. 3. Loonee. We found a Captain [illegible] at the Rest House, and he passed the evening with us and was a great bore. He staid so long; we wanted to go to bed early, and he would not take a hint.

Jan. 5. We started early this morning to ascend the Parbutty Hill, where are two famous Pagodas of the Peishwas, and were allowed a peep at two of their gods.

The Dome and Minarets of one were gilt. The ascent is very easy, as there are stone steps all the way, and the view very extensive and pretty, when you see 300,000 Mango trees which the Peishwa made a vow to plant, and which cost him a lac of Rupees a year to water. We returned to breakfast with Col. Elvington of the 47th, who hires the Peishwa's

Garden House, a lovely spot, certainly the prettiest thing I have seen since I have been in India.

Jan. 6. Yesterday Mr. and Mrs. Simson, Col. Elvington, Capt. Powell, and Mr. and Mrs. and Mr. J. Morris dined here; the latter gentlemen are the best style of civilians, and Mrs. Morris the prettiest and nicest woman I have seen since my arrival.

Jan. 7. We had intended to leave our kind friends yesterday, but as passing so much time at the Rest Houses is dull, we have agreed to stay till to-morrow night and then travel by torchlight (Dawk), taking 3 stages at once, having a relay of Hamauls on the road, and we shall hope to sleep well in our Palankeens.

Jan. 9. Karlee. We arrived here this morning, having travelled 35 miles.

Jan. 12. We got into Boat at Panwell, had a very pleasant sail by moonlight, arrived at the Court House at 11 and, not being expected, did not find things very comfortable.

Jan. 13. We have had visitors all day, the Commodore, and Officers without end. We went at 4 o'clock to see the Races. The Race stand is a handsome new building, where all the world were assembled.

Jan. 16. Captain Alexander dines with us to go to the Play.

Jan. 17. The Play was really very well acted, Mr. Keppel [1] (Lord Albemarle's son) and a few others very good. The Ladies are always the worst. Mr. Keppel sat two hours with us this morning. He is uncommonly good-humoured and pleasing, and we enjoyed our chat about Norfolk ex-

[1] Mr. Keppel, afterwards Lord Albemarle—elder brother of Sir Harry Keppel, the late genial Admiral of the Fleet, and godson of Charles James Fox—writes thus in his "Fifty Years of my Life":— "In the month of Jan. 1824, Mr. Ker Baillie Hamilton, Mr. Lamb, and myself met from different parts of India at the Presidency of Bombay, and resolved upon an overland journey to England. We were assisted in this arrangement by Capt. Alexander, who kindly granted us a passage to Bussorah in His Majesty's ship *Alligator*. We were invited to dine with His Highness Futteh Ali Khan, who embarked the following morning. I had seen His Highness at Calcutta, when as Aide-de-Camp to the Marquis of Hastings, Governor-General of India, I had an opportunity of conversing with him."

A day's riding seems to be more dangerous to a sailor than a week of storm, and Capt. Alexander was confined to his bed after a fall from his horse, and the voyage was delayed.

tremely. I fear he cannot dine with us. He goes away with Capt. Alexander on Monday, if he (Capt. Alexander) is well enough, but He has had a bad fall from His Horse to-day. He also takes the Persian Prince, who is staying here, to Persia, and goes home by land. We should like to be of the party.

Jan. 21. Everything went off very well in Court yesterday with the One Barrister, and We hear there is more business than ever there was. We learn that at Madras every one thinks Edward has acted right in everything. At Calcutta, of course, there are two opinions, but conscience tells him he has only done his duty, though painful, as he really feels for the Individuals, though they behaved in so ungentlemanlike a manner. Mr. Elphinstone and others called to-day. Captain and Mrs. Mariott are here; he is on the Station in a Frigate. We have called and shall ask them to dine. It is but charity, so far from Home.

Jan. 24. We dined yesterday at Mr. Warden's, a large party. In the evening they had a Dance. Edward prevailed on me to join the dancers. I felt quite nervous as a young lady just come out, I had not danced for so long, but I was made so much of, I enjoyed it, and almost fancied myself again Lucretia ffolkes. It was the least formal Party I have seen in India. The exertion of going out certainly does us both good.

Feb. 2. The long-expected *Sibbald* arrived. Thank God all my Family and Friends well. Edward heard from Mr. Wynne that he would send out the Charter as soon as possible, and that Mr. Chambers and Sir Ralph Rice come here, and Edward's friend, Mr. Baley,[1] goes to Penang. Mr. Wynne and Mr. Forbes introduced a Mr. Pitt to us, son of the member for Cricklade. I forgot to notice that we are no longer to be called Griffins, as we have been here a year on Monday.

Feb. 16. Edward is better from his excursion to the Deccan, but still so altered it makes me quite wretched, . . . a sad prospect for this country. I do not think that we shall be able to stay long.

Feb. 27. Edward dined on Wednesday with Mr. Goodwin, a Bachelor party. It is ridiculous how every one now courts Edward, many eagerly looking for the loaves and

[1] See note, page 84.

fishes. We used to believe that Recorder was equally great, but it does not appear so here.

March 7. We went on board the *Sibbald*, to sail out with the Stewarts. It was melancholy thinking They were perhaps the only real Friends we had here. It made it very painful to see them in such distress about their son.

March 18. We heard with much regret and horror from Dr. Wallace that poor Col. Darwin had shot himself this morning at Mr. G. Forbes's Bungalow on the Esplanade. Ill-luck in promotion, and the death of his mother, occasioned a great depression of spirits. He was an excellent Officer, beloved by his Regiment, the 47th, and by every one who knew Him. A Coroner's Inquest, of course, sat, and he was buried at 5 in the afternoon. One, to me, of the most horrible things of this Country is, that you are put into the Earth almost before you are cold, and soon forgotten. Edward was invited to attend the funeral, and he wished it, as a Compliment, but as he was not very well, and had sat in Court for two days, I persuaded him not to go. A mournful thing at all times; doubly so here. . . .

March 19. A sociable day, like England. Mrs. Baker and I working and talking, tho' plenty of morning visitors.

March 25. Mrs. and Miss Baker have left us this morning. I am quite sorry, as it was sociable and pleasant. We dine at Mr. Elphinstone's to-day. He called yesterday and is quite overpowering with his civilities. I believe he regrets His past conduct. We had a party yesterday of 35 to dinner, only one excuse. It seemed to go off well. Batt dining out with the Leggatts, Lady Maria West's[1] friend, at the jail.

April 6. We dined yesterday at Sir Charles Colville's, and had a most unpleasant day, as Mr. and Mrs. Norton were there, and Edward had not His proper rank assigned, and was placed so that when the Ladies left the table He was between Mr. Norton[2] and Mr. Wedderburn.[3] In consequence he found it necessary to go away; this is the 2nd time it has happened there, which is highly improper. Edward has spoken to Sir Charles, and I should hope it

[1] Sister-in-law of Sir E. West.

[2] Mr. Norton, the Company's Advocate-General, took every opportunity of annoying Sir E. West, and "was followed into Court by a crowd to witness his insults." (Letter to *Oriental Herald.*)

[3] A friend of Erskine.

would never occur again, but certainly here every one almost has tried to make it as unpleasant as possible, from Edward having conscientiously dismissed Mr. Erskine, one of the officers under his own Court. Also to be attributed to Mr. Elphinstone handing the laudatory address to Him.

April 7. We dined yesterday at Col. Leighton's, about 34, and passed a very pleasant day. This morning there was a general Meeting at the Church to examine the Boys and Girls, and give them the Prizes for the year. Sorry am I to say that it fell to my lot to distribute them; luckily there was little to be said. There were afterwards a few Speeches; decidedly Edward's was the best, and a warm discussion about building two new School Houses in the Country for the Children.

April 8. The Suspension of the Barristers was over yesterday, and the Government Paper, the *Gazette*, very improperly made remarks upon it; a continuation of their very reprehensible conduct.

April 9. Many People are in a great fright, as Lieut. Jervis has died in a few hours of the Cholera; for my own part, I never think about it.

April 10. Yesterday we had a snug little party at dinner, the Archdeacon, Mr. Goodwin,[1] his nephew, Mr. Kerr, Mr. Ferrier, Capt. Stratton, and a Mr. Page, a man of information, though he annoyed me by smoking a Hooka the whole time. Dr. Ducat has been very ill at Poona, and is just arrived here for change of air. He looks ill and out of spirits, as most people seem here.

April 14. The Sessions open to-day to call the Grand Jury; two of the Barristers, Mr. Irvin and Mr. Parry, came in, and behaved most properly.

April 15. Mr. Norton and Mr. Le Mesurier also made their appearance in Court, and all behaved much more respectfully to the Court than they ever did before. I hope now the past will be forgotten, and all things may go on quietly; a few Cases were tried and the Sessions adjourned for a few days on account of Easter.

April 17. Edward breakfasted at Malabar Point with Mr. Elphinstone, to talk over Political Economy and show Him his MS.,[2] which I wish he had published, but he always

[1] A member of the local government who loyally supported the decisions of the King's Court.

[2] It was published in 1826. See page 20.

waits to make things too perfect, and loses the proper moment.

April 25. Mr. Elphinstone has a ball and supper and fireworks. Sessions finished. We shall go and spend two or three days with the Bakers, as the change will do Edward good, and it is impossible to be dull with Col. Baker, and she is pleasing and ladylike, and we shall see trees and hear birds sing.

CHAPTER VI

The years 1818–1828—Dark years for India as for England: both countries ripening for reform—Over-taxation—The Company's faulty administration—Power in Parliament—Monopolies—Suttee —Press Licensing Laws—Suppression of the *Calcutta Journal*—Liberal-minded Company's servants—Courtenay Smith's defence of natives—Impending expiration of the Company's Charter—Lord Lansdowne's speech—English merchants prepare for the abolition of the Company's monopoly.

THE ten years between the Mahratta wars and the arrival of Lord William Bentinck as Governor-General of Bengal in 1828, are apt to be passed over by historians as an "uneventful" period, "a term of profound peace broken only by the siege of Bhurtpoor, and by the first war with Burma in 1824." But they were dark years for India, as they were for England.

The early part of the nineteenth century in Great Britain is thus described by Sir George Trevelyan in his Life of Macaulay.[1] "For the space of more than a generation, our country had, with a short interval, been governed on declared reactionary principles. We, in whose days Whigs and Tories have often exchanged office, and still more often interchanged policies, find it difficult to imagine what must have been the con-

[1] "Life of Macaulay," p. 159.

dition of the kingdom when one and the same party almost continuously held not only place, but power, throughout a period when public life was exasperated by hatred, and the charities of private life soured by political aversion! Fear, religion, ambition, and self-interest—everything that could tempt and everything that could deter—were enlisted on the side of the dominant opinions. . . . The county representation of England was an anomaly, and the borough representation little better than a scandal. The constituencies of Scotland, with so much else that of right belonged to the public, had got into Dundas's pocket. . . .

"In the year 1820 all the towns north of the Tweed together contained fewer voters than are now on the rolls of the single burgh of Hawick, and all the counties together contained fewer voters than are now on the register of Roxburghshire. So small a band of electors was easily manipulated by a party leader who had the patronage of India at his command.[1] The three Presidencies were flooded with the sons and nephews of men who were lucky enough to have a seat in a town

[1] Henry Dundas, Lord Melville, had been President of the Board of Control. His impeachment for "Malversation" as Treasurer of the Navy, and acquittal on technical grounds, took place in 1806. The management of Indian affairs was practically in his hands for sixteen years ("Dict. Nat. Biog."). Mill says: "I know no advice he gave to the Government of India which was not very obvious or wrong." He died in 1811. His son, Robert Dundas, 2nd Lord Melville, was also President of the Board of Control. He was First Lord of the Admiralty at the fall of the Duke of Wellington's Ministry in 1830.

council, or a superiority in a rural district. . . . The Press was gagged in England, and throttled in Scotland. Every speech, or sermon or pamphlet, the substance of which a Crown lawyer could torture into a semblance of sedition, sent its author to the jail, the hulks, or the pillory."

Such an age could not be expected to produce civil servants possessing either capacity for office, or that high ideal of honour and true patriotism which in modern times has distinguished those who have done their country's work in India and in Egypt.

Colebrooke describes the incapacity of the magistrates under a system "which allowed the veriest dolts to be sent to India to discharge duties of the highest importance,"[1] and the fact that official posts were interchangeable, and professional training considered unnecessary, must have added to the general inefficiency of the Civil Service.

It was at this period when, under most imperfect government, England was becoming ripe for the Reform Bill of 1832, that India, under a still more imperfect rule, was ripening for still greater changes.

But the reform was not to be complete. Reform of any kind was difficult enough in a country, governed as India was by an association of men with the influence over parliament, which

[1] "Life of Elphinstone," vol. ii. p. 79.

accompanied the mere fact of their being patrons of many hundreds of profitable posts for younger sons. But maladministration had now reached breaking point.

Not only in the newly acquired provinces of Western India, but all over the Company's territory, an impalpable autocracy, soulless and bodiless, was destroying with merciless taxation the very life of the country.[1] Natives were leaving the Company's dominions for the native States, or flocking to the Presidency towns to escape the anarchy of the provinces. Rickards, in an able history of the land system,[2] published at this time, wrote: "In the three Presidencies the despotic power of the Government is in some respects controlled. The King's Courts of Justice, besides the protection afforded by their judicial acts, are wholly independent of the Government. . . . They have the power to reverse many of the decisions" (of the local Government), "and the consciousness of such power being always present and alert, will restrain many of those arbitrary proceedings which occur beyond the limits of its jurisdiction . . . these favoured spots [the Presidency towns] not being subject to so uncontrolled a power, or so grinding a system of taxation, as that which crushes every vital spark

[1] "Their (the Company's) exactions from the agricultural population were equivalent to one-half of the produce of the soil."—Col. Stanhope, India House debate, March 19, 1828.

[2] R. Rickards, "Native Life in India." Smith Elder, 1829. 2 vols.

of prosperity in the interior, have gone on to rapid improvement."

Elsewhere misgovernment was at its worst. Commerce had come to bear no relation to commerce rightly understood;[1] for ship after ship was bringing to England the produce of India's taxation, without corresponding return.

And although in no country in the world were capable men of all kinds more wanted, the Directors were refusing Englishmen permission to proceed to India without a grudgingly granted licence, or to remain without their approval; while at the pleasure of a local governor a licence-holder could be transported 15,000 miles in a sailing ship, a proceeding which in some cases involved the confiscation of his entire fortune.

Although it had been repeatedly shown that the hideous custom of burning women to death on a funeral pyre—women of nine years old and upwards[2]—could be suppressed with little risk; that the best Brahmins detested it; that it had been discountenanced by the Company's predecessors, the Mogul Government, Dutch, French, and Portuguese,[3] the crime was flourishing under the sanction of the Directors. Two thousand six hundred suttees were said to have taken place in

[1] "All commerce consists in the exchange of commodities of equal value."—W. S. Jevons, "Money," p. 83. 1878.

[2] In a debate at the India House, it was stated that children of only eight years old were sometimes burned; often under circumstances of hideous cruelty. March 22, 1827.

[3] Buxton in House of Commons, June 1823.

two Presidencies during three years, and permission for a suttee given by the Company was looked upon by the people as an "approval"[1] and even an order to carry out the sacrifice.

"Suttee is kept up," said a writer of the time, "by pretended regard for native religion, but the Company impose taxes on pilgrims and seize idols for payment of revenue."[2]

Subscribers to missionary societies were hearing with dismay that the temple of Juggernaut at Orissa was rented by the Company, who paid the priests, kept the idol in clothes, and made a revenue out of the pilgrims.[3]

The Press, which had been subject only to ordinary law under Lord Hastings, was now in Calcutta made subservient to the Company by the passing of arbitrary licensing laws.

Mr. John Adam, temporary Governor-General of Bengal, and his successor, Lord Amherst, had been persuaded to suppress the *Calcutta Journal*, an independent but well conducted newspaper, and to banish those responsible for it. In 1823 the editor, James Silk Buckingham, having shown that the appointment of the head of the Presbyterian Church, the Rev. Dr. Bryce, to a clerkship in an office for supplying the Government with pens, ink, and pounce, was not only unusual but contrary to law, was at once deported by

[1] *Bombay Courier*, October 16, 1824. *Oriental Herald*, vol. i. p. 557.
[2] *O. H.*, vol. ii. p. 71; idem., vol. xiv. p. 43.
[3] Idem., vol. xx. p. 525.

Mr. Adam.[1] A rule was then passed subjecting the whole Bengal Press to a licence, to be granted or withheld at the Governor's pleasure, and prohibiting the publication or selling of any print of which the Governor might disapprove.[2]

A further attack was made on the *Calcutta Journal* after Lord Amherst's arrival. Some allusion had again been made to Bryce's pluralities, but the editor was now a half-caste, and could not be transported without trial. A sub-editor, Arnot, therefore, was imprisoned; and though released at once on applying to the King's Court, was again seized by the order of the Government, transported in the *Fame*[3] by a circuitous route to England, and though kept a prisoner, charged for the expenses of his long voyage. A vindictive sentence—the captains of no less than three ships sailing directly for England having offered Arnot a free passage—while the captain of the *Fame* was a personal friend of Arnot's enemy, Bryce.

The *Calcutta Journal* was then suppressed until a son-in-law of a member of Council accepted the editorship, together with Buckingham's house, and a salary of £1000 a year.

Buckingham appealed to Directors and Parliament against such tyranny; but it was many years

[1] Mr. Adam was by nature a benevolent, well-intentioned man, and convinced that he was doing his duty.

[2] The *Edinburgh Review* was said to have been among the prints disallowed.

[3] The *Fame* was on its way to Bencoolen to call for Sir Stamford Raffles. It was burned at sea. See chapter viii.

before he obtained as compensation an annual pension of £200, although a committee of the House of Commons decided in his favour in 1834.

Extravagance meantime and mismanagement, war with Burma, and the universal thirst for gold, were so impoverishing the country that in 1827, at the time of Lord Amherst's departure, the annual deficit amounted to more than a million sterling.

Men there were in the East India Company who, against their own interest, tried to stem this flood of selfishness. And the term "Company" must, of course, be understood to mean only the majority of East India Company officials, and of those who used their votes either as directors or proprietors of India stock.

In the minority were Sir Charles Forbes, Joseph Hume, and Rickards.

Head of a great mercantile house in Bombay, Sir Charles Forbes had made a fortune in India—had spent it in India for the good of India—and the name of the wise and benevolent merchant will be remembered by Indians when the names of many governors are forgotten.[1]

Forbes alone among Europeans had been able to borrow from the natives money to support Sir Arthur Wellesley's campaign. But now, Tory though he was, a sense of justice and right made him an ardent advocate of reform.

[1] See chapter iv.

In the House of Commons (in 1825) he contended that the conduct of the Government in India loudly called for the interposition of Parliament—that things could not be allowed to remain as they were; that natives were continually imprisoned without trial, and without hope of appeal; that he knew of a rajah who had been confined for fifteen years, "whose only offence was that he was beloved by his subjects"; that though an unrestricted Press was undesirable, the present restrictions were "absurd and useless."

Joseph Hume, a man who would answer well to Sydney Smith's description of a "manifold" man,[1] had been at the same time an efficient army surgeon, interpreter, paymaster, and postmaster to the forces in the Mahratta war. Like Sir C. Forbes, intimately acquainted with the natives and originally a supporter of the Company's government, his love of good management and order made him detest the increasing extravagance, waste, and arbitrary incapacity of the Chartered Company. With Sir Charles Forbes he held that nothing tended more to the promotion of good government, to the progress of knowledge and morality than the legitimate liberty of the Press;[2] but that "now no one could speak his sentiments in India without running a risk of being deported," that the system of intimi-

[1] "The meaning of an extraordinary man is that he is eight men, not one man" (Sydney Smith).

[2] India House debate, December 22, 1825.

dation had been "carried to a monstrous excess," that "proscription had followed proscription," and that the despotism exercised by the Indian Government was unexampled in English history.[1]

Robert Rickards, once on the Council of Bombay, had years before sacrificed his position in order to protest against the oppressive trade of the Company, and the high rate of the land revenue. The Company had requested him to resign his membership of the Council; but before leaving Bombay he had been entertained at a public dinner in consideration of his "great talents and eminent public worth."

In Parliament his exertions now helped to procure the abolition of the exclusive trade of the Company to Indian ports. In one of his parliamentary speeches Rickards proved conclusively that, save during a single exceptional year, the revenues of India were more than equal to all expenses in war and peace, and that the Indian debt was due to the Company's trade.

In 1829 he published an important work on India, showing clearly that twenty-one million sterling were annually drawn from the labour of an impoverished people "by as grinding a system of taxation as ever was inflicted on the human race."[2]

By a strange irony of fate, one of the three

[1] House of Commons debate, May 13, 1825.
[2] Rickards' "India," vol. i. Smith & Elder.

rare brethren, of whom Sydney Smith and Percy (Bobus) Smith are the best known, was a Company's judge in Calcutta at this time, and though his position must have been even more unenviable than that of a King's Judge, and though the Company in a panic suspended him for mentioning the fact that their charter might not be renewed, Courtenay Smith maintained his moral independence; and when the Governor-General (Lord Amherst)[1] and the Council of Calcutta were known to be in favour of allowing the miserable rite of widow burning to continue, Courtenay Smith, who knew and understood the natives, expressed fearlessly a deliberate opinion "that the toleration of the practice of suttee" was "a reproach to our government," and that "the entire and immediate abolition of it would be attended with no sort of danger."[2] Mr. Harrington, member of the Council, Mr. Gordon Forbes, judge of the Calcutta Circuit Court, Sir C. Forbes, Joseph Hume, and many others competent to give an opinion, were of the same mind, and it is impossible on reading the letters written at the time not to come to the

[1] It was said, no doubt with truth, that Lord Amherst declared that if he had to begin his career again, he would be more independent of the Council, and "act a very different part to that which he had taken in this as in other matters."—*O. H.*, vol. ii. p. 345.

[2] The Company's answer to Courtenay Smith's Minute was: "The Governor-General in Council cannot concur in the policy . . . of the measure proposed . . . and he is of opinion that the authoritative interposition of government with a view to abolish the right of suttees, either in the manner recommended by Mr. Smith, or by the adoption of partial measures . . . would produce very serious consequences." —*O. H.*, vol. xv. p. 409.

conclusion that Courtenay Smith and those on his side were right; and that Lord William Bentinck's most difficult tasks, requiring the highest courage throughout his Governor-Generalship, lay in his dealings, not with natives, but with Europeans.[1]

As was to be expected from his independence of thought and speech Courtenay Smith was "cut" by Calcutta society. But the following extract from a letter written at the time shows that at last he had his reward:—

". . . To illustrate the invidious construction put on a fearless and upright line of conduct, I shall only instance the case of Mr. Courtenay Smith, brother of the late Advocate-General, Percy Smith, and of the Rev. Sydney Smith, who incurred the hatred and bitterest invectives of all his brother civilians, for presuming to consider the natives entitled to redress, and protection from extortion, tyranny, and insult. Mr. Smith was in consequence scarcely visited by any European gentleman; his character was represented in the vilest colours; he was obliged to fight a duel; but, notwithstanding this, the Government acknow-

[1] One of the many letters to Indian papers brings home to us vividly both the brutality of the custom and the absence of any deeply rooted religious feeling connected with it. The writer witnessed a suttee in 1823. The fire was burning so slowly that the wretched woman could not endure it, and escaped. Her relations carried her back, and held her down till they were driven away by the heat. The poor woman then escaped to the river, where her friends tried to drown her; but on appealing to some Englishmen she was rescued and taken to the hospital, the crowd in the meantime making no remonstrance nor disapproving of the action of the Europeans (*Bombay Courier*, October 4, 1823). Other instances are given in which the wretched woman was taken back and held down by pieces of timber.

ledged his zeal, talents, and integrity; and although, in pretended vindication of its own dignity, it has more than once suspended him from all employ, for the too warm and unqualified declaration of his sentiments respecting the interests of the public, yet he has been again restored to high appointments.[1] Wherever his name is mentioned it is with respect and praise; the natives speak gratefully of his patient investigations, just decisions, his urbanity, his open intercourse with the natives of all orders. . . .

"Never did I hear a whisper of himself or his servants being accessible to bribes; yet of many I have heard it who are deemed in European society. . . ."

Colonel Robison, too, of the 24th Regiment, met with still harsher treatment. He had written a letter to the *Calcutta Journal* (May 16, 1822), to say that the former free Press had done more to check abuses of power, foul play, flogging, illegal trading, cheating, than all the regulations of the Bengal Code. For this he was dismissed from his command, ordered out of the country, forced to make a long journey through unhealthy districts in the hot season, and died on his way home.

But the year 1833 was approaching, and with it the expiration of the Company's charter, and louder became the voices of those who cried that

[1] His case was brought before the House of Commons by Mr. Brougham, and before the India House by Mr. Stanhope and Sir Charles Forbes.

the time had come for a stronger hand to take command of India. As traders, as conquerors, the Company had done a great work. They had subdued kingdoms; they had carried the name of England through the East. As rulers they had failed.

And now clouds were gathering on their horizon, and a coming change—possibly a forced abandonment of their guardianship—was felt to be near. Their day of reckoning had come. Silk Buckingham, editor of the *Calcutta Journal*, whom the Company had banished and tried to ruin; Sir Charles Forbes, who had spent his fortune for the good of the India he loved; Joseph Hume, and Rickards, in the House of Commons, and the short-lived King's Judges in the Presidency towns, were their Eumenides.

Both Canning and Wynn, President of the Board of Control, admitted that the management of India was defective; and early in 1827, in the House of Lords, Lord Lansdowne, at the close of a speech, stated that "the future system of government by which the affairs of India were to be managed was one for which the Legislature must prepare itself, the present one being inadequate to advance the interests, intelligence, and happiness of the millions subjected to our sway."

Liverpool merchants were at once on the alert for the opening of the China trade; Manchester, Birmingham, and Leeds prepared to trade with the interior of India; while many fervently hoped that England herself would at last take charge of her great empire in the East.

But the wheels of great changes move slowly—the pathway is full of obstruction; and the great reforms of Lord William Bentinck postponed for a quarter of a century the greatest reform of all. The French proverb was in this case reversed, and "the good" became the "enemy" of "the best." So in 1833 the Company, with its monopoly gone, obtained a renewed charter and a slightly lengthened lease of life.

India's time had not yet come—that Time of Transition often linked to Disaster—as we see it in the change of dynasties, in the expansion of nations, in the growth of wider and wiser religion, throughout the great world, as in the microcosm man—the birth-throes preceding a better tomorrow.

And it was destined that the tragedy of our interference in Afghanistan, and the greater tragedy of our blindness to the coming sepoy rebellion, were to be enacted before, in mourning and distress of nations, India's new day dawned.

CHAPTER VII

The third Mahratta war and its results—The Pindarees—Mountstuart Elphinstone—His settlement of the Deccan, 1818-19—Governor of Bombay—His great literary and social qualities, diplomatic skill, and Oriental profusion—His fatal love of popularity—Visit to the Deccan—Optimistic report on the condition of the country—Revelations of the official report of the administration of Bombay, 1893—Case of Narroba—His bequest to Bombay.

On the western side of India the Mahratta states, long coveted by the Bombay Government, had in 1818 all become territories or dependencies of the Company. The Peshwa, the Company-supported head of the Mahratta confederacy, had in his turn been at war with, and had been conquered by the Company. Poona, his capital in the Deccan, had been taken with but little bloodshed by Sir Lionel Smith,[1] and the Peshwa's country had been added to the Presidency of Bombay.

The war which led to these results—the last of the Mahratta wars—began as a campaign against the Pindarees.

The Pindarees were wandering freebooters, who plundered at large over wide tracts of country. Mounted on good horses, accompanied by women and children, and carrying with them

[1] See page 50.

lances and cooking-pans, they must—allowing for the difference in the animals they rode and the face of the earth over which they roamed—have had much in common with the Tuareg of the Sahara, and the chiefs of India paid them backsheesh, as the Arab traders still pay the Tuareg, or as Highlanders paid Rob Roy.

Descendants, many of them, of small land-owners driven from their homes by Mahometan exaction, they were recruited in later times from men of the same class, whose estates had been sold under the same exactions, enforced with greater energy by the Company. Not that the Company was entirely to blame for this. The Land Tax, with its rapacious "collections," was found already existing in India. But the "collectors" of the Chartered Company, under pressure from home, aware that the "proprietors" and "directors" in London expected large dividends on their India stock, allowed the middleman—sometimes the known villain of the community—to tax in his own way, until land-owners and peasants alike were ruined. As Rickards[1] pointed out, "it was officially certified that owners of estates of which the annual land tax amounted to £187,500, had in despair abandoned their property from inability to pay the over-assessment. Thousands of landed proprietors have been driven by the zeal of the

[1] Rickards, "India," 1829, vol. i. pp. 146, 573.

Company's collectors to relinquish patrimonies more cherished than life itself." And "in Madras many districts into which a settlement had been introduced, land put up for sale for arrears of taxes found no purchasers at any price." And so the Pindarees and Dacoits found their recruits among the ruined landowners and peasants of the Company's dominions.

In all ages the freebooter's life has been a refuge for the disinherited man. Each Esau outwitted by a Jacob becomes an outlaw. Hating the laws by which he has been deprived of his inheritance, he lives by the sword, and serves his brother while he exacts his ransom. Until at last the cunning of those who supplanted him, the growth of the resources, good and bad, of civilisation, the knitting together of the very ends of the earth by undreamed-of magic, leave the Ishmaelite no place of rest.

Though freebooters, the Pindarees were countenanced by Mahratta chiefs, and it was known by the Company's agents that war with them would bring on war with the Mahrattas, and end in the annexation of the territory most convenient to Bombay, and in the making of new arrangements with Scindia and Holkar.

To quote from Kaye's "Life of Metcalfe"[1]: "It was determined that at the commencement of the cold season in 1817, war should be declared

[1] Vol. i. p. 456.

against the Pindarees. . . . No neutrality on the part of the Mahratta states was to be permitted. They were to be called upon to operate with us against the Pindarees; and perhaps the expectation entertained that some reluctance would embroil us with the states in such a manner as to make new distributions of their territory, was not much unlike a hope. . . . It was hard to say who would not come within the scope of the chastisement we were preparing. Preparation on a large scale was made."

The Peshwa did as he was ordered, and collected troops, who soon threatened the British Resident and burned the empty Residency, and war began at its appointed time.[1] The British fought with their usual courage. The Peshwa was routed, Scindia forced to sign an agreement with the Company; the Rajah of Nagpore and Holkar were beaten, and the Peshwa was eventually taken prisoner.

The Pindarees were destroyed. New and more advantageous treaties could be enforced on almost all the Mahratta states. Treasure was taken for the Company's shareholders, and the Poona territories were at once absorbed into the Company's dominions.

Mountstuart Elphinstone, British Resident at Poona, was now made Commissioner of the newly

[1] The chapters "Trinbukjee" and "Kirkee" in Colebrooke's "Life of Elphinstone" throw light on this period.

conquered territory, with full authority over all civil and military offices; and he issued a proclamation that the country would in future be held by the Company; that "all property real and personal" would be secure; that only a "moderate revenue" would be collected, and that "cultivation of the soil would be encouraged." A supposed conspiracy was dealt with promptly by him, and the reputed leaders, Brahmins of high rank, were blown from guns.[1] "British rule was established with rapidity and apparent ease,"[2] and if we judge only by official letters, of which Elphinstone was an accomplished writer, the settlement was conducted with wisdom and liberality, and the ungrateful country of the Deccan entered on a period of unusual prosperity.

In 1819, in order that he should continue his superintendence of the conquered country, Elphinstone was appointed by the directors, Governor of Bombay.

Mountstuart Elphinstone was a man of great social qualities, profuse in entertainment, generous to friends, and possessed of both diplomatic skill and literary ability. He had found time, with the legal help at his disposal, to prepare a useful code

[1] Mr. J. S. Cotton mentions that Elphinstone was not the first, as has been stated, to introduce this form of punishment into British territory. It had been adopted by Sir Hector Munro in 1764, from the Mahrattas.

[2] Forrest, "Mountstuart Elphinstone," p. 57.

of laws; and to cultivate both European and Oriental literature. Lord Albemarle speaks of his conversational power;[1] and Bishop Heber, when his guest, was overwhelmed with Elphinstone's "unremitting kindness and splendid hospitality, and the bishop's warm testimonial to his hospitable host given originally in Heber's journal is known to readers of any "Life of Elphinstone." "He possessed," said Heber,[2] "great activity of body and mind, remarkable talent for, and application to public business, a love of literature and . . . almost universal information. . . . He was one of the ablest men, possessing a degree of popularity, as well as an intimate knowledge of every person within the Government which I never saw before, except in the Duke of Richelieu."

Elphinstone even impressed the gentle bishop with his devotion to the Church, with the lowness of taxation in the country, and almost convinced him of the expediency of abolishing the freedom of the Press, and adopting "decided and vigorous measures" in dealing with it.

His biographer, Colebrooke, has written his life with biographical enthusiasm; and my friend Mr. J. S. Cotton places his name first among the "rulers of India."

Elphinstone's great attributes, like those of

[1] "Fifty Years of My Life," G. T. Keppel, 1876.
[2] Heber's "Journal," iii. 132.

his successor Malcolm, and unlike in every essential point those of Lord William Bentinck—soon to transform for ever our rule in India—appealed at once to the Anglo-Indian public of the day; and the amiable weakness of character, omitted by biographers, but always there—his great love of applause—served only, in a man of his ability, to feed his popularity. But it led him, as will be seen, into methods too clever to be fair. It caused a loss of that scrupulousness in word and deed which has happily been an attribute of most great Englishmen. It tempted him to support the actions, however doubtful, of all friends and subordinates; to overtax for the supposed commercial interests of the Company the poorer natives of the Deccan; to be as lavishly generous with the wealth of the country as with his own; and to encourage a love of profusion and extravagance, public and private, at a time of India's greatest need.

Some allowance must be made for the difficulties of the task Elphinstone had set himself. It was no easy thing to be Governor of Bombay, with its newly annexed states; to take all available treasure from the country in order to please directors and proprietors of Indian stock; to make and reward many friends; to stand well with all parties; and at the same time to be fair to those whose voices, after all, England might never hear.

Some light is thrown on Elphinstone's character by an entry in his diary,[1] when during this settlement of the Deccan he was appointed Governor of Bombay:—

"If I go to Bombay, I must not hope to be near so happy as I have been here. The climate will certainly not agree with me. . . . The society will be new and awkward to me; lawyers, merchants, sailors, instead of officers whom I am used to, and with whose ideas I sympathise; I shall not be able to keep up the constant entertainments I have here, even on a much more limited scale. I shall exceed my means. . . . I shall have the constant occurrence of business with which I am ignorant; I shall have all the trammels of established custom, and the restraints of English law, and the odium of keeping up economy here and of occasioning expense in Leadenhall Street.[2] . . . One honourable path to popularity is to attend to public claims in the distribution of patronage. . . . Another is not to court popularity directly; but to aim at the esteem of the public by study and able conduct."

Much of Elphinstone's strength and weakness is shown in this entry.

A year or two later, Silk Buckingham, writing of him said: "He has the merit of great

[1] Colebrooke's "Life of Elphinstone," vol. ii. p. 39.
[2] India House.

talents and many social virtues; but the great blemish in his public character appears to have been that, while professing the utmost regard for freedom and liberal opinions and affecting to relieve the Press of Bombay from a censorship, he was acting in direct opposition to his professions, supporting Mr. Adam in his restrictions at Bengal, and exercising an influence over the Press at Bombay quite as great as an acknowledged censorship, and suffering it to be used for the purpose of bringing the only authority which existed as a check upon the abuse of his own, namely the King's Court, into contempt."

And again: "There can be no doubt that Mr. Elphinstone has more talent and more knowledge than Sir John Malcolm. Mr. Elphinstone's abilities and attainments are of the very highest order; but he is himself a very striking instance of how little these contribute, unaccompanied by wisdom, to the formation of a great man. Acted upon by surrounding circumstances, rather than referring to permanent principles, and consulting the convenience of those around him, rather than following the dictates of his own judgment, he has committed the same sort of inconsistencies as Sir John Malcolm." [1]

Arrived at Bombay, Elphinstone put himself

[1] *O. H.*, vol. xii. p. 326. Sir J. Malcolm's name had been connected with the Mahratta states for many years. See chapter xiv.

into the hands of Mr. Warden, a member of the Council and proprietor of two local newspapers, and created additional posts with salaries attached to them, to which he appointed during his pleasure servants of the Company. Warm-hearted and generous to his friends, and loyally supporting members of the Civil Service in their dealings with the natives, he entertained with Oriental profusion and splendour. All men spoke well of him.

The Commissioner who succeeded Elphinstone continued the management of the Deccan on the lines laid down by his chief, and Elphinstone himself made visits of inspection—one of them in 1822–23, lasting five months; but not much is to be learned from his diary during his visit. "The journal," Colebrooke tells us, "is a record of sport, and of the air and climate of the Deccan." "I have had," he says, "pleasant society and abundance of amusement, and I go (to Bombay) to dull formal parties among strangers."

During the whole of Elphinstone's governorship there was profound peace in that part of India, and nothing to interfere with a just settlement of the conquered provinces.

His report on that "settlement," a volume containing much information and irreproachable sentiments, was sent home. In it Elphinstone states his belief that there would be no further trouble, though he regrets the disaffection and ingratitude of all classes in the Peshwa's territory, even of the agricultural class, which, he says, had been so "lightly assessed."

"The general disposition of the agricultural class," he writes, "is in favour of tranquillity. They are the first sufferers by wars or by assemblages of banditti; and as they were by no means favoured under the Brahmin government, they cannot, whatever pride they may take in Mahratta independence, seriously wish for its restoration. But even among them there are many drawbacks on the gratitude we might expect from our light assessments and protection. . . . The village authorities, who lose power by our care to prevent exactions, have probably influence sufficient to injure us with the very people in whose cause we incur their odium."

While Elphinstone's report was being read with approval by the Directors at home, the following letters written by Englishmen in the Deccan to friends in England appeared in the *Globe* and *Oriental Herald*:—

Letter, dated Oct. 1824, *from a Station in the Deccan.*

"We shall have a famine all over the Deccan. Government must know it, and could soften the misery by laying out five lacs of rupees in grain; for there is plenty in the country but all getting into the hands of forestallers, and if Government came into the markets against them, many thousand poor wretches would be saved . . . but no; they

[1] *Oriental Herald*, vol. v. p. 124.

would lose, and that tells in Leadenhall Street.[1] . . . This country has been going to the dogs ever since it was conquered, and it must ever be the case under such a rapacious revenue system. In 1823 there was grain enough raised for five years' consumption; it was then of so little value that the Ryots could not realise enough to pay the Collector; but the Company insisted on cash, and the consequence was the sale of five times the usual quantity of grain . . . and now the people have neither money nor grain. God help the poor inoffensive wretches, they deserve something better."

A letter written from the Deccan in 1824, published in the *Globe* newspaper, states that those who had "got the Company into the scrape of the Burmese war begin to apprehend resistance in other quarters; but they have no occasion to be afraid of the Deccan, for the whole country is in a state of famine from two years' drought. The cattle are all dead, and the people must die also, for Government will give them no assistance; and though there is plenty of grain in the country from the over-abundant harvest of 1822, the poor wretches have no money to buy it from the forestallers. *In poverty and universal wretchedness this country has retrograded one hundred years owing to the severity of our collections in hard money, which, in consequence of the immense sums taken out of the country and sent home after the war, the poor devils really have not the means of finding*. This year they have nothing left for it but to quit the country or die. The *white* people in Bombay eat and drink much the same as usual,

[1] India House.

and I do not think you will hear much of the sufferings of the black caste, but I know you will pity them."

This letter, although anonymous, could not have been pleasant reading at the breakfast tables of "directors and proprietors," who must have waited with some anxiety for the Governor's next report.

That report, "grateful and comforting," was a lesson in diplomatic letter writing. In the account of his visit of 1825, Elphinstone says:[1]—

"A continuance of quiet . . . has reduced their (the chiefs') retinue since my last visit. Some of them were then attended by as many as fifteen hundred men with several guns; now none had more than an escort of three hundred horse, and they often rode with one attendant. These chiefs are no doubt in a much better situation than they were under the Peshwa, but they are in complete subjection to the Government. . . . General advice is sufficient to prevent great oppression [by the chiefs!] . . . The tranquillity of the country has surpassed expectation. . . . In the meantime the burdens of the people have been much lightened, and, in spite of bad seasons and redundant produce, their condition is probably much better than in the best years of the Peshwa's government."

Mr. Warden, member of Council, accompanied Elphinstone in the Deccan; and two

[1] "Life of Elphinstone," vol. ii. pp. 190–92.

years later, when the usual address given to every departing Governor was being prepared, and signatures were being obtained by Mr. Warden, the address from Europeans was made to say that Elphinstone had rendered "the unavoidable extension of British power the source of unknown felicity to the inhabitants of the conquered countries;" and the address for the native chiefs was made to say that "until you became Commissioner in the Deccan never had we been enabled to appreciate correctly the invaluable benefits which the British dominion is calculated to diffuse throughout the whole of India."

And so for half a century many believed that the Company's rule in the Deccan had been one of which Englishmen could be proud.

Our feeling of indignation that these plausible reports of the "light burdens," "bettered condition," and "unknown felicity of the conquered countries" should have been sent to England from a misgoverned land, becomes one of shame when we read a more complete account of the Company's rule in the Peshwa's country, given to the world by an authority from which unfortunately there can be no appeal. In the "Official Report of the Administration of the Bombay Presidency," published by the British Government in 1893,[1] we read :—

[1] "Official Report of the Administration of the Bombay Government, 1892–93," p. 76.

"The revenue survey of the Bombay Presidency has been in progress for a period of fifty-seven years. . . . When the present survey was commenced the Deccan had been for seventeen years under British rule. In that space of time it had been reduced from a comparatively prosperous condition to the extreme of impoverishment and exhaustion. Two causes had been mainly instrumental in bringing about this state of things: one was the continuous fall in the money value of agricultural produce" (all available money had been taken by the Company's agents!) . . . "the other was a settlement effected in connection with the previous survey. This had been carried out under the direction of Mr. Pringle of the Civil Service.[1] His settlement attempted to fix the Government demand at about half (55 per cent.) of the net produce, and therefore entailed not only estimates of the yield of various crops, but of the cost of cultivation.

"The execution of the different operations . . . was entrusted entirely to native agency without either the experience or integrity needed for the task, and at a subsequent period the results obtained were found to be nearly worthless. . . . From the outset it was found impossible to collect anything approaching the full revenue. In some districts not one-half could

[1] Under Elphinstone.

be realised. Things now went rapidly from bad to worse. Every year brought its addition to the accumulated arrears of revenue. The state of confusion in the accounts . . . was taken advantage of by native officials to levy contributions for themselves. . . . Every effort, lawful and unlawful, was made to get the utmost out of the wretched peasantry, who were subjected to torture, in some instances cruel and revolting beyond description, if they would not or could not yield what was demanded. Numbers abandoned their homes and fled into neighbouring native states. Large tracts of land were thrown out of cultivation, and in some districts no more than a third of the cultivable area remained in occupation. . . . At the end of 1835 an examination and correction of Mr. Pringle's survey was ordered."

The administration of the Dutch in Java never sank to a lower level!

Of all nations on the earth that one most capable of dealing justly and wisely with a subject race was—as she herself has the splendid strength to admit—for seventeen years—during Mountstuart Elphinstone's and Sir John Malcolm's governorship—depopulating the Deccan; and that not in the time-honoured game of war, but in a peaceful "settlement"—carried out in the spirit of Shylock, and recorded in the language of Pecksniff!

But the good as well as the evil that men do lives after them; and when in thirty years' time natives whose parents had experienced these merciless methods of providing high dividends for the Company's shareholders joined the notorious Nana Sahib, the disappointed heir of the Peshwas, in his orgy of hate, and drank to the very dregs the cup of revenge their gods so unexpectedly held out to them; when a new generation of innocent English men, women, and children suffered horribly for the mistakes of those who had gone before—in that dark hour the Presidency towns of India, which for half a century had known true English justice, administered by independent Englishmen, stood by us in our need.

An action which arose out of this settlement of the Deccan, and came before the King's Court in 1825, may be mentioned in this place. It was brought by the heir of Narroba, who had been a Mahratta banker of importance, and private banker to the Peshwa before the war—for the restoration of his property.

Narroba's house had been broken into, and treasure seized by the Collector, Lieut. H. Dundas Robertson, some months after Poona had been in the possession of the Company, and after civil law had been established.

The King's Court of Bombay returned a verdict against Elphinstone and Robertson for the restoration of the property with interest to Narroba's heir.

The case was referred to the Privy Council; and in 1831, when Elphinstone was in England, and the two judges, West and Chambers, in their graves, the judgment was reversed. It was decided by Lord Tenterden that as some forts a hundred and twenty miles from Poona, held by refractory Arabs, had not surrendered in 1818, the country was still at war, and the King's Court had therefore no jurisdiction.

The account of it by Elphinstone, and the report lately published by the State Trials Committee,[1] give, as might be expected, very different aspects of the case. Elphinstone wrote:[2]—

"About the end of the war a Governor of one of the Peshwa's forts, who was also one of his treasurers, surrendered his fort, but broke his capitulation, and ran away with a good deal of treasure. The hue and cry was raised by the officer commanding, and by the Government of Bombay. The fugitive Governor came to Poona, where I was Commissioner, and the Collector, Captain Robertson, seized him, found a good deal of treasure in his possession, and accounts that showed he had still more to account for. After paying a part of this he was released, and

[1] "Reports of State Trials," New Series, London, 1889, vol. ii. p. 379–458.

[2] Colebrooke's "Life," vol. ii. p. 180.

he continued to claim sometimes part and sometimes the whole of the property as his own. On his death he constituted a Bombay banker his executor. This man prosecuted the Company. . . . The counsel[1] for the plaintiff declaimed against the Government in the most unmeasured terms, and promised to expose the misgovernment of the Company.[2] . . . The Chief Justice, though he observed great caution, showed so evident a wish to criminate the Government and its agents, that there can be no doubt that many more suits will be filed. I do not know any vulnerable points in the management of the Deccan, but there must in all new settlements be many faults."

Elphinstone wisely adds: "This letter" is to be "used with discretion, more with a view to defence than attack."

The following is an abstract of the evidence given before the King's Court, and published in "State Trials":[3]—

In 1818 Lieut. Henry Dundas Robertson was made by Elphinstone Collector and Magistrate at Poona, and also appointed to the political and judicial departments. Elphinstone then issued the following proclamation:—

"To the inhabitants of the Peshwa's former

[1] Mr. Morley. [2] An exaggeration, to judge from the report.
[3] Vol. ii. p. 379. The evidence occupies more than fifty columns. Great pains were taken by the Chief Justice to arrive at the truth. Sir Lionel Smith, as can be seen by Lady West's "Diary," came to Bombay to give evidence, and the trial lasted many days. See Lady West's "Diary," p. 259.

dominions. . . . the country will be held by the Honourable Company; the revenue will be collected for the Government; but all property, real and personal, will be secured, . . . officers shall be forthwith appointed to collect a regular and moderate revenue, . . . and to administer justice."

Thereupon Narroba surrendered to Colonel Prother the Mahratta fort of Rajpur, which he was holding, came to Poona and lived for two months under British protection. No evidence of "breach of capitulation" was given at the trials, except the confessions extorted under a mild form of torture; nor of any "hue and cry." It was even pleaded, on behalf of Robertson, though not proved, that Narroba was sent from Rajpur to Poona in custody.

On the 17th of July, some months after the proclamation, Lieut. Robertson ordered Narroba's house to be broken into. Narroba was found sitting with his wife and children, and was brought to Lieut. Robertson. Twenty-eight bags of gold mohur and venetians found in the house were also carried away, and every endeavour was made, though without success, to induce Narroba to confess that the money taken from him was the property of the Peshwa. Narroba was then sent to the common jail. Elphinstone, on being referred to, decided that the money should remain with his friend, Lieut. Robertson.[1]

[1] Who claimed five per cent. of it as his own share

Narroba, who at first refused food, was kept three months in jail in solitary confinement, during which time attempts were continually made to force an admission from him that the money seized was the property of the State; and he was promised his liberty if he would sign a statement to that effect, and also contribute five more bags of venetians to those already taken.

At last, after three months of imprisonment and discomfort, Narroba was induced to sign a document handing over "State" money "to the Honourable Company," and submitting to "whatever their Honours may please to order to be done to him."

Narroba's head clerk experienced even harsher treatment. He was confined in another part of the jail; and on his asserting that the money seized belonged to Narroba, a blacksmith was sent for; the wretched clerk was put in irons, and was kept in solitary confinement for two months, when the required admission was made, and the required document signed.

The King's Court rejected on the ground of "duress" both the promise and admission wrung from Narroba and his clerk, and as no further evidence could be obtained that Narroba was not the rightful owner, gave a judgment against Elphinstone and Robertson for the restoration of the treasure. This judgment, as has been shown, was reversed, and thus more than a hundred thousand pounds, of which at least five thousand was claimed by Lieutenant Robertson, was extracted from the distressful country of the Deccan.

Shortly after gaining his case in India Narroba's heir died, and left by will a lac of rupees towards liberating the imprisoned debtors of Bombay.[1]

[1] From advertisement columns of *Bombay Gazette*—No notice was taken by the local papers of this generous bequest.

CHAPTER VIII

Ceylon : a contrast to India—Sir Alexander Johnstone's wise administration : slavery renounced ; loyalty of natives—Sir Stamford Raffles in Java—The island ceded to the Dutch—Rise of Singapore—Cession of Sumatra—Sir S. Raffles' brilliant administration : his natural history collections—Burning of the *Fame*.

It is a relief to turn for one moment from the Government of Bombay to that of Ceylon and Singapore. Ceylon had been fortunate both in its Governor, Sir Thomas Maitland, and in its Chief Justice, Sir Alexander Johnstone.

Johnstone, inspired by an interview with Charles James Fox, had his mind set, early in life, on improving our rule in the East. In 1805 he had been appointed member of Council, and Chief Justice of Ceylon ; and in a few years' time through his influence that island was in the van of Indian reform.

Three things must have contributed to this result—the comparatively long life of the Chief Justice, the sympathy of the Governor, and the fact that Ceylon was a Crown colony, not a Company's possession.

And so, under Sir A. Johnstone's guidance, religious liberty was established, a system of universal education was set on foot, Europeans were freely permitted to settle, public employment was opened to natives, and, more important still, natives were tried by a jury of their own countrymen.

Innovations such as these could not have been possible had not the judge himself gone to England, and laid his plans before the Government of the day. The result is seen in a letter written by the Chief Justice to Mr. Wynn, and published in the Indian papers in 1827. "The old system of administering justice," the letter points out, "was dilatory, expensive, and unpopular. Natives had no interest in a system they did not understand, and in which they had no share; consequently they attached no importance to veracity." Sir A. Johnstone thereupon consulted the chief Buddhist and Brahmin priests, prepared a scheme of law reform, left for England, and returned with a new charter, granting to every native the right to be tried by jurymen of his own caste, chosen by lot.

The native jurymen thus deciding matters of fact, and the justices matters only of law, one judge was able to do the work formerly done by three. Native jurymen, from knowing the degree of credit to be given to each witness, decided promptly, and trials which had formerly lasted a month were despatched in a day. The natives became educated in English law. Excellent magistrates were made out of former native jurymen; the efficiency of the courts increased;

prisoners and witnesses were relieved from the hardship of protracted sessions; and a sum of ten thousand pounds a year was saved in the expenses of the Court.

One of the results of Sir Alexander Johnstone's wise legislation was that, in 1816, the natives of all castes resolved of their own accord to renounce slavery. And in 1820, Sir Hardinge Giffard, Sir A. Johnstone's successor, found that the people had changed "from revolt and disaffection" to "attachment and loyalty."

Our invaluable possession, the City of Singapore, sprang into life at this time. Few probably of the thousands who visit the Zoological Society's Gardens in Regent's Park are aware how great was the man who looks down on them in marble from the wall of the Lion House. Founder of the Zoological Gardens in London, Thomas Stamford Raffles was also founder of the city which commands the Eastern seas. A clerk in the India House—where Charles Lamb was still leaning against the desk like "Philomel against a thorn"—Raffles had been sent by the Directors to Penang, thence to Java—half conquered, and wholly misgoverned by the Dutch. Here he had reorganised finance, abolished forced labour, and introduced trial by jury; and just at the time when by his personal influence the rest of the island had been brought under British control, Raffles was summarily recalled, and Java in all its newly acquired prosperity handed over to the Dutch.

In 1818 Raffles found himself Governor of Bencoolen, in Sumatra, where there was little security for either life or property. Here, as in Java, he showed his extraordinary capacity for successful benevolent administration. He made friends with the chiefs, organised the police, emancipated the Company's slaves, and suppressed the Company's gambling houses, established schools, imported missionaries, explored the island, but tried in vain to persuade the Company to unite their settlements in the Straits. The Directors, who mistrusted equally his energy and his philanthropy, denounced Raffles and all his works.

But the Dutch in the meantime were occupying every port in the Straits; and as England was being shut out of the Eastern seas, Raffles himself set off in a small boat for India, and though shipwrecked at the mouth of the Ganges, reached Calcutta, and obtained permission from the Governor-General, Lord Hastings, to secure a harbour for the Company on the way to China.

The Dutch had no claim whatever to Singapore. And so—for about the price of a small house in Piccadilly—Singapore was purchased; and the Union Jack floated over the harbour.

The Dutch protested and threatened. The Company's Governor at Penang refused help of any kind; and pressure was put upon Lord

Hastings to counter-order the occupation of the port if its transfer were still incomplete. The letter from Lord Hastings arrived some six weeks too late.

But while the fate of Singapore was hanging in the balance, the administrative genius of Raffles was doing its work. Though a servant of the Company, Raffles abolished monopoly; and Singapore became at once a free port to all ships. Magistrates were appointed irrespective of colour or nationality. Native chiefs were invited to assist in legislation, on the condition that no regulation should be inconsistent with British law. Gambling houses were prohibited. Slavery was suppressed; and respectable citizens, of all religions and nations, admitted as jurors. This, too, at a time when even in England no Deist, Mohammedan or Jew could serve on a jury. Small wonder that Raffles was mistrusted by the Company.

Singapore sprang into prosperity. And a seaside village of a hundred and fifty natives—a nest of pirates—became within a year a law-abiding prosperous community with a rapidly increasing trade.

But that Singapore to-day is not a Dutch Colony, and that the key to China seas is safely kept in a British Admiral's pocket, thanks are due to Sir Stamford Raffles, not to the Directors of the Company.

For five years Singapore was governed from Bencoolen. It was then decided that Sumatra should be handed over to the Dutch, and Raffles left for England. He sailed from Sumatra on February 2, 1824—the first anniversary of Sir E. West's arrival in Bombay—taking with him an enormous Natural History collection, made chiefly by himself. His ship, which resembled a Noah's Ark, never reached its destination. Its loss was described by an eye-witness in a letter to the India *Gazette*. The letter, written by a Dr. Tylor, appears to have escaped the notice of Sir S. Raffles' biographers. It is worth recording.[1]

"About 9 P.M. a red light was seen gleaming faintly, then vividly, over the atmosphere in the direction where the *Fame* had last been observed. At 10 P.M. all the boats were despatched in the direction of the supposed fire. At 2 A.M., on the 3rd, a column of clear white light[2] shot up into the atmosphere and illuminated the whole shore of Bencoolen, and then all was darkness. At 11 A.M. boats were seen filled with people far out at sea. As a boat reached the shore, 'Is Sir Stamford safe?' was shouted from all mouths, and 'Yes' in reply hailed with delight; and then we learned that the carelessness of the ship's steward had set the ship on fire fifty miles from

[1] The letter has been slightly abbreviated.

[2] The explosion of the magazine.

land. The fortitude of Sir Stamford alone was the means of preserving all their lives. He gave his orders with the utmost promptitude and coolness, and ordered the boats to be lowered at the critical moment, for one instant later would have been attended with total destruction.

"All on board the ship were then admitted into the boats, with only one compass, and scarcely any clothes; and they all reached Bencoolen in safety, after having been about thirteen hours at sea in two open boats. Had the current set off the land and carried them to sea, they must have been driven to Engano, where their fate would have been worse than death. Not a jot of property, with the exception of one or two small bags, has escaped the flames, and the whole of the splendid collections made by Sir Stamford Raffles and his invaluable MSS., plate and jewels have been destroyed. His total loss is estimated at £25,000. Sir Stamford Raffles wore the same clothes as those in which he had departed twenty-four hours previously, but all soiled. Lady Raffles wore a borrowed gown. The pleasure I received at seeing them rescued from destruction was inexpressible. In every face, European and Native, Hindoo and Malay, appeared to beam gladness and joy. Not a murmur of complaint escaped Sir Stamford Raffles' lips, and in reply to an address of condolence he said that his reception on landing was a complete compensation for all his losses;

that he had placed too much value on his collections, and depended too surely on his future success; that the check was necessary, and he was resigned to the will of Heaven."

Besides suffering this disaster, he had lost eight members of his family at Bencoolen since his arrival on the coast.

Nothing daunted, Raffles seems to have formed a second collection with extraordinary energy. With this he arrived safely in England, in August 1824, and with the help of Humphry Davy and others, founded the Zoological Society with its Regent's Park menagerie the following year. In a biographical notice of him, Sir Humphry Davy said, "Having lost one splendid collection by fire, he instantly commenced the formation of another; and having brought this to Europe, he made it not private, but public property."

CHAPTER IX

Arrival of Sir Charles Chambers at Bombay—Establishment of the Supreme Court at Bombay—Mortality among the King's Judges—Deportation of Mr. Fair; true cause of Elphinstone's action; a side blow at the King's Judges.

Lady West's Journal (May 1824–March 1825):—Prevalence of cholera; trials of Europeans; water famine; deaths of Sir Christopher Puller, Sir Willingham Franklin, Sir Francis Bayley, Lady Franklin; arrival of Sir Ralph Rice; murder of Mr. Thackeray; expedition to Goa; return to Bombay.

To return to affairs of Bombay. Friendship between Mr. Elphinstone and Sir E. West, strained on one hand by the Erskine testimonial, and on the other by the determination of the Recorder to be impartial in all suits between Europeans and natives, was now partly restored. Elphinstone, Lady West tells us, "courts Edward in every way,"[1] and the judge is ready to meet the Governor's advances. The prospect, too, of place among the many offices of the new Supreme Court helped to lay party spirit; and in the meantime there was always at hand, for the consolation of antagonistic Bombay society, opportunity for petty annoyance; such as sending the judge into dinner at the tail of the guests, and placing him so that when ladies left the table he should find himself between Mr. Norton, the aggressive

[1] Letter to Mrs. Lane.

Advocate-General, and some other member of the hostile faction. Still, on the whole, life at Bombay went smoothly during the spring of 1824.

On the 6th of May 1824 the ship *Duke of York*, with the second judge on board, was sighted. Sir Charles Harcourt Chambers (Fellow of Trinity College, Cambridge, and nephew of Sir Robert Chambers, Dr. Johnson's friend) was an able lawyer, and, like West, free from taint of time-service. His arrival had been anxiously expected by the Company's officials, and before his landing messages and invitations were sent to him, and attempts made to prejudice him against his brother judge—all to no purpose. Sir C. Chambers examined for himself the state of the Law Courts, and cordially supported his colleague.

On the 8th of May the Supreme Court of Bombay was "established." Oaths were taken; guns were fired; and the two judges, wisely wearing "their small wigs" on a hot May day, began at once the work of the Court.

The arrangements for the Court of Small Causes, and all the measures carried out by Sir E. West, received the approval of Sir Charles Chambers; and the newly appointed Chief Justice had the gratification of receiving letters from the President of the Board of Control in England, on his "meritorious exertion and praiseworthy conduct in regard to Mr. Erskine."

But to counterbalance this came news of the serious illness of Sir Charles Grey at Madras, and of the sudden deaths of Sir Christopher Puller at Calcutta, of Sir Willingham Franklin at Madras,[1] and of Sir Francis Bayley, two months after his arrival, at Penang—all King's Judges and friends of Sir E. West—and of Lady Franklin and her infant daughter.[2]

Meantime, as Lady West says, "the judges were to have no rest." In July 1824, during a long lawsuit, an incident occurred which ended with the banishment of Fair, editor of the *Bombay Gazette*. Sir. E. West has been credited with this severe sentence;[3] but Fair, as will be seen, was sent home by Elphinstone, not by the judges—ostensibly, because he refused to apologise to Sir Charles Chambers for misrepresentation—in reality, because the Directors had refused to renew his licence some six months before!

It appears that when the Court was sitting a young civil servant, Shaw by name, ordered a native usher to bring him pens and paper.[4] The official replied that he had been stationed where he was by the judge's orders, and could not leave, but that a sepoy would bring what was required. Thereupon Shaw struck the usher

[1] See "Diary," June 11, p. 156.
[2] "Diary," Oct. 3, p. 160, and Dec. 2, p. 161.
[3] The case is reported both in the *Bombay Gazette* and *Oriental Herald*, and gives a good idea of life at Bombay at this time.
[4] See "Diary," July 12 to 22, August 25, and Sept. 10 and 11.

a heavy blow on the temple. A writ for contempt of Court was issued against Shaw, and as a matter of course Norton, the "loud-voiced" Advocate-General, was asked by the judge to conduct the prosecution. Norton replied in his accustomed manner that he was not bound to prosecute offenders against the Court unless ordered to do so by the Governor, and that he had accepted a retainer for Mr. Shaw—thus gaining not only a fee which he would have missed, but an opportunity of attacking the judge. The trial proceeded. Shaw was found guilty, dealt with leniently by the judges, and fined one rupee.

Throughout the trial the *Bombay Gazette*, of which Mr. Warden, Member of Council, was the chief proprietor, put its own colour and made its own comments on the proceedings. To this Sir E. West called the attention of the Governor, and the Governor undertook to reprimand the editor. The latter part of the trial was presided over by Sir Charles Chambers, who wrote to Elphinstone complaining that he had been misquoted and misrepresented in the *Gazette*. As honourable men the judges themselves could not prosecute Fair in the King's Court, and act at the same time the part of plaintiff and judge.

Elphinstone upon receipt of the letter demanded from Fair an immediate and public acknowledgment of the misstatements, and an ample apology to Sir Charles Chambers. Fair offered to insert an apology in the *Gazette*, together with a report of that part of the trial which had been omitted.

The Governor replied that the apology was not sufficiently explicit, and that Fair consequently had forfeited his claim to the protection of the Government, that his licence to reside in the East Indies would be withdrawn, and that he must leave at once, or give security in 30,000 rupees to leave within three months. Fair replied that it was impossible for him to give such security. He was then handed over to the magistrate of the police, hurried on board the Company's ship *London*, and within a month of receiving the first letter from Bombay Castle shipped for England by a long sea route.

Fair fired a shot as he left Bombay and published the Governor's letters.[1]

The following extracts give the pith of the correspondence:—

Extracts from the Correspondence between the Bombay Government *and* Mr. Fair.

Bombay, *Sept.* 6, 1824.

In explanation of the circumstances that have led to my compulsory removal from this country . . . I have thought it expedient to strike off a few copies of the correspondence

[1] The whole correspondence is given in the *Oriental Herald* of the time.

that has passed between the officers of the Government and myself for distribution among my private friends. . . .

C. J. Fair.

General Department, Bombay Castle,
Aug. 13*th*, 1824.

To C. J. Fair, Esq.,
Editor of *Bombay Gazette*.

Sir,—The Governor in Council has observed with surprise the publication in the last number of the *Gazette* of a report calculated to lower the character of the Honourable the Supreme Court. In addition to the disrespectful insinuations apparent on a mere perusal of that article, he is informed by the Court that it contains many misrepresentations of the proceedings, by the omission of some passages and the insertion of others, tending altogether to give a very false impression of the spirit in which those proceedings were conducted.

If this article was prepared subsequently to the receipt by you of my letter of the 9th, it must be considered as an open defiance of the Government, and will leave the Governor in Council no choice but immediately to enforce the penalty, announced in that letter, by cancelling your licence to remain in India. . . . Although he is not prepared to proceed at once to the full extent which the case might justify, he can only exercise this forbearance on condition of an immediate and public acknowledgment of the misstatements, and an ample apology for having given them publicity.

The acknowledgment and apology must be full and explicit, and must be transmitted to the Secretary's Office within three days.—Your obed. servant,

J. Farish, *Sec. to Gov.*

Bombay Castle, *August* 19, 1824.

To C. J. Fair, Esq.

Sir,— . . . The repeated declarations of the Court that there was no intention to treat Mr. Shaw with harshness are omitted [in the *Gazette*], and the whole of the latter part of the proceedings in which he was shown particular indulgence is suppressed. The result of these omissions, together with other passages imperfectly reported, is to produce a false impression as to the temper and feelings of the Court, and this effect is still more directly attempted by an allusion to the personal demeanour of the Judge[1] on the bench; such an allusion which in all circumstances would have been disrespectful, could only have been introduced for the purpose of lowering the character of the Court, and is considered by the Governor in Council to be peculiarly reprehensible. . . . —Your obed. servant, J. FARISH, *Sec. to Gov.*

BOMBAY CASTLE, *Aug.* 24, 1824.

To C. J. FAIR, Esq.

SIR,— . . . The Governor in Council cannot discover in your replying to his desire that you would send a draft of an apology for his consideration, by requesting that he would propose one for yours, any sign of that anxiety to meet his wishes which is professed in another part of your letter. . . . The Governor in Council observes that you have in this letter acknowledged a considerable omission; and that the publication of your opinion as to the feelings of the Judge[2] was obviously neither requisite nor respectful. He is therefore at a loss to conceive on what ground you can refuse to acknowledge that your report was inaccurate, and to express your regret. . . .

The Governor in Council expects that whatever apology you make may be so explicit as to effectually remove the impression above alluded to, and he directs me to inform you, that unless such an apology is immediately transmitted to me he will proceed, without further notice, to remove you from this country.—Your most obed. servant,

J. FARISH, *Sec. to Gov.*

Bombay Gazette Office,
Aug. 25, 1824.

To J. FARISH, Esq., *Sec. to Gov.*

SIR,— . . . Having been so unfortunate as to add to the displeasure of Government in every endeavour I have hitherto made to explain the difficulty of my situation, and remove the disapprobation of the hon. Board, I shall abstain from doing more on this occasion than enclosing an apology

[1] Sir Charles Chambers. [2] Ibid.

to the effect you require, and which I am ready to publish either in an appendix to my paper, or an extra *Gazette*, if the hon. Board should so desire it. I regret extremely that it was not in my power to transmit this document so immediately as appeared to be expected by your present communication, and I can only assure you that the delay has not arisen from disrespect to the hon. the Governor in Council, or disregard of his commands.—Your most obed. servant,

C. J. Fair.

Bombay Castle, *Aug.* 28 (1824).

To C. J. Fair, Esq.

Sir,— . . . I have received instructions to inform you that the apology offered by you is entirely unsatisfactory. . . . I have, therefore, in command from the hon. the Governor in Council, to declare and notify to you, that you have in the judgment of the Governor forfeited your claim to the countenance and protection of the Government of this Presidency, and I am directed to declare to you that permission to remain in India is withdrawn from the 30th of this month; and that after the 30th of this month you will, if residing in India, be proceeded against according to law. —Your obed. servant,

J. Farish, *Sec. to Gov.*

Bombay, *Aug.* 29, 1824.

To J. Farish, Esq., *Sec. to Gov.*

Sir,— . . . I was honoured last evening with your letter advising me that the hon. the Governor in Council has been pleased to declare my licence to reside in the East Indies to be void from to-morrow. . . . To this decision of the Government I have, of course, no alternative but to submit myself without reserve; but it is of so much importance to me to know whether I am expected to embark by the first opportunity that offers, or if a reasonable period will be allowed me to settle my affairs, that I trust I shall stand excused for requesting you will have the goodness to obtain for me the necessary information on these points; in order that I may not by a longer residence in India than the hon. Board may think expedient, infringe the orders you have been directed to transmit to me. . . . —Your most obed. servant,

C. J. Fair.

Aug. 31.

To W. A. Morgan, Esq., Hon. Company's Solicitor.

Sir,—I have to acknowledge the receipt of your letter advising me of the instructions you had received from the hon. the Governor in Council . . . respecting my transmission to the United Kingdom, and proposing me certain conditions, on complying with which permission will be given me to remain in India until the 30th of November, subject however to the contingency of being obliged to quit this country before that period.

For the fulfilment of this engagement you require security in the penalty of twenty thousand rupees for myself, and ten thousand rupees for two securities, who must be inhabitants of Bombay.

It is my duty to state that the security you have thought it right to require of me is of such a nature and amount, that I feel it not only impossible to comply with it in my own person, but equally so in respect to the few friends I have at this place, and that I must in consequence prepare myself for the only other alternative left me. . . . —Your most obed., C. J. Fair.

Sept. 6, 1824.

H.C.S. *London*, Bombay Harbour.

Sir,—Following the orders of Government, and Warrants of the hon. the Governor to the Magistrate of Police, I am now a prisoner on board H.C.S. *London*. And though I have considered it desirable on every account not to offer any sort of resistance, or to raise any question of law, I should be wanting in justice to myself if I were not thus to avow my belief that the whole of the proceedings against me on this unfortunate occasion are illegal, and more particularly my transmission to the United Kingdom, in a ship not bound direct to that quarter. I desire therefore to enter my protest against these proceedings. . . . —Your most obed.,

C. J. Fair.

Elphinstone's sudden friendliness to the King's Court, his anxiety to uphold its dignity, and extraordinary harshness to the editor of a paper on the side of the Bombay Government, must have puzzled the judges. Neither Sir Edward West nor Sir Charles Chambers had demanded the deportation of Fair. In a letter written shortly afterwards from Bombay, "An Old Indian" says: "Why Mr. Elphinstone should have preferred sending the unfortunate editor home to the obvious one of requiring Mr. Warden to dismiss him, it is difficult to understand; for it is certain that Sir Charles Chambers never suggested any measures for the adoption of the Government. He merely stated the fact of the misrepresentation to the Governor, who of his own accord adopted the measure of sending Mr. Fair home."

Nor is there any evidence that an apology was insisted on by the judge.

Then there is the extraordinary silence of Warden, chief proprietor of the paper, and friend of Elphinstone. The whole proceeding remains incomprehensible until we turn to a letter in Colebrooke's "Life of Elphinstone."[1]

There Elphinstone confesses "The truth is he" [Fair] "was before" [the Shaw trial] "under orders from the Court of Directors to be sent home unless a licence arrived for him by a certain day, which had elapsed." So the true history of the banishment of Fair, like that of Elphinstone's settlement of the Deccan, only comes to light in these latter days.

[1] Vol. ii. p. 166.

It was an act of considerable diplomatic skill, not of a very high order. It is impossible, for instance, to imagine Lord William Bentinck being capable of such subtlety. Fair was sent home because Elphinstone had received an order to that effect sent out from England some months before, but Elphinstone seized the opportunity of transporting him with considerable harshness,[1] ostensibly because Sir Charles Chambers complained that the newspaper of which Fair was editor had attacked him, and misreported the proceedings of the Court.

By this piece of finesse Elphinstone was enabled to wave a rod over the Anglo-Indian Press; to appear in the light of one who magnanimously upheld the rights of those who were often opposed to him; and, at the same time, to transfer all the great odium of an unwarrantable proceeding on to the heads of the judges of the King's Court. So that even Silk Buckingham wrote of Sir Charles Chambers: "What! a British judge, sent expressly to India for the purpose of protecting individuals from tyranny . . . to ask that law be set aside, and an act of despotism exercised."

And years afterwards Colebrooke, after quoting Elphinstone's letter, concludes rather illogically: "It has been seen that one of the first acts of the Court was to appeal to the Executive to deport an unfortunate editor."[2]

[1] The harshness, nevertheless, was not quite so great as it seemed. Elphinstone's letter shows that the proprietors of the paper were ready to provide for Fair at home if he refused to apologise. Elphinstone's "Life," vol. ii.

[2] Vol. ii. p. 178.

And still further from the truth, the author of "Glimpses of Old Bombay" deliberately states that Sir Edward West himself "deported Fair."[1] So history is made!

FROM LADY WEST'S JOURNAL

May 8, 1824. Sir Charles and Lady Chambers landed yesterday. He is a plain man, and his wife was never out of Scotland till she married; . . . having been sea-sick all the way, so weak and delicate. We have also a Cousin of hers, a little child of eighteen months old, staying with us; a Mr. Hopkins (his wife died on board), two English maids—soldiers' wives—an English clerk, so that we are over full.

May 10. The Judges have been in Court, and decided the Precedence;[2] they wore their small Wigs, not becoming, but I think quite proper. They must meet every day to settle Fees, and look into business. Edward received a delightful letter from ffolkes, announcing dear Charlotte's[3] safety in the birth of a third son in December.

May 15. Lady Chambers drove out last night, and seems all the better for it; she seems very good-humoured, and pleasing, and to be delighted with our attention. I hope she will be able to see some People on Monday.

May 16. Martin West is here. He is very little grown, but has the same expression of countenance, only looking more healthy and weather-beaten, and most polite and pleasing manners; he seems to have met with universal kindness and attention at Calcutta, and everywhere.

May 20. The Small Cause Court held to-day, and Sir Charles much pleased with it, and astonished at the Barristers' presumption in finding fault with it.

May 25. Sir Charles has a smart attack of fever; he has been bled, and takes calomel every two hours; the poor soul has been much frightened. I have sent my

[1] See page 54.

[2] The barristers had a long dispute as to the precedence of Mr. Morley, who had not been called to an Inn in England.

[3] Lady Ffolkes, Lady West's sister-in-law.

letters by the *Isabella* to ffolkes, Anna, Lady Bridport, Lady Adare; and the Wests[1] have written to their father.

May 31. We had a man attacked last night with cholera. Edward went himself with him to the Dispensary, saw him bled, and take 20 grains of Calomel; it is now raging dreadfully amongst the Natives, 60 die in a day, but it has at present attacked very few of the Europeans. The want of water is now very great.

June 1. Our poor man is better, quite safe. The Government have opened medical Depots in many Places, and stationed Native Doctors to be in constant attendance. Yesterday we dined again at Parell,[2] to meet Colonel and Mrs. Macdonald just arrived from Madras. He expected to go to Persia, but the king will not receive a Company's servant. She speaks very pleasingly both of the Greys and Franklins, and is a pleasing woman; we having no finery made the day pass much less formally than usual.

June 3. Our servant is quite recovered, and so are our invalids,[3] but they never come down to breakfast, and as visiting begins here soon after 5, I know not what they will do.

June 8. The *Dunera* is just come in, and has brought us innumerable letters, one from Mr. Wynn, the most flattering and complimentary that could be written on Edward's meritorious exertions and his praiseworthy and steady firm conduct in regard to Mr. Erskine. It is quite delightful to see how well the two judges get on together; Sir Charles approves of everything Edward has done.

June 11. We were panic-struck yesterday, for within one hour Edward had letters from Calcutta and Madras to announce the deaths of Sir Christopher Puller[4] and Sir

[1] Martin and young Edward West.

[2] About five miles from Bombay; the Governor's country residence. Elphinstone also built a bungalow at Malabar Point.

[3] Sir C. and Lady Chambers.

[4] Sir C. Puller, a scholar of high attainments, of "singleness and simplicity of mind and high morality," left a large practice on the Oxford circuit; arrived as Chief Justice in King's Court, Calcutta, April 14, 1824, and died five weeks after landing. (*Calcutta Weekly Messenger.*) He had taken the University prize for Latin verse at Oxford.

Willingham Franklin,[1] the former from fever and the latter from cholera. I have great apprehensions for his poor wife, they were such an attached couple. In this insulated place I cannot express what our sensations have been to lose two Friends in one day, and Sir Willingham had been so kind in writing to Edward in all his difficulties.

June 13. A Fire in the Bazaar yesterday; 16 lives lost by the explosion of gunpowder and huts innumerable destroyed. The accounts of cholera are most alarming at Madras; and also the progress the Burmese are making. It is said that Lord Amherst is in a fright, and gives up everything to Sir Ed. Paget, and the merchants want to put their money into Fort St. George.

June 16. Took a long drive to Malabar Point to call on Mr., Mrs., and the Miss Elphinstones.

June 17. Sir Charles Grey, Edward hears, has had a severe attack of cholera, but is out of danger. Poor Lady Franklin tolerably composed, but cannot leave India before January, on account of her confinement. Lady Chambers still invisible from prickly heat.

June 20. We have had 21 guns fired for the taking of "Rangoon," and the *Gazette* as pompous as if it had been a second battle of Waterloo. Young Puller very ill at Calcutta. It is to be hoped that he will recover, or what will become of poor Lady Puller.

June 23. Delightful letters, but I grieve to hear of a contested election again for Lynn, by the death of Lord Titchfield. Everything goes on agreeably in Court, and Edward in very good spirits.

June 30. People like to foretell evil, and now talk of there being no Monsoon, which would occasion a want of water; the Cattle will die and there will be a famine; but I dare say it will come in time to avoid such calamities.

July 6. The Monsoon is, I am happy to say, set in, and the thermometer only 80°. We dined yesterday at Mr. Prendergast's, and met the usual party.

[1] Sir W. Franklin, judge in the King's Court at Madras, scholar of Corpus, and fellow of Oriel, Oxford, was like his brother, the intrepid Arctic explorer, and like his friend Sir E. West, a man of energy and of honour. His diary, in the possession of his grandson, Mr. Willingham Rawnsley, shows that he arrived at Madras in Oct. 1822, and during his short life there did what was possible to promote the efficiency of the Court.

July 12. A long tiresome case came on in chambers, of the Leckie family; the Judges seem to have no rest.

July 21. To-day a Mr. Shaw, a Civilian, a witness in the Leckie case, struck one of our Chobdars in Court for no reason. This is called a Contempt, which deserves punishment, and the Sheriff is ordered to bring up the Gentleman to-morrow.[1]

July 22. Mr. Shaw has been in Court, and the Advocate-General has accepted a Retainer for him, which has produced an inquiry to the Government as to his duties. All these things make me very nervous, though they are quite necessary. Sir Charles is, if possible, more particular and anxious for the rights and dignity of the Court than Edward. We heard yesterday of an elopement between Miss Elphinstone and Captain Macdonald, which had taken place the evening before. To-day a licence has come for them. They were married by a Catholic Priest, and were, I understand, assisted by the Mother.

July 24. To-day the Sessions commenced. Edward made a very short Charge to the Jury, alluding chiefly to the increase of gentlemen for the Grand Jury, as the Mayor and Aldermen are now liable to serve; and also to a murder committed on a (Bheel) robber by Lieut. Fenwick. Under other circumstances he might have made a fine speech, but all subjects are tender ones, and Mr. Norton took the opportunity of making a motion to abuse the Master in Equity, Mr. Fenwick,[2] in which he was quite wrong, and was so told by both the Judges.

July 26.. The Judges were in Court from 11 till ½ past 5, and were quite tired. The *London* just arrived from St. Helena and England; 10th of March; no letters; but we heard that the Stewarts went on to England. I quite rejoice on their account that they have not returned to this nasty place, and Mr. Stewart seeing Mr. Wynn will be very satisfactory to all parties.

July 27. 15000 Moorsmen [illegible] have met this morning to pray on the Esplanade for rain, and this is their 4th day of fasting. It is a very pretty sight from the Windows, as they are all habited in white, except

[1] This case was followed by the banishment of Fair. See p. 145, chapter viii.

[2] Mr. Fenwick had been appointed Master in Equity in Erskine's place.

their turbans, and have numberless colored flags. The Arabs have also prayed and fasted. I wonder the Archdeacon has not thought of a fast day.

July 30. To-day was the trial for murder against Lieut. Fenwick for having hung a Bheel. The trial lasted from 11 to a ¼ past 6. The Jury found him guilty, but the Judges will not hang him, and indeed think he may get off on something of the jurisdiction. I am told that Edward summed up uncommonly well, and will give Judgment when the Sessions are over. A very crowded and hot Court. There was so much curiosity and anxiety about it, as it was so cool and cruel a murder, hanging the Man to a Tree like a Dog; but I regret to say that many of the young men seem to treat them as such.[1]

July 31. To-day the Sessions finished; a work of hard labour in this country. Edward *sifts* all the cases so completely. Batt[2] was at a delightful Dance last evening; it was a meeting of good company, good music and excellent supper. Batt opened the Ball, and was handed to supper by the host and danced 11 dances, and seems to have been made as much of here as a pretty Woman is in England.

Aug. 12. The weather very cool and pleasant, but not enough rain to be of any use. The Governor begins to be alarmed, and consulted Edward as to what Government could do in the event of a famine, which he begins to dread.[3]

Aug. 17. The misrepresentations of the proceedings in Court continue in the *Gazette* newspaper; last Wednesday Sir Charles was attacked. He has commenced a correspondence with Mr. Elphinstone on the subject. I think some curious discoveries as to the proprietors will be made. Edward had often complained, now I trust it will be rectified.

Aug. 21. The Chambers' have hired a very nice cool House in the Country 4 miles off. I hope they will not leave us till very near her confinement, as we shall miss them

[1] The judges decided that the event occurred outside the limits of their jurisdiction.

[2] Lady West's maid. A faithful servant, who afterwards accompanied the orphan child of the Wests to England.

[3] Elphinstone afterwards repaired the tanks, and opened some new wells in the Island, and a native address headed by Hormajee Bomangee, a genuine vote of thanks, was presented to him.

very much. The weather now wet and damp enough to please any one. We have been quite busy putting up a Punka in one of our drawing-rooms, but now the weather reminds me of dear Tunbridge Wells, so damp and chill. I long for a fire—thermometer 75°.

Sept. 3. A French Ship has just come in. As I feared, ffolkes has lost his Election again, tho' he seems to gain in popularity. The Norwich papers are very gratifying.

Sept. 6. The *London* Indiaman sails to-day, and takes away Mr. Fair, the editor of the *Gazette* newspaper.

Sept. 8. Edward has been to attend a meeting of the Native School, and has been elected Vice-President of it. We heard yesterday of the death of poor Commodore Grant at Penang on the 25th. I really regret him, he seemed such a friendly and worthy man. People in England will think India quite fatal, as a Bishop,[1] two Judges, and a Commodore have died since our arrival.

Sept. 10. Term began to-day, and Mr. Shaw's business was again brought on, and as usual Mr. Norton was excessively insolent, and the Judges obliged to put him down. Edward was, I hear, cool and firm, but Sir Charles a little warm.

Sept. 11. To-day Edward gave judgment on Mr. Shaw very coolly and deliberately. He was only fined a rupee. He and his party did not seem much pleased, as it was proved a contempt of Court. I am glad it is concluded.

Sept. 13. Term seems to be going on quietly. The barristers are so frightened at Edward having received an official letter from the E.I.C. Directors to know how many barristers he would wish to have licenced.

Sept. 16. Another dreadful, close, hot night. I was devoured with Mosquitoes, which now swarm in the country and still consider me a delicacy. I never escape them. Poor creatures are arriving from Cutch, where there has been a want of grain and water—and will sell you a child for three rupees, or for rice. What a horrible idea.

Sept. 28. We dined yesterday with the Governor at Parell. I sat at his left, as the Bride, Mrs. Macdonald,[2] was at his right, and was introduced and talked a good deal to a Persian, who was just arrived. He is nephew to the last

[1] Bishop Middleton, first Bishop of Calcutta, arrived November 1814, and died July 1822.

[2] *Née* Elphinstone. See "Diary," July 6.

ambassador we had in London, and seems to have travelled a great deal and to be an intelligent man.

Oct. 3. Lady Chambers confined to-day. I felt dreadfully tired and anxious. I never left her for 18 hours. Edward has heard from Sir Ralph Rice at Madras. He is coming from thence by Land, and hopes to be here in a month. He mentions with sorrow and dismay the death of poor Lady Franklin the day before (Sept. 22), six days after the birth of her infant. Poor thing—the loss of her Husband and Child had quite broken her heart. What a sad annihilation of that family; to herself I doubt not a happy event. The two poor little children must be taken home. To-day Mr. Norton purposely drove against Sir Charles Chambers, no doubt to insult him. However, I hope it will pass off, as I long for a little peace, and so does Edward; difficult with such an A.G.[1]

Oct. 14. To-day the Sessions begin, and Edward paid Sir Charles the compliment of making him charge the Jury. They tried 5 prisoners out of 8, all slight offences. It appears that the slight punishments Edward inflicts diminishes the number of the prisoners.

Oct. 15. Sessions finished to-day, unparalleled in shortness. We send for *salt* water for our ablutions. I wish every one would do the same.[2]

Oct. 23. Edward has been unwell for a day or two. This morning he has been profusely bled, and has taken plenty of medicine. These attacks in this country make one very anxious. In another fortnight we hope for cool weather. We have had wind, thunder, lightning, and what they call "Elephanta"[3] four or five nights.

Oct. 27. Sir Ralph Rice arrived this morning at a quarter past 6. He has taken the Oath and his seat in Court, and has gone to the Archdeacon's.[4]

Nov. 1. We dined to-day at Sir Charles Chambers, and rejoiced to see Lady Chambers at the head of her table. Only Sir Ralph Rice met us, who did not make himself at all agreeable. I fear we shall find him a little troublesome. Edward has gone this morning to call on Mr. Elphinstone on his return from the Ghauts, and to return Col. Rupert's visit.

[1] Advocate-General. [2] During the water famine.
[3] A Portuguese word for the wind which terminates the monsoon.
[4] Archdeacon Barnes.

Nov. 16. One hears of nothing but disturbances all over the country. Poor Mr. Thackeray murdered at Kittoor,[1] and the people rising in many Places; all, it is supposed, in consequence of the ill-advised attack on Rangoon.

Nov. 25. Capt. Tucker of the *Ganges* dined with us yesterday to talk over our going down with him as far as Colombo, as he has 3 best Cabins vacant to that Place. We should enjoy it amazingly if we could ensure getting back for the Sessions on the 26th Jan.

Dec. 1. The Chambers arrived to-day bag and baggage for Lady Chambers to be churched and the young lady to be christened. I am to stand godmother. Poor Mr. Ayrton is dead, having just settled his affairs, and taken his passage to England.

Dec. 2. We heard to-day of poor Sir Francis Bayley's[2] death at Penang on the 20th of October; really quite awful and melancholy to Edward, as this country seems the grave for all his Friends. How thankful we ought to be for our health and happiness. Edward has just received a letter from Gilbert[3] to tell him how highly his conduct is approved and appreciated by the Board of Control, and, as a proof, Mr. Wynn has written to offer him the Chief Justiceship of Madras; and that Mr. Norton is unequivocally condemned. I need scarcely add how happy and light this has made our minds, and we are not a little anxious for the next Ship from England to bring us Mr. Wynn's and many other letters.

Dec. 5. On board the *Ganges*. We are a small party. Everything about the Ship seems neat, well arranged, and comfortable.

Dec. 7. Had it not been for Mosquitoes, Cockroaches, and Ants I should have slept very well. We sailed so quick, we arrived off Goa[4] at 12 o'clock; at 2 o'clock the

[1] Kittoor, a small principality in the Deccan. The dispute arose on a question of successor to the Chief. A considerable amount of treasure was taken out of it.

[2] Sir Francis Bayley was appointed Recorder of Penang, December 10, 1823. He arrived about August 24, 1824, and died in two months' time.

[3] His brother.

[4] The Portuguese possession of Goa, before the appearance of the Dutch in India, was celebrated for its military and ecclesiastical splendour. By the middle of the eighteenth century it was deserted by nearly all but its ecclesiastics.

Adjutant-General and the Governor's Aide-de-Camp arrived in two fine boats; one talked bad English, the other nothing but Portuguese. At 4 we left the ship and had to sail and row 18 miles. The Sea so rough that I really felt some degree of alarm till we crossed the Bar and got into the river. Luckily it was moonlight and the view beautiful. We found Palankeens ready, and were brought to a very excellent House, with a guard of Soldiers, and were ushered upstairs quite in Royal style, preceded by 6 wax candles, escorted by our Beaux. We had our Tea and passed a most comfortable night, almost cold.

Dec. 8. Before we were up we had an Invitation to go and dine with the Governor at 4 o'clock. We have had visits from 3 of the great gentlemen, who are all oppressively civil and attentive and were desirous to offer us every possible Compliment. Edward has been to pay his Compliments to the Governor and his Lady, and reports them both very pleasing People. The view from our Window is beautiful, a peep of the River and a Magnificent group of Cocoanut Trees beyond. The Government House is a large White Building much handsomer than any of the Houses at Bombay, with a large space in front of it. The Palankeens we have are like Sedan chairs, the bearers carry the Poles on the top of the head, instead of the shoulder as they do at Bombay. Some are like Boats with a straw roof to them and windows to open in the side of the roof.

Dec. 9. We dined yesterday at the Governor's and were received with the greatest possible state. He talks English extremely well, and, having served under Marshal Beresford throughout the Peninsular War has quite English manners grafted on the politeness of a Foreigner. The *Governess* is a Woman of high rank from Portugal, daughter of the Marquis de Sabouqorza, a very lady-like, interesting, pleasing Woman. She talked English very tolerably. They have 4 very handsome little girls. She was the only Lady. We had an abundance of gentlemen, almost all Portuguese. The room where we dined was very large with a domed ceiling, and the Pictures of all the Governors hung round—the view from it quite beautiful—French windows opening into Balconies and almost overhanging the River—a magnificent expanse of blue Water with banks of Cocoa Nut trees, and distant views of Islands and hills of all shapes, towering one above another, covered with Wood, and White buildings, at the foot of them, and at the summit to enliven the already cheerful prospect.

Our dinner in quantity exceeded anything I ever saw, not an inch of Table Cloth to be seen and all the Dishes cut up and brought round, that it makes it endless. This was all removed, and then an equal quantity of fruits, cakes and sweet things were put on. The whole ceremony took up about an hour and a half. The Gentlemen moved from the Table with us and took a Segar, so I believe did the lady slyly, as she invited me to do so. A Band played in the evening, almost all English airs, to which the Children waltzed and sang and we became great Friends. There is a magnificent Causeway, I suppose 25 ft. broad and 3 miles long, with long views of wood and Water. It must resemble parts of Italy, the beautiful clearness of the sky and the calm serenity of the whole scene; but too quiet, I should think, as there can be no society; they are all very poor, and there is no Trade, not a Horse or a Carriage in the Place. A little misery—receiving visits of form from Portuguese Gentlemen, who can speak and understand no other language, and sit smiling at each other for a quarter of an hour.

At 4 o'clock we sailed down the river to the Bar and landed to see a church on the Banks, beautifully situated. More visits from Brigadier-General, Secretaries, etc., all wishing to show us some mark of attention. The Governor heard me say I liked Music, so the Band plays every evening, and it is really quite annoying; the Guard turns out and beats the drum whenever we pass, and as we are great fidgets, I think they must wish us back again at Bombay. No Ladies have called—poor Souls—they are not presentable I believe, and say they are sick. The Governor says a convenient excuse.

Dec. 10. We took our Coffee this Morning at 6 and went in a boat down to Old Goa, attended by one of the Governor's Aides-de-Camps. At St. Francis de Xavier we saw a splendid Monument of Marble, and were introduced to the Priest, who was the Chief Inquisitor. He seemed a sensible man and could talk a little French. I only wonder he could talk at all after 45 years' residence in such solitude.

Dec. 11. Three years to-day since I had the Misfortune to lose the best and kindest of Fathers. God bless him, and that we may meet in a better World. This morning we called upon the Governor and his Lady, and found them so polite and pleasing, that we stayed two hours. Nothing can exceed their attention, fancying what we can want and sending it.

Dec. 12 (*Sunday*). We got up this morning at 6 o'clock to breakfast with the Brigadier-General de Mello, who lives on the Bank of the river near Goa, and for Him to escort us to hear grand Mass at the Cathedral. We found a daughter of his, about 30, who could not speak anything but Portuguese. We had breakfast, and went in palankeens to the Cathedral, where the Service was badly chanted, and no congregation. It is a fine large Building, 300 years old, as Goa was taken by the Portuguese in 1510. I saw the Grand Inquisitor again, and enquired how long it was since any one had been burnt. He said about 60 years, and there used to be from 12 to 20 sacrificed every year. I was glad to get back to the boat, and had a cool row home and ate a good luncheon at 1 o'clock. There are a few Tygers about here, eight leagues off; they are so numerous not a week passes without a Child being carried off. Kittoor [1] is only 50 miles from here. We understand that the Fort has Surrendered to the English with very little bloodshed: the Governor's Secretary, a Portuguese who talks very good English, called upon us to show us a splendid view at the top of a Hill, I should suppose as beautiful as anything could be; distant mountains, hills covered with wood, Forts on their summits; the Sea, various rivers, and Islands, in every prospect, with a wildness in some parts quite beautiful. I had no idea that there were so many as 300,000 souls in the Portuguese territory here. The wages are marvellously low, one Rupee a month to most, four to a good servant. The People are stout made, and ugly and dreadfully naked.

Dec. 13. Edward went out in a boat to Goa, and from thence two hours in a Manchille (Palankeen) to a fine Lake to shoot Wild Ducks. He came home covered with mud, and with three Herons as his afternoon's sport, but delighted with the views he saw. I hope he has not suffered from the Sun, but he was rather imprudent in shooting at 4 o'clock.

Dec. 15. We went and sat an hour with the Governor and his Lady, who are both particularly well bred, pleasing and obliging. He told us his Salary was only 10,000

[1] Kittoor—a small principality in the Deccan. Taken during this year.

Rupees a year, but 6,000 Rupees a year on his return. The Adjutant-General, Don José de Castro, called this morning again, and brought his Wife to pay *ses devoirs;* quite immense in size, fair and unassuming, and not speaking a word of either French or English. He is a really sensible man.

Dec. 16. At 4 o'clock we started with the Governor, and a cavalcade of People, to visit Cabo, an Island, where there is always a fine breeze, and so healthy. There is a Hospital kept in repair by the English Company. We had many soldiers there 7 years ago. Upon our return we took the Governor's Family dinner, and Edward played a rubber of whist, and saw some beautiful Chess-Men made from the bones of the Hippopotamus from the Mozambique.

Dec. 18. Edward got up this morning at 4, to go with the Governor to shoot at a Lake where he said there were an abundance of Wild Ducks, but they all turned out to be Birds like Moor Hens,[1] with green legs and brown plumage, and another large bird, with beautiful purple plumage, red legs and beak, and called here Gallino,[2] all said to be good eating and which the Sportsmen in this country all shoot *sitting*. They breakfasted at an old House near the Lake, and were home at Eleven o'clock.

Dec. 19. The Governor sent a Portuguese to show us a curious animal called here a wild cat;[3] a hideous black thing, with a face like a bat, and an immense long tail, and flaps at the sides between the legs, which pull out to a great width, which make it resemble a bat, and it seems to jump so high, almost as if it flew, and looks wild and savage. The man said not; it seemed fond of him and feeds on bread, milk, rice. We have had a long and interesting visit from the Chief of the Marine here. Our Parsee Servant was obliged to be the Interpreter.

Dec. 20. Edward rose early and took a walk. I went with Madame de Camera to return Donna Curita's visit, the Adjutant-General's Lady, a sad-mannered person, as they all seem to be, who have been born here; Edward also went to return some of his visits. We dined at 3, and sailed about from 5 till 7; it was very cool and pleasant.

[1] The common moorhen has a wide range, and is found in Indian, as in English rivers and pools.

[2] Indian Purple Gallinule (*Porphyrio poliocephalus*), one of a family of beautifully coloured moorhens.

[3] A large flying squirrel (*Pteromys oral*).

Dec. 24. Yesterday we left Goa, and really with regret, having passed a fortnight so pleasantly; we had a salute given us, which Capt. Pepper returned to the Governor.

Jan. 1, 1825 (*Saturday*). Not a cheerful New Year's Day; I laid in bed all day, the ship rolls and pitches, and annoys me more than the *Milford* ever did. I shall hope never to take but one more voyage, and that to dear Home.

Jan. 2. We arrived within sight of the Lighthouse early in the morning, but had such light and contrary winds that we did not arrive at the Court-House till past seven in the evening, and the last four miles rowed in a Boat.

Jan. 3. We hear from Sir Lionel [1] that Little Edward [2] has been very unwell with fever. We have written to desire him to come to us as now this climate is better. Mr. Newnham called, and innumerable visitors.

Jan. 14. We were woke this morning with letters from England, just arrived by our dear *Milford*. Edward has had a most satisfactory letter from Mr. Wynn in regard to the Barristers. About the C. J.[3] of Madras he knows not how to decide. We have had good health here and have many friends. Edward has done and is still doing so much good. The Natives say they shall petition Edward to stay if they think he is likely to go away, which is very gratifying.

Jan. 18. We have just received more letters by the *Sarah* from Mr. and Mrs. Stewart and Sir Charles Forbes, with extracts from newspapers, etc. Every letter seems most gratifying. We only regret that the Debate in the House of Commons has not appeared in the papers, as I understand it was very flattering to Edward.[4] We had 34 at dinner yesterday, The Governor, Sir Keith Jackson, Captain Seton, General Short, Mrs. and Misses Wilson, Mr. and Mrs. Morley, and others. The party stayed till 12, so I hope it was not very dull.

Jan. 25. Last night was Sir Ralph Rice's [5] gay Ball and Supper. I opened it with him with a country dance, and

[1] Sir Lionel Smith, Commander of the Fourth Division of the Army of the Deccan.

[2] Edward Stamp West, nephew of Sir E. West.

[3] Chief Justiceship.

[4] This debate lasted two hours, but was not reported. See p. 72.

[5] Sir R. Rice left India the following year, and seems to have died shortly afterwards.

began the quadrille with Mr. Newnham, and I hope I did my duty. He took me down to supper and gave some silly bad toasts. But on the whole the thing went off cheerfully and well.

Jan. 29. A trial of some Chinamen for a murder lasted nearly all day. Edward did not get home till half-past 9 at night, and really did not seem very tired, he is always so interested in business.

Jan. 31. A long day, Edward not out of Court till 6. We then took a drive and a walk on the Esplanade by moonlight.

Feb. 3. Two years yesterday since we landed. Sir Charles has a holiday to-day, and Sir Ralph has not attended since Saturday. Edward says the Barristers behave well. The Court cannot be in better order, and he thinks the Criminal Court and the Small Cause Court are complete.

Feb. 7. Edward to-day gave judgment on several of the most important cases he tried at the Sessions, and was obliged to condemn one man to death, which is always a most painful and dreadful duty, and one he feels very much.

Feb. 14. Valentine's Day, and the Lynn Mart proclaimed. Here one day and one season are much like another, and the time passes very rapidly.

March 2. Edward still engaged every day from 10 to 6 framing and settling the new rules.

March 12. A beautiful bird was brought in dead. It is very large, white with a long neck, long red legs, and tips of the wings scarlet and black.[1] I long to have it stuffed, but that could not be done. The servant says it is good eating. We shall see.

March 13. The bird was voted strong and not good.

March 29. Last evening we drove a new horse. It went quiet but rather ungainly, as one would say in Norfolk. Edward heard to-day from the Bishop of Calcutta[2] declining both ours and Sir Charles Chambers' invitation to stay, as he thinks it right to occupy the really furnished house Government have prepared for him. We have two poor Hamauls very ill with small-pox. We have sent them

[1] The European Flamingo is found at the Cape, Ceylon, and Bombay.

[2] Bishop Heber.

to the native hospital, and I hope they may recover. The Cook's mate, a Portuguese, has it, also a horse-keeper. They were vaccinated, but I suppose it was badly done, and so many are now ill who fancied they were safe, that I believe they will not be easily persuaded to have it done to their children.

March 30. A poor Hamaul is dead, and will I suppose be burning this evening as is the custom of their Caste.

CHAPTER X

Bishop Heber at Bombay—Expedition to Bassein—Portuguese ruins—Death of Bishop Heber: and of his successor.

Lady West's Journal (April-October 1825):—Details of Bishop Heber's visit; foundation-stones of Central Schools laid; expedition of the Governor, Hebers, Wests, Chambers, to Salsette; Tannah; Kennery Caves, Bassein; Elphinstone an excellent host; Sir Ralph Rice; murder trials; embarrassing gifts; illegal flogging.

In 1825 the newly-appointed Bishop of Calcutta, Dr. Reginald Heber, formerly Fellow of All Souls, Oxford, held a visitation at Bombay, and remained four months in the island. His appointment to India had been well received. It was known that he had taken "the Newdigate"—the prize for English verse at Oxford—and the Calcutta and Bombay newspapers had published with approval some lines written by him for a missionary meeting. They began with the words "From Greenland's icy mountains." Little could the good Bishop have dreamed of the coming generations of school children who would chant those verses!

Friend of Sir E. West and Sir C. Chambers, the Bishop had received invitations from both; but he was accompanied to Bombay by another friend, Archdeacon Barnes, an old resident at

Bombay, who had seconded the Governor's vote of a testimonial to Erskine, and as might have been expected, the Bishop was induced to decline the invitations of the judges, and to stay in the house prepared for him by the Governor. Still, though Bishop Heber must have come to Bombay with some prejudice against the judges[1] and in favour of the Governor, his visit was a blessing to all. Lady West, sitting at dinner between the Bishop and Sir Charles Chambers, finds it "almost England again from the manner and style of behaviour and conversation—unlike the Goths here." Elphinstone treats Lady West with marked consideration, expresses his regret at having invited her to meet ladies of doubtful reputation, and entertains the Bishop "with unremitting kindness, splendid hospitality, and agreeable conversation."[2] A picnic, lasting five days, is arranged for the Bishop and Mrs. Heber. Archdeacon Barnes, the two judges, Lady West, Lady Chambers, and eleven others join the party.[3] Visits are made to the Island of Salsette, the caves of Kennery, and the ruined city of Bassein.

Lady West's diary here makes an interesting

[1] They are only mentioned once (as "acquaintances") in Heber's long account of his visit, though in a letter to Mr. Wynn the Bishop speaks of Sir E. West and the other two Chief Justices in India as "old friends."

[2] Heber's "Journal," vol. iii. p. 91.

[3] Sir Ralph Rice, the second puisne judge, does not appear to have taken part in this expedition, nor is his name mentioned in Heber's "Journal."

supplement to the Bishop's "Journal." The expedition was enjoyed by all. Lady West says: "Nothing could exceed Mr. Elphinstone's attention; he was my devoted cavaliere servente the whole time. He certainly shines in these parties, and I am sure we all regretted that it was Saturday and that we must return home."

It was after this visit to the ruined churches of Bassein that Bishop Heber made the remark —made before by Burke in other words—made since by others, "They are melancholy objects to look at" (the Portuguese churches), "but they are monuments nevertheless of departed greatness, of a love of splendour, and of a zeal for God, which, if not according to knowledge, was a zeal still and a sincere one. It was painful to me to think how few relics, *if the English were now expelled from India, would be left behind of their religion, their power, or their civil and military magnificence.*"[1] There was some foundation then, perhaps, for the Bishop's reflections, though surely there is now an answer that England has raised monuments more lasting than these in the permanent lifting up of the Indian races. "We make our appearance," says Sir W. Hunter, "in the long list of races who have ruled that splendid empire, not as temple builders like the Hindus, nor as palace and tomb builders like the Musalmáns, nor as fort builders like the Mahrattas,

[1] Bishop Heber's "Journal," vol. iii. p. 91.

nor as church builders like the Portuguese; but in the more commonplace capacity of town builders; as a nation that had the talent for selecting sites on which great commercial cities would grow up, and who have in this way created a new industrial life for the Indian people."[1]

Never before in recorded history have conquerors of an Asiatic race raised the conquered in intellectual independence, in morality, in national aim and ideal. These Portuguese ruins, splendid though they are, seem after all but the bones of gross ecclesiastical materialism; unhealthy at its best and destined to perish. "The Portuguese," writes Vambéry,[2] "came to India as robber-knights and crusaders, and looked upon all heathen people as enemies of Portugal and of Christ. Their conduct in India was marked by fanaticism and cruelty which put even the actions of a Pizarro and Cortes in the shade. The Christian Catholic missionaries did not hesitate to use the most cruel measures in the service of their Church, for these pious men had more regard for the treasures than for the souls of the poor Hindus. It is, therefore, easy to see that Portugal carried the seeds of decline and destruction in its own bosom, and was bound ere long to disappear from the scene."

Monuments, therefore, these ruins surely are,

[1] Sir W. Hunter, "The Indian Empire," p. 440.
[2] Vambéry, "Western Culture in Eastern Lands," p. 131. London, 1906.

not of departed greatness but of departed littleness—beacons rather—not without their warning.

With much ceremony, soon after the Bishop's arrival, the foundation-stones of the Central Schools were laid by Elphinstone, the Archdeacon, Mrs. Heber, and Lady West; and the gentle Bishop had caught just a little of his host's spirit, when, addressing Elphinstone, he said that "it was a grateful sight to see the high, the talented, the valorous, and the fair unite to grace with their presence the education of the poor"; and that he might "indulge an honest pride" in expressing his belief that the "British are the only people among whom such a scene could be exhibited."[1]

Still, though the Bishop sat at the feet of Elphinstone, and though Archdeacon Barnes, who conducted him through the Deccan at the very time when its inhabitants were being driven out by over-taxation,[2] persuaded the Bishop that the "burdens of the peasantry" were "less in amount, and collected in a less oppressive manner, than under the old Monarchy";[3] and that the popular Governor was always in the right and the King's Court in the wrong; the fresh moral atmosphere

[1] "In the above national eulogy he forgot to mention that at Bombay 1200 children are educated by the American Missionary Society, and only 1000 by the Education Society on the British system."—*Oriental Herald*, vii. 555.

[2] See "Official Report of Bombay Government of 1893," p. 76, quoted in chapter vii. p. 128.

[3] Heber's "Journal," vol. iii. p. 121.

created by his four months' visit must have been welcome to all. Well that it was so, for no second visit was to be paid. During this unhappy decade the lives of bishops were as short as those of King's Judges.[1] Six months after leaving Bombay, on a day on which he had visited a native school, Bishop Heber was found dead in his bath.

Death was said to have been due to apoplexy, and it may have been. But those who know how difficult it frequently is, even at the present day, and in England, to be certain of the cause of sudden illness; and how often opinions of excellent physicians are contradicted by examinations made after death, must agree that eighty years ago in India, where Company's surgeons were few, scattered, and imperfectly trained, where sudden death frequently followed sudden illness, and was always followed by immediate burial, statements as to cause of death must often have been mere conjecture.

Lady West says: "We were dreadfully shocked to hear of the death of Bishop Heber on the 3rd April. I always feared that he would fall a martyr to these visitations. I have such a horror of travelling in this country. May God preserve my husband to me."

Later pages of the journal will show that Lady

[1] Bishop Middleton, first Bishop of Calcutta, died in 1822. Bishop Heber arrived in India in 1823 and died in 1826. Bishop James arrived in India in 1827 and died in 1828.

West's forebodings were true. It is worthy of note too that Heber's successor, Bishop James, was seized with fatal illness during his first journey.

FROM LADY WEST'S JOURNAL

April 2, 1825. Term begins to-day. There was very little business, only a motion from Mr. Irwin for Mr. Norton. He (Mr. Norton) and one of the Attorneys having had a quarrel; and a challenge which Mr. N. refused. Mr. N. will soon be cut by every one.

April 3. Water will, it is feared, be very scarce. We had sixty-three bottles filled yesterday at the Caves of Elephanta for drinking. We had mangoes for the first time to-day.

April 17. Edward has sent the new Rules of Court, and a long official letter to Mr. Wynn,[1] and gave a very interesting judgment on a long pending case, a native with the Government, and gave it in favour of the former. Poor creatures, I believe since Sir William Syer's[2] time they have rarely had justice. The Court has been so subservient to the Government; but now it is free and independent, and they daily feel the blessings of it.

April 20. Little Edward has hurt his arm and has twice had leeches put on to it. I am inclined to think that it will be best to send him home, as he seems never quite well. It will make a sad blank to me, as he seems to me like my own child. Mr. Carr, the padre, asked me to lay the foundation stone for the Girls' School next month, and the Governor is to lay that for the Boys'. I was obliged to say "yes," but I so much dislike all those exhibitions. We were awakened this morning by the salute for the Bishop.[3]

April 24 (*Sunday*). The Bishop preached this morning to an overflowing Congregation whose curiosity took them there. Usually the Church is quite deserted. The dis-

[1] President of the Board of Control.

[2] Sir William Syer, the first Recorder of the King's Court of Bombay, seems to have been an excellent judge, though little is known of him.

[3] Bishop Heber, born 1783, arrived in India in 1823 and died in 1826.

course was long and the matter pretty good, but the delivery bad, and the voice harsh and unpleasing. He is thin, and looks ten years older than Edward though exactly the same age.

April 25. The Sessions commence to-day. Sir Ralph Rice charged the Jury. I understand it was very long and bad. We drove in the evening to look at the new Penitentiary, as we did not feel inclined to go to the Ball and supper at the Governor's.

April 27. Mrs. Heber arrived last night from Calcutta.[1]

April 28. We dined yesterday at Government House. I passed a pleasant day, as I sat between the Governor and the Bishop, who is, of course, a perfect and polite gentleman (a rarity here)—and talked much of Edward's talents and the good he is doing, and that he would be Chief Justice of Calcutta. We also found Mrs. Heber pleasant and ladylike. I shall gain the character here of a "*spirit*," as I wrote to the Governor, having met several times at his house ladies of spotted reputation, and who are not visited by any one. Of course I had a polite answer pretending ignorance on the subject.

May 1 (*Sunday*). Church was very full, as the Bishop preached. He is not to me at all a very fine or interesting preacher. We dined yesterday at Sir Charles Chambers'—a large party for the Bishop. I found it pleasant, as I sat between Sir Charles and the Bishop, and almost found it England again, from the manner and style of behaviour and conversation—so unlike the Goths here.

May 2. Quite a storm of fine Sea-air. I cannot believe that we are in the dreaded month of May.

May 4. We were from 10 to 2 in the church to-day—the examination of the children of the central school. I gave the prizes to the Girls; the Governor to the Boys. We had a large meeting and some little speechifying and thanking.

May 5. This morning at 7 we went to lay the foundation stones of the two new Central Schools for the boys and the girls.[2] Lady Chambers and myself for the Girls,

[1] Bishop Heber's "Journal," April 26: "My dear wife and elder girl arrived in Bombay after a tedious and distressing voyage."

[2] Idem., vol. iii. p. 78: "On May 5th the foundation of a Free School on the same plan with that of Calcutta was laid. The ceremony was numerously attended."

the Governor and Archdeacon for the boys. The children sang the Hymn of Praise, we then laid the stones, depositing an engraved brass plate and some coins, and with our silver trowels I hope performed our work elegantly. After this the Bishop gave us a prayer, the children sang again, at 8 o'clock we all partook of a breakfast given by the Archdeacon, which I really enjoyed, as I had a very pleasant seat between the Governor and the Bishop. He made a very appropriate speech, and one knows him so good and so superior a man that every word has, I hope, a good effect. But he cannot be eloquent, having a little hesitation. Afterwards the Bishop, the Governor, and ourselves walked over the new penitentiary, which is just finished. We then returned home quite tired, but Edward is so indefatigable that he is gone into Court.

May 8. At 6 this morning we saw the *Regalia* sail out with poor little Edward. We all feel quite unsettled and odd without him.

May 11 (*Wed.*). We hear by way of Madras that two of the China ships left the Cape on the 14th of March. We may now hourly expect their arrival. We had yesterday a party of 28 to dinner. The Bishop took me to dinner, and Edward Mrs. Heber.

May 15. We attended church this morning. The Bishop preached and gave us an excellent sermon.

May 16. Mr. Elphinstone tells me that he has inquired as to the two ladies' characters I named to him, and finds them both so very bad, that he shall never ask them again to his house. He thanked me, but in his heart, I am sure, must hate Edward and me, as he worships popularity, and he cares for no one, and wishes to make no distinctions. I thought it my *Duty* as the head of Society not to countenance meeting such people, and am rejoiced that I did it, as one of the ladies has had the assurance to come and call on both Mrs. Heber and myself. I luckily called out *not at home*, and we shall not return the visit. This is the consequence of her being invited by the Governor.

May 19 (*Thursday*). Yesterday a poor sepoy came to Edward to complain, and to show the cuts on his back inflicted by his master (Mr. C——) of the European regiment. He investigated the case, found that Mr. Snow, the magistrate, had done his duty, and had ordered the case to be brought before the Petty Sessions, and I sincerely hope that the gentleman will be severely punished, and the poor man get his 6 months' wages, which was the occasion of the beating, because he asked for it. These poor creatures are gaining courage, knowing Edward's wish to protect them, and Mr. Fenwick[1] says that flogging has very much decreased since Edward arrived here. We dined yesterday with Mr. Fenwick, a pleasant party. The Bishop took me to dinner, and Edward took Mrs. Cowper, as people pay the Bishop and Mrs. Heber the compliment of precedency, which I quite approve.

May 23. Edward attended a meeting at the Church—the establishment of the Society for the Propagation of the Gospel. Edward gave 3000 rupees donation, and R.100 a year annual subscription. Naturally the poor natives and the Hamauls bless Edward's exertions, as the poor sepoy whom Mr. C—— flogged will now get his 6 months' arrear of wages in the Court for Small Causes, and he received 70 rupees which Mr. C—— was fined at the Petty Sessions. This will, I hope, make the young cadets more cautious.

May 24. To-day we left Bombay in a hired barouche with our own horses to Parell, where Hormajee Bomanjee[2] lent us a pair of horses which took us to Corler,[3] six miles. We had to pass over a very narrow road, two miles long, which joins the island of Salsette to Bombay. I am grown so timid, I had a Palankeen waiting to take me over. Mrs. Heber and I travelled in company, and the Bishop and Edward rode to Toolsey, where we found Mr. Elphinstone waiting to receive us and all our tents pitched in the most picturesque spot in a valley, with fine mountains nearly all round, and fine banyan trees which hung over us to shade us.

Our party consisted of the Hebers, the Chambers, Col. and Mrs. Macdonald, the Archdeacon, Major and Mrs. Hardy, Mr. Young, Captain Gillespie, Sir Keith Jackson, Capt. Burrows, Mr. Seton, Martin West, Col. Rienzi (a Frenchman). We had one magnificent tent for our drawing

[1] Master in Equity, Supreme Court—originally appointed to Recorder's Court in Erskine's place.

[2] An enlightened and philanthropic Parsee merchant.

[3] Probably Kurla.

and dining room. We did not dine till 8, and in the evening played at whist.[1]

May 26. Edward got up early and took a ride. At 3 we started in our Palankeens to see the Kennery Caves, picturesque scenery, but the path sadly steep, rugged, and bad for horses. The caves are certainly very curious, one very much in the same style as the Karlee Caves, but not so large or in so perfect a state.

May 27. We were up this morning at a quarter to 4. At 5 Edward got on his horse and Batt and I in our Palankeens to go 6 miles to Tannah. But at the top of the Vear Hill I found the Governor's carriage, which he had sent for me. I could not do otherwise than use it, and was much delighted with the drive to Tannah.[2] The descent of the hill is exceedingly steep, and the scenery very wild and beautiful. Tannah seems a pretty place, and they are now finishing a fine church there.

We believed ourselves and the Chambers' as we travelled together to be the first at Tannah, but we found that the Governor, the Hebers, and Macdonalds had embarked in one Bunda Boat,[3] and had gone off to the Governor's yacht, and not a moment was to be lost on account of the tide. To my dismay I was obliged to go and leave Batt to follow with Major and Mrs. Hardy in another Bunda boat. We had a very long row, and reached the yacht at 9, and found an excellent breakfast on the table. At 2 we had again to get into Bunda Boats to row to Gorabunder, as the yacht got aground. The views all day were very beautiful, and employed the Bishop and Sir Charles Chambers in taking some pretty sketches.

We arrived at Gorabunder at 3, a Portuguese church, beautifully situated at the top of a high mountain, to which you ascend by an immensely long flight of stone steps. The encampment was at the foot of the hill, and was voted too

[1] Bishop Heber's "Journal": "We accompanied the Governor and a large party on a tour through Salsette. This is a very beautiful Island, united with the smaller one of Bombay by a causeway built in the time of Governor Duncan, a work of great convenience to the natives, but so narrow and with so inconvenient an angle that many Europeans object to pass it in carriages."

[2] Bishop Heber's "Journal": "Tannah is chiefly inhabited by Roman Catholic Christians, either converted Hindoos or Portuguese who have become as black as the natives and assumed all their habits."

[3] Bunder boat, *i.e.* Harbour boat.

hot, and all the ladies were lodged in the church, where we had a fine large room for eating, which was not forgotten anywhere. It would make an excellent dwelling-house, and the views from it quite magnificent, on one side overhanging the water, which had the appearance of a fine lake.

In the evening Col. Rienzi harmonised us by singing to an ill-strung fiddle. He has a good voice, and some execution.

May 28. We breakfasted early this morning to go and see the old ruined city of Bassein 8 miles off, and were to go in the yacht and sent our Palankeens on to await our arrival. But we had so little wind we had to tack about so much it was thought advisable to get into the Bunda Boats and row to Bassein. When we arrived there the Palankeens were not arrived. We all got out to walk under the umbrellas, and I believe I may say that no one ever felt greater heat or more scorching sun at 12 o'clock under a high wall, with the black sand half over one's shoes, which literally blistered our feet, it was so hot. After half an hour's walk apparently 3 sides round a large castle, we saw a bullock cart with a little tilt; we were gladly (Mrs. Heber, Lady Chambers, and myself) lifted into and squeezed into this machine, and really no chaise and four would have been more welcome to us at that moment.[1] We were driven very dexterously through ruined gateways and walls to a church, a fine and complete ruin, and saw some tombstones, of 1606, of Portuguese families. Soon after this the Palankeens arrived and we went to see a Hindu building not at all decayed, and a most perfect fine carved stone cow which they worshipped. We went to another church where there were remains of fine stone carving, and the entrance very fine. The arches and Corinthian pillars and some of the iron of the gate very finely embossed with iron nails. There are the remains of innumerable fine houses and streets.

It really fills one with melancholy when one reflects

[1] Mrs. Heber's "Journal": "We walked for nearly two miles, exposed to the noon-day sun, the heat increased from the reflection from the white walls, with the sand ankle deep, so hot as to be painful to our feet, while to the barefooted natives it was insupportable, and they fairly ran off." . . . "On our return to Gorabunder we found all things ready for our journey to Bombay, where we arrived late at night, much interested and gratified by all we had seen and done."—Heber's "Journal," vol. iii. p. 86.

that this once magnificent place is now a perfect desert with not one single inhabitant, and it is not accounted for except that it is thought that the Mahrattas drove the Portuguese out of it. We were much pleased with it, and only regretted that we could not stay longer, but we were too tired and hot to prolong our researches, and as we had 2 Palankeens I took Lady Chambers into mine, and Sir Charles took Mrs. Heber, and in half an hour we got back to the yacht, where we found an excellent dinner waiting for us, and to that, and claret and water, we did ample justice. We sailed back so soon that we found ourselves at Gorabunder by the time dinner was over, and by the time our adventures had been related the carriages and horses were ready, and at 5 o'clock our agreeable and cheerful party dispersed. I think I may say that every one enjoyed it extremely; nothing could exceed Mr. Elphinstone's attention, civility, and wish of obliging; he was my devoted Cavaliere Servente the whole time. He certainly shines in these parties, and I am sure we all regretted that it was Saturday and that we must return home. Hormajee's horses took us the first 12 miles to Ambole; the hired horses took us to Bandora, where we had to ferry over to Mahim, and by driving very fast we were soon home, as we found our horses the other side of the water, and drove the 10 miles in an hour and 20 minutes.

The ferrying over is a curious process; there is a large Cage put upon two boats, the horses are taken off, and one is pushed up the inclined plane into this Cage in one's carriage. The horses stand by the side, and in a quarter of an hour one is rowed over. We saw the chief part of the island of Salsette. The whole of the drive to-day was very rich, almost like a gentleman's park with large mango trees where I suppose there have been houses, and now and then ruins of them and also churches with a Cross in front; it is indeed sad to think that all this fine country seems nearly depopulated; the Governor has tried to do what he can, but it does not seem to answer, in fact I suppose it is hot and unhealthy. In some degree Bassein reminded one of Goa, though there the Churches were kept in repair, and inhabited by the Monks. The view of Bassein [1] was very pretty from the water; walled all round. I regretted then, as I always do, that I cannot sketch.

[1] Bishop Heber on Bassein, see p. 171.

May 21. Yesterday we dined at Mr. John Elphinstone's, a party of 28. I went with him to dinner, and Edward had to Beau Mrs. Prendergast.

June 4. We were to have dined yesterday at the Wardens, but so violent a storm of thunder, lightning and rain came on at the time that we were obliged to send an excuse.

June 6. Two letters from dear Charlotte. One from Caroline Dunraven. The poor dear old house in Mansfield Street is sold. All our family well, thank God.

June 13. Davidass,[1] a rich Hindu native, called and told Edward he hoped he would not go to Madras, as no one had ever done so much good here before. This is very gratifying.

June 15. We hear that Sir Ralph Palmer[2] is arrived at Madras in 85 days from England, and that Sir Charles Grey is appointed Chief Justice at Calcutta. Edward has written to them both to congratulate them.[3]

June 22. Edward did not get home till past five yesterday, and brought me a curious letter from Mr. Warden, M.C.,[4] to read, bona fide taxing the judges with sending accounts to Buckingham for his *Oriental Herald*, which attacks him [Warden] upon being chief proprietor of the *Gazette*, which has been libelling the Court; but Edward's fault since our residence here has been not writing to his friends to tell them of his difficulty, and to avoid misrepresentations. He had also a letter from Sir Charles Grey telling him he [Grey] was appointed Chief Justice of Calcutta, and that Sir Ralph Palmer had arrived as Chief of Madras, but if Edward likes to go there he will come here. I had a long visit from Col. Macdonald.

June 27. Edward has written a letter to Mr. Elphinstone mentioning Mr. Warden's paper, and has received a very handsome answer on the subject.

[1] The principal Hindoo in Bombay. See chapter xiii.

[2] Sir R. Palmer succeeded Sir Edmond Stanley as Chief Justice of Madras.

[3] Bishop Heber, in a letter to Mr. Wynn, says: "You have added much to my comfort by sending Grey here. . . . It happens just now remarkably that all the three Chief Justices were my contemporaries at Oxford, and that I have always been on terms of friendly intercourse with all; though Grey was the only one with whom I was intimate."—"Journal," vol. iii. p. 452.

[4] Member of Council.

June 30. A signal of a ship coming in. I think a large Indiaman. The *Farquharson*, Captain Cruikshank, has come in. Little news except the dreadful account of the Indiaman blown up in Falmouth Roads; part of the 31st Regiment on board and 90 lives lost.[1]

July 12. A close day and heavy rain. Edward has been in Court to settle an equity case, Sir Ralph not there. A Hindoo who has lost his caste, to regain it is to measure his length for 7 miles in the dirt, and was to begin his undertaking on Tuesday. Oswald saw him performing it.

July 20. Edward has been in Court a short time on the Prendergast case, and the whole day yesterday. We went this morning to call upon the Hebers and found them at home, and now Edward has gone to the Court House to ascertain a law point for the Bishop.

July 22. The Bishop breakfasted with us, and was anxious to consult Edward on some law matters as to his charter, and a case before him of Mr.——, and I doubt not that it will have been of great use, or he might have done more than he ought, as his mind has evidently been prejudiced, and he might have got himself into a scrape, which Edward will I hope prevent.[2]

July 26. Sir Ralph Rice was not at the opening of the Sessions yesterday, but came up to-day, and was I fancy very perverse about trying the causes; like a dog in the manger, would not help himself, and yet did not like Sir Charles to do so. Edward was not home till six. Bad accounts from Colonel Cowper; and the cook's mate attacked with cholera. We dined at General Wilson's; all the grandees except the poor Bishop were there; he was not well. I had Mr. Warden for my beau, and Edward took Mrs. Warden. I passed a cheerful evening talking to Mrs. Heber.

July 29. Edward was in Court from 10 till after 7 trying an Englishman for the murder of his wife. He had the painful duty of condemning him to death. Edward says

[1] Evidently the first rumour of the destruction by fire of the *Kent* in the Bay of Biscay, with a loss of 85 lives out of 600.

[2] Bishop Heber's "Journal," vol. iii. p. 128: "The remainder of my stay at Bombay was disagreeably . . . occupied in examining into the conduct of one of my chaplains, a man of talent and high pretensions to austere piety. The inquiry ended very unsatisfactorily; still nothing was actually proved against him."

he never heard of a more brutal and savage murder; he almost cut her in pieces, and assigns no excuse for it. The Bishop sat some time with me, and gratified me extremely with his high opinion of Edward's talents, independence, integrity, etc., which he says is the universal opinion here even amongst his opponents, in fact they could not say otherwise.

July 30. Another murder to be tried to-day. Edward is quite knocked up, and as the two Puisne Judges were there he did not think it necessary to attend in Court, indeed two murders tried two successive days is too harassing in this country. Poor Colonel Cowper was released on Thursday afternoon, and buried yesterday; Edward could not go, but sent his carriage to follow the hearse.

July 31. Went to Church, the Bishop preached a Sermon about the Unjust Steward; it is always an obscure and difficult subject to understand, and he in my opinion did not enlighten it at all.

Aug. 3. Edward and Sir Charles and all the grandees dined with Colonel Williams and the mess of the Queen's Royals, and returned home in high glee, having had toasts and bumpers without end.

Aug. 8. The wretched man was hung this morning for the murder of his wife; he could not be saved, but it is a sad duty for Judges who have any feeling.

Aug. 13. Edward had a long take leave note from the Bishop, who goes to-morrow. I have had a kind note from Mrs. Heber; Edward is gone to say adieu, and now I hear the salute, they must have embarked. Edward went on board to see the Hebers, and heard from the Bishop that nothing could be proved against Mr. ——. I hope, therefore, that Edward will from authority circulate this, that Party spirit and ill-will will die away, of which there is always an abundance here, people love gossip and ill-humour.

Aug. 20. Edward has gone into Court. He received yesterday a letter from Major Hardy to explain something about his wife's evidence in this unfortunate affair, with some letters of the Bishop's, etc. But as we wish to take no part in the business Edward very properly begged to return them all unread. I wish others would do the same.

Aug. 25. We dined yesterday at the Bakers; a small

party, only sixteen. Some new arrivals were there, the Misses F.—dashing, vulgar-looking girls, but one sang delightfully; a fine voice, and she accompanied herself well. As I do not feel quite stout we have sent an excuse to Parell, where we were to have dined to-day. I wished Edward to go, but he kindly will not.

Sept. 2. Nothing but rain, the esplanade looks like the environs of Ely, but it is very cool. Edward heard from Sir Charles Grey at Calcutta; Lady Grey and children going home.

Sept. 9. Edward was at the Court House. I had a visit from a rich Hindu from Surat,[1] and his little nephew, a child of five years old, with a gold tissue turban and gold tissue pantaloons, and immense earrings, who brought me a present (a dish of sugar candy, and a handsome white shawl), both of which I thought it necessary to decline accepting, and had it explained as well as I could that it was not mine, or the Chief Justice's custom to take presents, that I felt extremely flattered and obliged. I fear that they were hurt, as they cannot understand our feelings on the subject.

Sept. 11. Term commenced yesterday. Sir Ralph Rice did not come to look at the books of the Officers of the Court, which the other Judges investigated by appointment.

Sept. 12. Sir Roger de Taria has sent me 2 Sheep and a Keg of Humps, Tongues, etc. As he is a great Portuguese Merchant I thought I could not refuse all, and therefore accepted of the dead stock.

Sept. 13. Even Portuguese Merchants are not to be depended upon, for yesterday a Cause came on in Court in which Sir Roger de Taria was interested. It taught me not to put any trust in man.

Sept. 19. Edward, I understand, gave Mr. Norton an excellent reproof to-day, so mild and to the purpose. Sir Ralph behaved very well. Sir Charles completely concurred in all Edward said about the Government.

[1] Surat. The first factories of the old East India Company were started here, in spite of the opposition of Portuguese in 1612. As Bombay rose, Surat declined. An interesting account of Surat is to be found in Forrest's "Cities of India."

Sept. 21. A Syrian Bishop, who is here on a Mission from Antioch to Travancore, called upon Edward; he wants to get money to build a church, I suppose at Antioch.

Sept. 22. We have just heard the melancholy news of the death of a poor young man here, a Mr. Bax, so sudden that he was dead before his friends even knew that he was ill. He was to have dined with us to-day, and the bell tolling was the only way that we heard of it, also the death of Captain Macdonald.[1] This prevented Mr. and Mrs. Elphinstone dining with us.

Sept. 24. Mr. Elphinstone has very politely offered us his bungalow at the top of the Ghaut, and Mr. Chaplin [2] one of his at Poona, but I am inclined to think we shall only go into our own Tents.

Sept. 29. Michaelmas Day. A name almost forgotten with those who have been long here. We must have a Goose to keep up all our English happy recollections.

Oct. 2. Martin, as Registrar, has had some very insolent notes from a civilian here, a Mr. Norris, Secretary to the Government, who is compelled to make an ample apology, which he did. I hope this spirit will prevent its occurring again. This is the consequence of the conduct of Government, and also of Sir Ralph Rice. I luckily did not hear of it till it was all over. Mr. Fenwick is the adviser, and a sensible, manly man he is, and yet cool. I have had a visit from Capt. Forbes of the *Sibbald;* little English news, except the appointment of Sir Thomas Bradford as our Commander-in-Chief.

Oct. 4. Edward is quite engrossed preparing his Charge for the Grand Jury, in which he means to state facts as to the illegal course of the Police Magistrates in flogging and banishing, etc., known to the Government from an official letter of Sir James Mackintosh's as he was leaving this place, when he says: "I take shame to myself for not having noticed or prevented it during my residence here."[3]

Oct. 5. Edward went in the evening to visit the gaol and to see the poor man who had been flogged the day

[1] Capt. Macdonald had married a Miss Elphinstone. See "Diary," 22nd July 1824, p. 189.

[2] Mr. Chaplain was Commissioner of the Deccan under Elphinstone.

[3] See page 188.

before the Petty Sessions. He was not out of Court till 6 o'clock.

Oct. 13. I received a packet of letters brought by Miss Webb, strongly recommended by the Duchess of Leeds, the Townsends, and other friends.

Oct. 14. Sessions commenced to-day; few prisoners; but one for murder.

CHAPTER XI

Sir James Mackintosh on illegal punishments—Sydney Smith's sermon—Sir Edward West's Charge to the Grand Jury on illegal and brutal flogging of natives and Europeans, on illegal banishment of natives, on illegal private imprisonment in guard-rooms.—Reply of the Grand Jury.

Lady West's Journal (October 18–December 31, 1825):—Death of Mr. Peacock; journey to the Ghauts; tigers; death of the Viceroy of Goa and of Mr. Adam; a fracas; Christmas festivities; Sir Lionel Smith; prisoners as labourers.

It will be seen from Lady West's diary that the arbitrary flogging of natives—incapable alike of resistance or appeal—had exercised the mind of Sir E. West for some time, and in an exhaustive report upon the practices of police courts and petty sessions, delivered as a Charge to the Grand Jury, the Chief Justice pointed out the severity and the illegality of many sentences pronounced by Company's judges and police magistrates.

Attention had already been called to these abuses in an official statement by Sir James Mackintosh—a Parthian shot as he left Bombay—but during the eleven years which intervened between the resignation of that able judge and the appointment of West, little notice seems to have been taken of Mackintosh's report. In that short interval no less than five judges had held the Recordership, or Acting-Recordership of Bombay. Life there had been too brief to enable any King's Judge to do more than carry on for his short term the routine duties of the office.

By a curious coincidence, many thousand miles away, in the great Minster at York, Sydney Smith had just preached before the Judges of Assize his well-known sermon on the "Judge that smites contrary to law."[1] In Bombay there was more material for such addresses than in York.

Sir E. West's charge was an important one, but it must be given in an abbreviated form.[2] The charge shows the lawless state of the Company's law courts, the hopeless antagonism of the old order to both justice and mercy as Sir E. West understood them, the courage of the Chief Justice—whom no prospect of wealth could bribe, nor unpopularity intimidate, in upholding the honour of the Crown and English justice and honour.

SIR E. WEST'S CHARGE TO THE GRAND JURY

Fourth Sessions, 1825.

"Gentlemen, it has long been my anxious wish to make some observations upon the subject of your duties as magistrates, and upon the pro-

[1] "Sittest thou to judge me after the law, and commandest me to be smitten contrary to the law," Acts xxiii. 3. The sermon is given at length in his published works.

[2] The charge in its original form occupies fifteen pages of octavo in small type.

ceedings of the stipendiary or police magistrates. I have however been obliged to defer the performance of this duty, partly on account of my incessant occupation in revising the Rules of the Supreme Court and reducing the practice of it to order and system, and partly on account of the want of complete judicial information upon the various topics upon which I am under the necessity of addressing you, but which at length I have been able to obtain, so far at least as to show you the necessity of a thorough reform in the proceedings of that department of criminal judicature.

"It is scarcely necessary to inform you that the magistrates and justices and Courts of Quarter and Petty Sessions are by law placed under the control and superintendence of the Supreme Court, and that it is the bounden duty of the Supreme Court to see that they do not abuse or exceed the authority by law vested in them.

"The charter of the Supreme Court, in addition to the general powers which it gives when it vests them with the same authority and jurisdiction as the Court of the King's Bench in England, points specially to this jurisdiction over the magistrates."

Having quoted the clause referring to this, Sir E. West continued:—

"By this clause of the charter, as well as by the general law of England, the magistrates are responsible to this Court, and to this Court alone, and no other authority than this Court has any control over them, except that the police magistrates hold their offices in the police at the pleasure of Government.

"It is then one of the most imperative and sacred of our duties to point out any irregularity in the proceedings of those courts and of the magistrates; and I know of no occasion so fitting for that purpose as a charge to the Grand Jury; not only on account of its publicity and solemnity, not only because many of the gentlemen who attend the Grand Jury fill also the office of magistrate, but because the Grand Jury is composed, as by the charter it is directed to be, of the principal inhabitants of the place, and who have therefore the most weight and influence in society. Above all, because you have, as a Grand Jury, the means and the right of inquiring into and presenting any abuses.

"I shall therefore proceed to call your attention first to the origin, the constitution, and powers of the Court of Petty Sessions; secondly, to the actual proceedings of that Court; thirdly, to the powers of the police magistrates, sitting singly or jointly; and lastly, to *their* actual proceedings.

"First, with respect to the origin, constitution, and powers of the Court of Petty Sessions.

"In tracing the origin of the Court of Petty Sessions, I shall have to request your attention to some very extraordinary facts with respect to the police of this island, and I trust that in so doing you will not suppose that I am endeavouring to excite any prejudice against the gentlemen who at present fill the office of police magistrates. Those facts may now be considered as matter of history, and they constitute a history pregnant with instruction. It will impress upon your minds with tenfold more force than any arguments of mine the necessity of a vigilant superintendence over those intrusted with the immense powers of the police. It will prove to you that for want of such constant superintendence nearly the same course of illegality has continued for nearly fifty years, in spite of the occasional interference of judges and Grand Juries.

"Gentlemen, I wish to state most explicitly, and to have it understood most distinctly, that in all my observations it is the system that I am assailing, and not the gentlemen who are now police magistrates. They have, it is but justice to them to state, but trodden in the footsteps of their predecessors. Strange as it sounds in the ears of Englishmen, of those at least who have lived long enough in England to imbibe the spirit of her constitution, the system of police here has been, as far back as it can be traced, a system of discretion, and never a system of law. I will do the present police magistrates the justice of saying, that I believe that none of the abuses, to which I shall draw your attention, have originated with them."

Sir E. West then briefly summarised the singular history of the police of Bombay, relying chiefly on the document framed by Sir James Mackintosh.

He pointed out that in 1779 the Grand Jury had "presented one James Todd (then Lieutenant of Police) as a public nuisance," and his office as "of a most dangerous tendency;" and had "earnestly recommended that it should be immediately abolished." . . . "The office, however, was not abolished . . . but continued in force during eleven years afterwards, when the same Todd was tried for corruption and convicted, and the name of 'Lieutenant of Police' abolished."

Later on, in 1794, however, the same office was vested in an officer called "Superintendent of Police," and this, in spite of the fact that the system had been explicitly annulled by a Royal Warrant of George III. The last holder of this office was convicted of corruption in the Recorder's Court, the trial bringing to light an extraordinary story of fraud, cruelty, and oppression.

Sir James Mackintosh had pointed out that the summary convictions and punishments by the police were illegal on four distinct grounds:—

(1) Because they were inflicted under rules possessing no authority.

(2) Because they were inflicted by a single magistrate (contrary to 47 Geo. III.).

(3) Because cases of felony cannot be dealt with by justices of peace.

(4) Because the punishments were such as could, under no circumstances, be inflicted by any court of summary jurisdiction.

"Gentlemen," continued the Chief Justice, "it is to Sir James Mackintosh, I repeat, that we owe the abolition of this office. That eminent person, in this remote and then obscure spot, commenced that course of alleviation and correction of our criminal law which he has since pursued in England. His exertions in that cause will hand his name down to posterity as one of the foremost in that honourable race of humanity and philanthropy in which so many of our countrymen are now engaged. Soon after this representation of Sir James Mackintosh, the present regulations were passed by the Government, and registered in the Recorder's Court. These regulations are very imperfect and scanty, and, in some instances, most unskilfully drawn; but they were intended, I presume, merely as an outline, and to be filled up by other regulations, which longer experience might prove or new exigencies render expedient.

"Gentlemen, it is only from these regulations and others which have since been duly passed and registered that the Petty Sessions and magistrates can derive any authority, except, indeed, such power as they are invested with by the English law respecting magistrates in England. In communicating this power of framing regulations, and to a certain extent, therefore, of legislating, the British legislature has proceeded with becoming caution and circumspection, and has provided every possible security that such regulations shall be conformable to the law of England. After they are passed by the Government, they must, before they have legal effect, be registered in the King's Court, with its approbation and consent. It is expressly provided that they shall not be repugnant to the laws of the realm; and it is the duty of the Court to reject any proposed regulations which should be repugnant to the laws of the realm. Further, an appeal lies against any such regulations to his Majesty in Council, who may disallow them; and copies of all such regulations are to be transmitted to one of his Majesty's principal Secretaries of State."

After criticising the careless and unskilful way in which these regulations had been framed, Sir Edward West proceeded to point out in detail the illegality of the punishments inflicted by the police magistrates, first dealing with the flagrant cases of illegal banishment.

Sir E. West continued:—

"I shall confine myself strictly to those facts of which I have judicial knowledge. By one of the regulations the Court is required to lay a summary of their convictions and punishments quarterly, before the Quarter Sessions of the Peace, the Court of Oyer and Terminer, and the Honourable the Governor in Council. The object of this rule was, of course, to give the Government, the King's Court, and magistrates, information as to the proceedings of the Court, in order to prevent, by means of their superintendence, a recurrence of the abuses, upon the discovery of which these rules were passed. This rule, when first I arrived in the country, was not complied with; no summaries were ever handed up to the Court of Oyer and Terminer. I therefore ordered that in future the senior magistrate of police should comply with the regulation; and to the convictions and punishments, as they appear on the face of these summaries, I shall almost entirely confine my observations. The first is as to the punishment of

"BANISHMENT.

"In the summary (the first which I have) which extends from the 6th of January 1823 to the 31st of March of the same year, a period of about three months, there are thirty-five instances of such punishment; and, in the next summary, extending from the 7th of April 1823 to the 30th of June in the same year, there are thirty such instances. You will observe also the proportion which these punishments bear to all the offences tried by the Petty Sessions. The whole number of cases tried by the Petty Sessions during the first period is sixty-one, including many offences of a trivial nature, such as 'driving without badges upon hackeries,' 'using abusive language,' 'and selling liquor without a licence.' Out of these sixty-one cases there are thirty-five sentences of banishment. . . .

"Gentlemen, in the regulations there are some provisions, which passed in 1813, respecting the sending *aliens* off the island. The first is in the case of an alien's non-payment of a fine imposed for not entering his name with the muccadum of his caste. The second is, where aliens live idle without work; in which case they may be committed to jail, and be flogged, and, upon a second conviction, upon production of the former record, they may be sent off the island. This punishment, however, has been constantly and indiscriminately inflicted upon all persons, without inquiry as to their place of birth, or domicile; and not one of the sentences of banishment in the summaries has proceeded upon the above-mentioned provisions.

"To warrant this punishment, a punishment inflicted upon summary conviction, there is not a shadow of authority, even for any the most heinous offence. But for what is it inflicted?—'for being found in suspicious situations,' 'for being bad characters,'—and that by a Court of which two out of three of the judges are stipendiary or police magistrates.

"But, gentlemen, you may wish, and it is necessary for you to know how this sentence of banishment is carried into effect, and what is the precise meaning of the sentence—'that the prisoner do receive a pass-note.'

"Upon the sentence being passed, a note is sent by the police to the Custom-house; that note is signed by the officer at the Custom-house, and a police sepoy takes the note and the prisoner to the passage-boat, which passes over to the mainland. The prisoner is placed in charge of the tindal, who has directions to land the prisoner at Panwell or the nearest mainland; and the prisoner is accordingly there landed and turned loose. The prisoner is also threatened, in order to prevent his returning, with severe punishment in case he should be found again on the island; nor is this a mere idle or vain threat, as you have seen—'three months' solitary confinement,' and 'three dozen lashes,' are the penalties for returning from banishment."

Quoting with approval Sir J. Mackintosh's dictum that "the greatest inconvenience that can befall any community is to be governed by a power without law," Sir E. West showed that since the sentence of banishment by the Company's magistrates was utterly illegal, it was no crime to return from banishment, and that consequently the heavy punishments inflicted for this imaginary offence were as illegal as they were cruel.

"Had the persons so sentenced," said Sir E. West, "petitioned the King's Court to be brought up by *habeas corpus* we must have discharged them. But in most cases the prisoners so sentenced had no opportunity of so petitioning, being confined in the police guard-room."

The Chief Justice then called the attention of the Grand Jury to another punishment, that of

FLOGGING.

". . . The power of the Petty Sessions to inflict this punishment must be derived from regulations made" [for Bengal] "under the Statute 39th & 40th Geo. III., c. 79, s. 18, which enacts 'that it shall be lawful for the Governor-General and Council . . . to order . . . such *moderate and reasonable* corporal punishment . . . as to them shall seem fit and expedient, for the breach . . . of any rules . . . by them made, subject nevertheless to . . . registry, publication, approbation, power of appeal . . . Provided always . . . that no such corporal punishment shall in any case be . . . inflicted except only in case of due conviction . . . before two justices of the peace . . .'

"This power, subject to the same provisions, extended to the Governments of Madras and Bombay . . .

"Gentlemen, I shall proceed to consider, first, whether this punishment, as it is actually inflicted by the Petty Sessions, is reasonable and moderate;

and secondly, whether it has been limited to those offences for which it can by the regulations be inflicted.

"You are, perhaps, aware the punishment is inflicted with a rattan upon the naked back. The sufferer is tied usually, I believe, to a tree.

"Upon the subject of the severity of this punishment I shall beg to read to you a letter of the late High Sheriff, Captain Hughes, who, as you know, has the legal custody of the jail, and has been a military man, and has therefore witnessed the punishment of flogging as practised in the army.

"'My Lord, the infliction of punishment by rattan, as now practised in jails, being attended with extraordinary severity, drawing blood at every stripe, and sometimes taking off with it small pieces of flesh; and, in full assurance that a measure so extreme will not, when known, be sanctioned by your lordship, I beg leave, in consequence, respectfully to propose that a drummer's cat be made use of in the jail in lieu of the rattan, which, however formidable it may be in appearance, is far less severe and injurious in its effects. In support of this opinion, I may be permitted to state, that there is now in my custody a battalion sepoy, who, on the 3rd inst. received three hundred lashes on his left shoulder by the drummers of his corps; and on the 13th of the same month (being committed to jail) eighteen lashes with a rattan were inflicted on the other shoulder. The wounds on both are still unhealed. On being questioned as to the difference in point of severity of the two punishments, he declared with confidence, that they did not bear comparison, and was one or the other to be repeated, and a choice given, that he would gladly take the former.

"'Though I do not credit,' proceeds Captain Hughes, 'the sepoy's assertion to its fullest extent, still, as he speaks from experience, and has a further punishment hanging over him, his opinion may be deemed to deserve consideration.'

"Upon receipt of this letter, I immediately addressed the surgeon, who is appointed by the Government to attend the jail, Dr. Smytton, and requested him to give me his opinion in writing. It is as follows:—

"'My Lord,—In reference to your enquiries on the subject of certain punishments, I have the honour to state, as my opinion, that flogging with the rattan is a very severe punishment, in so far as I may yet be allowed to judge from my limited experience of such cases in the jail.' (Dr. Smytton had been but a short time surgeon of the jail.)

"'When inflicted,' continues Dr. Smytton, 'on the bare back, in the manner usual in the jail here, one stroke is equal, I think, to at least a dozen with the cat, as applied in military punishments, and it is liable to be much aggravated by any accidental splitting of the cane.'

"Upon receipt of these letters I immediately sent for the junior magistrate of police, mentioned these facts to him, and suggested the propriety of adopting some other mode of punishment, or at least of inflicting that punishment with more moderation. I desired him also to communicate my sentiments to the senior magistrate of police; and I also mentioned the subject repeatedly to some other gentlemen who are justices of the peace. These suggestions, I believe, have had some effect; the punishment of flogging is not, I believe, inflicted so frequently as it used to be, nor generally to the same extent, though, in the last summary, I still observe instances of prisoners being sentenced to two inflictions of three dozen each.

"In the Supreme Court, where of course the highest classes of offences are tried, I never sentenced, even before I received this information, any offender to more than two dozen stripes at one time; and since we have received this information, we have applied this punishment with much more moderation. In the Petty Sessions it used to be a very common sentence, and that sentence still occurs, that the offender do receive three dozen lashes before he go to jail, that then he be imprisoned one, two, or three months, and at the expiration of that time receive three dozen more. According to information which I have received, and upon which I can rely, the wounds of the first infliction are frequently scarcely healed before the second is suffered.

"Gentlemen, the scars of these wounds are never obliterated but by death, and consequent dissolution of the body; and you may observe the scars on many a native as he toils along the streets of the town under the burthen of a palanquin.

"The persons present at these punishments are generally, as Sir James Mackintosh observes, only a handful of timid natives. But it so happens that on one of the occasions of the infliction of this punishment at the office of the junior magistrate of police, a reverend gentleman . . . , Mr. Jackson, happened to be at the office. I heard of the circumstance, and requested him to give me his opinion in writing, which he has done, and permitted me to make this use of it. It is as follows :—

"'In reply to your note of the 10th, I have to inform you that I witnessed the punishment which you allude to, and which I will endeavour to describe.

"'I happened some weeks since to call on one of the magistrates, whom I found engaged in his office. A Hindoo was before him, charged with stealing some turban cloth; the theft was clearly proved, and the prisoner sentenced to be *publicly* flogged, and to receive six lashes, or, as I afterwards found to be the case, strokes to be inflicted by a cane.

"'The man was immediately tied up to a tree

in a yard adjoining the house, and one of the policemen proceeded to inflict the strokes.

"'The punishment was most severe, and to me most disgusting; and I confess I was much surprised to find that the spirit of prison discipline, as it is termed, and which is now a subject which engages considerable attention in England, had not found its way to her Eastern Colonies. . . .'

"The infliction in this case was but six blows; what must be the effect of six times six, or three dozen blows, some of them necessarily falling repeatedly upon the same place, upon the wounds made by the first blows?

"Gentlemen, in considering what is moderate and reasonable corporal punishment within the words of the statute, we must of course take into the account the nature of the offence; and I need not ask you whether for common assaults . . . three dozen lashes . . . is a moderate and reasonable corporal punishment? The rule itself is a most extraordinary one, which authorises flogging for assaults, affrays, and defamatory words; but even that rule cannot authorise the infliction of a punishment so disproportioned to the offence, and which is, consequently, in respect of the offence, so *immoderate* and *unreasonable.*

"This punishment of flogging, too, is often inflicted in its utmost severity for returning from banishment, which is no offence at all.

"We come now to another class of offences,

for which this punishment is inflicted by the Petty Sessions, in its utmost severity, upon British as well as native subjects of his Majesty. . . .

"By the statute 2d, Geo. II., c. 37, justices of the peace may punish seamen in the [Company's] merchant service, who shall desert or absent themselves from, or leave, the ship before they are discharged, by forfeiture of wages, and imprisonment for a limited period; but there is no power given to flog or inflict any corporal punishment except that of imprisonment.

"I shall not recapitulate the cases in which this punishment, as well as that of banishment, is inflicted upon persons for the offence of 'being found in suspicious situations.'

"The only further observations which I shall make upon this species of punishment is, that it is mostly inflicted not in jail, but by the police immediately after conviction, so that the prisoner has no opportunity of applying to the Supreme Court for a *habeas corpus*, should he, as is most improbable, be aware of its illegality, and have the means of getting his petition and necessary affidavit prepared.

"I now come to another species of sentence, 'that the prisoner do find securities for his good behaviour.' When such a sentence is passed, the Court should mention in it the kind and amount of the security; as, that he should find security for his good behaviour for such a time, himself in such a sum, with two such sufficient sureties in such a sum each. It is, however, almost always passed in the Petty Sessions in the manner I have mentioned; 'that the prisoner do give security,' without specifying the period for which, or the sum in which, or whether sureties are required or not. Upon such sentence not mentioning sureties, the Court have no right to require sureties, but must be satisfied with the prisoner's own security.

"Gentlemen, upon these sentences to find security, prisoners have been frequently confined for very long periods of time. Thus, on the 6th of October 1817, a man . . . was sentenced to hard labour till he should find securities. Under this sentence he remained in jail till July 1823, a period of six years, when he died in jail. There are almost innumerable other instances of prisoners being confined for very long periods under like sentences. I hold in my hand a list of a few of them, which I directed the Marshal to make out. I will trouble you with only one of them. On the 23rd of February 1824, one George Bartley was convicted by the Petty Sessions of an assault, and he was sentenced to three months' imprisonment in the county jail, and the last month to solitary confinement, and at the expiration of those three months to enter into a recognizance to keep the peace towards Louisa Bartley his wife. After the expiration of three months he applied again and again to the senior magistrate of police for his discharge, who refused it upon the ground that he had not found sureties. He proposed sureties more than once, but they were rejected. He petitioned me several times for his discharge, but as he never sent me a copy of the warrant, I presumed that he was legally imprisoned, and of course did not interfere. At last, however, I directed him, in answer to his last petition, to send a copy of the warrant, which he did, and it appeared by the warrant and sentence that no sureties were necessary. I accordingly intimated to the senior magistrate of police that he was entitled to be discharged upon his own recognizance; and that unless he was so discharged, I should order him to be brought up before me by *habeas corpus*, upon which he was discharged, but not till after he had been imprisoned eight months, during five of which he was illegally confined.

"Gentlemen, all I can say in excuse of the police magistrate upon this occasion, is, that I believe he thought he was acting legally; and there certainly is not the least ground to impute to him any malicious or improper motive.

"There is one other circumstance which I must bring to your attention, with respect both to the Petty Sessions and to the police magistrates, sitting either jointly or separately. It is the imprisonment of persons in the police guard-rooms, for long periods.

"Soon after my arrival in this country, I desired the Marshal to send me weekly a return of all the prisoners in jail, which has since been regularly done. I have been constantly much surprised at observing about a week or ten days before the sessions, scarcely any prisoners for trial mentioned in this weekly return; but when the sessions arrived, have found that we had fifteen or sixteen, or sometimes twenty or more prisoners to try; and upon inquiry I have learnt that the prisoners have been kept for weeks in the police guard-rooms, after the depositions have been taken, instead of committing them, as should have been done, immediately to the jail. I have mentioned this subject several times to the magistrates, and, I believe, with some effect. But let us look to the return I received last Monday week, and compare it with the present calendar. The return of last Monday week was two prisoners in jail for trial; the calendar contains nineteen prisoners for trial; and on looking to the depositions in one case, . . . the depositions and recognizances were taken on the 6th of September, the warrant of commitment, which I sent for, bears date the 29th of September. . . .

"With respect to the imprisonment of persons in the police guard-room, after conviction, I have not been able to ascertain whether it is a general practice; but one case, which appeared to me at the time to be a very aggravated one, came to my notice some time since. A petition was presented to me by a near relative of a man, . . . which stated that he had then been confined in the police guard-room for twelve days. I inquired into the facts, found that there was no warrant, and directed him to be brought up, by *habeas corpus*, and on the return to that writ it appeared that he had been convicted before the Petty Sessions of retailing tobacco without a licence, and the sentence of the Court was, that 'he should be fined under the sixth clause of the seventh regulation, and that the tobacco should be confiscated.' This was the whole of the sentence: there was no sentence of imprisonment; but, nevertheless, he was imprisoned, as I have mentioned, in the police guard-room for twelve days, and till he was discharged under the *habeas corpus*. This imprisonment was utterly illegal: it was illegal, because there was no sentence of imprisonment; and it was illegal, because, if there had been such sentence, he should have been committed, not to the police guard-room, but to the jail. . . .

"Gentlemen, the mischievous tendency of this practice of imprisoning persons in the police guard-rooms, instead of committing them to jail, is almost too obvious to require comment. The prisoners have no means of sending petitions for *habeas corpus* to the judges; the other magistrates have no means of visiting the jail; the grand juries never think of visiting or inspecting them; and the prisoners are entirely under the control of native clerks and constables, who, you well know, are to be trusted very cautiously with power.

"I should have thought that the abuses of this system, which were brought to public view on the trial of the head clerk, or purvoe, of the late junior magistrate of police,[1] would have operated as a sufficient warning to the police magistrates against the continuance of it. That person is still in jail under the sentence of the Recorder's Court. But this sentence has been as inoperative to check abuse as the presentments of grand juries and the protest of Sir James Mackintosh.

"I now come to the powers of the police magistrates, sitting . . . singly . . .

"By article fourth of Regulation I. of 1812, 'each magistrate shall ordinarily, within his own district, and occasionally elsewhere in the island, do all acts that a single justice of the peace may by the law of England do.'

"By article fifth of the same Regulation, 'each of them shall, in the same manner, apprehend, examine, and commit for trial, all persons charged before him with any breach or violation of any rule now legally passed, or hereafter to be legally passed, by the Honourable the

[1] Erskine.

Governor in Council.' These are all the powers of the magistrates, with the exception of those given by some of the Regulations with respect to servants.

. . . .

"I was not a little surprised, after Sir James Mackintosh's protest against the proceedings of the superintendent of police, to hear, some time since, that the police magistrates, sitting singly, were in the habit of trying and punishing felonies, of flogging, and banishing. As soon as I was made aware of these proceedings, I directed the Clerk of the Crown to order the magistrates, in pursuance of the Regulation before alluded to, to make a quarterly return of the crimes and punishments tried and inflicted in their respective offices."

Sir E. West then quoted cases from the returns made by the junior magistrate.

"Upon referring to the return of the senior magistrate made at these sessions, I find that he also has pursued the same course of trying felonies, flogging, and banishing.

"I need not repeat to you, that it is utterly illegal for magistrates to try felonies; . . . and that, by the statute, it is illegal that flogging should be inflicted by *one* magistrate. It is utterly illegal for the Petty Sessions, or magistrates, to banish, except under the single Regulation which I have before mentioned.

"You must be aware of the care, of the scrutiny, of the sifting of evidence, which are necessary in this country to arrive at justice. My experience has already taught me, that the most usual instrument of revenge among the natives, is a criminal charge in courts of justice. Malicious prosecutions are most common. The witnesses can in no case be implicitly relied upon, and the duty of the judges in administering criminal justice is a most arduous one. Notwithstanding the solemnity of a superior Court, which, as we well know, has a very considerable effect upon native witnesses in keeping them nearer to the truth; notwithstanding the time we give to each case, with our professional habits of sifting evidence, with the aid, too, of most intelligent petty juries, with the advantage of depositions previously taken before a magistrate, and which enable us to detect the witnesses in any variance of their testimony—we have frequently the greatest difficulty in eliciting the truth. Again and again, when the case for prosecution has appeared clear beyond contradiction, some variance, or other circumstance, has turned up at nearly the close of the case, which has given a different colour to the whole transaction, and, ultimately, the prisoner has been acquitted. Such being the difficulty in the Supreme Court, what security is there, or rather I should say, what chance is there of justice being done in a magistrate's office, in the hurry of business, with none of the experience or the aid which the judges possess?

"Upon this subject I shall again have recourse to Sir James Mackintosh.

"'It is,' says that eminent person, 'a still more melancholy reflection that this system is not only a continued breach of law, but contains no tolerable security for the observance of justice. Criminal charges are tried before a *single* person. His power cannot be limited by law, since it does not issue from law.

"'It is fettered by no rule or form of proceeding. It is exercised under no restraint from the public. The persons present are, in general, only a handful of timid natives. Nine-tenths of the condemnations are unknown to any man who would dare to utter or even to form an opinion.

"'If this uncontrolled magistrate deigns to record the case at all, he does it in a language unknown to those who are alone interested to correct him, and he may give any colour to the facts that suits his purpose.

"'He is not obliged or accustomed to lay even the most brief extract of such records before any superior authority.

"'There are no rules which allow time for defence, or prescribe limits to the punishment.

"'It is after such trial (if that word may be used on such an occasion) that many hundreds of men, entitled to all the privileges of British subjects, have been fined and flogged without limits, have been banished, and condemned to the condition of galley-slaves. In such a plan, it is surely great moderation of language to say that there is no security for justice. It is no reflection on any man to impute to him the common quality of human nature. We cannot have the least approach to a reasonable ground of belief that the majority of punishments so inflicted may not be unjust.

"'That absolute power corrupts every man who has the misfortune to exercise it, is an obvious and most certain truth which has been repeated very often indeed, but, unfortunately, not often enough to produce its due effect.

"'A precipitate, clandestine, and arbitrary jurisdiction, a power of trying as a judge pleases, of convicting for what crime he pleases, and condemning to what punishment he pleases, without responsibility to his superiors, restraint from law, or check from public opinion, would be a situation of danger to the highest human virtue, and is perfectly sure to corrupt common human integrity. When this is joined to the undefined jurisdiction exercised respecting castes; to the influence possessed over the appointment of the chiefs of castes; to the power extended, under various pretences, to mere questions of property; to the minute information supposed to be conveyed to the superintendent by his spies; and to the terror carried into the poorest hovel by his peons dispersed over the island, the whole forms an authority so terrible as to have few parallels in civilised society.'

"Gentlemen, Sir James Mackintosh was here drawing a picture of the police as it was in his day. I am sorry to say that, with a very slight alteration (I mean as to the sentences of prisoners to work in chains, and to the power of appointing heads of castes), the years that have passed have not destroyed, or even much impaired, the resemblance.

"With respect to questions of property, the Petty Sessions, long after my arrival here, were in the habit of deciding them without a shadow of right; and it is but very lately, if at all, that they have discontinued the practice of settling rights to land in a summary way.

"I think I have said enough to convince you that the whole system of police in this island is illegal; that it is such that palliatives can be of no use. It would be vain to attempt to reduce this system to one of law and justice by lopping and pruning. It must be entirely eradicated. A new system must be adopted.

"Gentlemen, I have now performed a very unpleasant duty. It cannot be pleasant to me to throw blame, even impliedly, upon any persons, and, least of all, upon gentlemen holding the respectable offices of police magistrates. I will again repeat, in justice to them, that the course which they have been pursuing is that in which most of their predecessors have, I believe, trod for many years. Indeed, I have reason to think that within these last two years the system has been considerably alleviated; and I know that, in many cases of cruelty to native servants, the magistrates have afforded them redress against their European masters. One case in particular, Gentlemen, I must mention to you. A few weeks since a native presented to me a petition, stating that he had been flogged most severely with a riding-whip by his European master for the crime of asking for his wages, which were six months in arrear. His back was scored with the wounds of the whip. I immediately sent him to the Petty Sessions, to which, indeed, he had before applied, but, by some mistake or misconduct of the native purvoe, without effect. The complaint was entered, the master summoned, and fined seventy rupees. Gentlemen, I must do the senior magistrate of police the justice to say that in all these cases between natives and Europeans he does his duty most impartially and most exemplarily, without respect of persons, without fear or favour. This is no mean praise in a country like this; and I trust, indeed I am confident, that he will take every means of repressing a system so disgraceful to the name and character of Englishmen as that of flogging servants. Gentlemen, I have already mentioned to you that this system of police has continued in much the same state for nearly fifty years; but the very inveteracy of the system, though some excuse to the magistrates, makes it the more necessary that I should take this public notice of it. Sir James Mackintosh in the very document, parts of which I have read to you, reproaches himself most severely, but perhaps without cause, for not having before interfered to prevent such a system of illegality. It was in the last year of his residence here that he framed that representation. But, as he therein mentions that he had before that time only suspicions and no judicial knowledge of the illegality of the system, it appears to me that he takes blame to himself without cause.[1]

"With these summaries, and the other facts which I have mentioned within my own judicial knowledge, I should have no such excuse. I am resolved that I will not, at the termination of my residence here, have any cause for self-reproach; nor will I afford occasion for my successor in office to blame me for supineness and neglect of the most important duties.

"Gentlemen, I have but a word more. It is to point out to you the parts of this system to which I would recommend you to direct your immediate

[1] Mackintosh had thrown up his judicial appointment, and had left for England in November 1811, a Madras judge, Sir J. Newbolt, temporarily taking his place.

attention. The subject will be renewed at every sessions when I have the pleasure of addressing you. I would propose then to you, that you should at these sessions direct your attention to the punishment of flogging, and that, should you not be satisfied with the evidence which I have already laid before you, you should call witnesses, and examine them upon that subject. With respect to many of these abuses (I mean those of which the Court can obtain judicial knowledge) we shall, after this public notice, use all the means in our power to prevent their recurrence. But I am confident that you, Gentlemen, will be most anxious to participate in the satisfaction and the honour of correcting the system which I have exposed to you, and of ameliorating the condition of the millions entrusted by Providence to our protection."

Sir Edward West's charge was not received with enthusiasm by his audience, many of whom were magistrates.

The Grand Jury thanked the Chief Justice, but considered that the police regulations, even if illegal, were expedient—that any reduction in the power of the police magistrates would be attended with the greatest danger—that, with regard to banishment and flogging, "no change was expedient either in the frequency or severity of those punishments, or in the instrument with which the latter is inflicted." They considered that there was no undue severity in the flogging witnessed by the Reverend C. Jackson, though it "might shock the feelings of a gentleman unaccustomed to such sights."[1]

The sentiments of the Bombay Grand Jury were happily not universal. A Calcutta newspaper reviewing the charge, says: "It reflected the highest honour on the learned judge who delivered it, not for its eloquence—that is evidently not aimed at—but for its subject-matter. In this country where, from the remoteness of all check over the actions of men in power, and the absence of the salutary control of the Press, there is a constant tendency to abuse power, and a union of all who possess it to support each other in unconstitutional conduct, it must be refreshing to every one whose love of liberty has not given way to servility, which a dependence on the nod of power engenders, to behold a British judge untainted by the atmosphere of corruption by which he is surrounded, laying open the abuses practised with impunity for years past, and announcing his determination to employ the power entrusted to him as the representative of his Majesty in the administration of justice, and in vindication of violated rights."

[1] *Oriental Herald*, vol. ix. p. 425.

FROM LADY WEST'S JOURNAL

Oct. 18, 1825. Last evening was a long and anxious one, having heard that Martin West[1] had called upon a gentleman for an apology for rude conduct. I am truly rejoiced to say that the man has made an apology, so there's an end of it; but here they are *such* a set, for Martin's is a very good temper, and is certainly not quarrelsome, though People might think him so from these things.

Oct. 19. The Sessions finished to-day; I quite rejoiced, as Edward looks fagged.

Oct. 21. Edward always busy all day at chambers. We drove in the evening to Colaba and witnessed the funeral of 2 privates of the Queen's Royals. The burying-ground was a melancholy sight—2 rows of new graves; I suppose about 50 since we last walked there. It made us reflect on the uncertainty of life, and particularly in this climate, where one ought to try to be prepared to leave this life whenever it may please the Almighty to take us. I see by the paper the death of poor Mr. Peacock at Madras (Sir W. Franklin's nephew). What a total and awful visitation there has been on all that family.[2] Those who remain in England must shudder at the name of Madras.

Oct. 27. We drank tea with the Bakers last evening on board their yacht. It was very cool and pleasant. At 6 we had to get into the bunda boat to cross to Panwell to commence our journey to the ghauts.

Nov. 2. We took a very pretty walk last evening in the Lonowlee wood,[3] where the creepers are the largest and finest I ever saw, as large round as my body, and twining from tree to tree. The noise of the jackals in the evening is quite hideous.

Nov. 6. We heard that a small tyger was killed here a few evenings ago, and a fresh skin is certainly to be seen. The guards are a great comfort.

Nov. 7. We are told that there are black bears here, and the soldiers say that they hear the tygers grumbling of a night on the hill. We hear wonderful stories of tygers. A month ago one attacking a cow, and though 50 men

[1] Nephew of Sir E. West. [2] See p. 156.

[3] At this time "the wood of Lanowlie was known to the natives as a favourite haunt of tigers."—"Memoirs of a Highland Lady," p. 433.

tried to rescue her they could not; the tyger eat half of her and then marched off. Edward has been answering letters from the Duke of Buckingham and Mr. Courtenay.[1]

Nov. 16.[2] Edward is busily engaged answering Mr. Wynn's letters of enquiries as to half-castes on Jury. He has also written a letter to Mr. Brougham.

Nov. 18. Edward has begun again his Political Economy. One of the soldiers has just brought us a cobra capello which he had but half killed. This is the fourth he has destroyed, but we must be more careful in our walking; it was 5 feet 3 inches in length.

Nov. 21. We heard yesterday that a tyger had the night before half eat up a cow, we therefore got the villagers to show us the way, and walked there; a most picturesque walk and sequestered wild spot, where we plainly saw the marks of the paws down the bank across the road and up another bank, where we saw the mangled carcase, which the people had put into a sort of trap covered over with heavy timbers and stones to fall upon the tyger when he goes in; in this way they caught one the week before our arrival. I have bespoke the skin should it be caught. I now begin to believe about tygers being here. We also saw 2 wild peacocks flying.

Nov. 24. A horrid animal was brought in alive by one of the sepoys, something like a tortoise with pig's face and human hands, the Portuguese and Hindoos eat them.[3] 3 wild hogs passed by our tents quite close.

[1] Charles W. W. Wynn, Joseph Phillimore, D.C.L. of Oxford, a distinguished lawyer and scholar, and Mr. Courtenay were the three members of the Board of Control until the advent of the Duke of Wellington's ministry.

[2] In Europe this day began a week of historic gales. The *Annual Register* reports that in St. Petersburg men, women, and children were drowned before they could escape, and that the street became full of wrecked ships and drowned animals; that for days no food was obtained, and all business ceased. On the 23rd Nov., according to the same authority, ships "foundered at Portsmouth in all directions." It must have been on this day (though local tradition says the 25th) that the sea broke through the Chesil Bank near Weymouth, and destroyed the village of Fleet; and that a sloop was lifted up and carried by the sea over a great part of the Chesil Bank, finally making its way to the backwater, and so to Portland by the most extraordinary overland route ever accomplished by a vessel of the royal navy.

[3] Probably the Indian pangolin, an ant-eater, covered with scales arranged like those of a spruce fir cone, and with long finger-like claws.

Nov. 26. The account of the dinner and speeches to Sir Charles Colville[1] at Bombay quite disgusting, really with such a set of people praise is quite a libel. Sir Charles Chambers says that Sir Ralph Rice was quite a mountebank. More thunder this afternoon and a very heavy shower of rain. I have heard from Sir Lionel Smith,[2] who cannot yet leave Poona, sending off troops to the South. Edward's purvoe has arrived to copy his Political Economy,[3] and made us laugh with the account of his journey. His "hackney came in two pieces." He "had to send back for a she-buffalo to bring his things, and he came by walk."

Dec. 1. We have heard to-day with real regret of the death of the poor Viceroy of Goa.[4] I know of no situation which can be so melancholy as that of Viceroy; I scarcely know how or when he can get away from Goa. We shall write and ask her [the Viceroy's widow] to come to us at Bombay if that will be of any use to her. They are certainly the people we have received the most delicate attention from, since we have been in India.

Dec. 6. We have heard with real regret of the death of Captain Alexander[5] at Calcutta, and that the Burmese war is commencing again.

Dec. 7. I am pleased to see extracts from one of the Calcutta papers praising Edward's Charge. It will, I think, occasion improvement at Calcutta; at all events investigation, which does good.

Dec. 9. The Chambers dined with us yesterday. We hear that Mr. Adam[6] died on his passage home, and that Mr. Graham has been horsewhipping Mr. Irwin at the billiard-table in the presence of Mr. Warden; this is the result of the barristers' conduct to the Court.

Dec. 15. Sir Lionel Smith and Captain Keith arrived unexpectedly, and took an early dinner with us, and at 6

[1] Apparently a dinner got up by a Mr. Crawford for party purposes. See Sir E. West's letter, p. 230.

[2] Commander of the army of the Deccan. See p. 83.

[3] The second pamphlet. See p. 20.

[4] The Governor of Goa, who had served in the Peninsular War, had lately entertained the Wests. See chapter ix. p. 162.

[5] See p. 93.

[6] Temporary Governor-General of Bengal. On this day the *Enterprise*, a vessel propelled by steam, managed to reach Calcutta from England.

proceeded on their way to Bombay in all anxiety to see Lady Smith and his daughters, whom he had not seen for 17 years. He was so pleasing, and cheerful, and gentleman-like, we quite enjoyed our day. I have been writing to Mr. Strickland[1] and Lord Nelson.[2]

Dec. 25. Christmas Day. The first we have passed at home since we married. We shall try and make it as cheerful as we can; I have ordered an English dinner, and we shall have champagne. Batt[3] will have as much party as she can, and I have a Snap Dragon in the evening. All our People have been to us to make *Salaam*, and we have ordered them all some Sheep for their Curries.

Dec. 26. Five boxes have come by the *Upton Castle;* I am quite anxious to unpack them. No one who has not been so far from England can imagine the delight of a box from thence and packed by those one loves.

Dec. 27. Two more servants ill; it is quite disheartening, but we understand it is the same all over the Deccan.

Dec. 28 (*Wednesday*). 36 Hamauls[4] just arrived, and a Troop of Bullocks as we are all off to-morrow. I regret it, as I always do, leaving home where one has been comfortable. I omitted to mention a circumstance Captain Keith spoke of, that he had seen 50 Prisoners from the Bombay gaol working in Sir Charles Colville's garden in chains about three years and a half ago. Can anything be so revolting to good English feeling? In a soldier, it surprised me, though Mrs. Warden once told Edward a more horrible story; a postillion had died from flogging—can it be possible?

Dec. 29. Packing up to leave Lonowlee, having been very comfortable for more than 2 months.

Dec. 31. Left Chowk yesterday, and arrived at Panwell at 10, the hamauls carried us so fast. Had our breakfast quietly, and then a visit from Sir Lionel Smith, who was at the Rest House with all his party. At 12 we went over to call—Lady Smith looking well. The young ladies very tall,

[1] Of Cokethorpe Park, Oxon.

[2] First Earl Nelson and Bronte. The admiral's elder brother, cousin of Lady West.

[3] Lady West's maid.

[4] Porters.

but all nature, happiness, and good humour. We arrived at our own house at 8, having had a nice sail, and though Bombay is not a nice place, I was glad to get *home*. The end of the year, always a melancholy reflection. May the next be equally prosperous, and may we become better people.

CHAPTER XII

Bombay society in quarrelsome mood; libels, assaults, and challenges—Attempt to inveigle the Chief Justice into a duel with the Governor—Correspondence between Sir Edward West and Mr. Elphinstone.

Lady West's Journal **(January 8–February 2, 1826):—Sir R. Rice; trials for assault and libel; death of Col. Baker; Col. Stannus calls on Sir E. West.**

Sir Edward West's Memorandum on Mr. Warden's conduct.

THE new year found Bombay society in quarrelsome mood. Mr. Norton, the loud-voiced Advocate-General to the Bombay Government, had been challenged by a Mr. Browne, but had refused to go out with him. Martin West (Sir E. West's nephew) had been insulted by Mr. Norris, a member of the Bombay Government, and had been obliged to demand an apology; Mr. Graham, an attorney, had libelled and had challenged Mr. Irwin, a barrister, and, on the challenge being declined, had horsewhipped him. Mr. Warden had circulated a defamatory paper, aspersing the character of Mr. Graham; and trials for assault and libel occupied the attention of the Supreme Court.

In this stormy atmosphere it must have occurred to those who were smarting under Sir E. West's recent charge to the Grand Jury, and to

P

whom an independent King's Court was a standing inconvenience, that the Chief Justice might with advantage be provoked into fighting a duel. There were difficulties in the way, no doubt, but the desired end might be attained; and Mr. Elphinstone, who, whatever his moral strength, was never deficient in physical courage, was obviously the right antagonist. So without a written challenge, which would remain as evidence, an attempt was apparently made to bring about a meeting.

The actual message sent by the Governor must remain a mystery; that delivered by his messenger is given fully in Sir E. West's letter, and in the following extracts from Lady West's "Journal":—

Jan. 3, 1826. We did not go to the Gala last evening, which was, I hear, thinly and badly attended. We have had visitors all day and but one subject of discussion, the late disgraceful fracas, but I prevent the discussion as much as I can. There is good news from Burma. A victory after three days' fighting, but the particulars not yet known.

Jan. 6. We dined yesterday at Parell; Mr. Elphinstone handed the Bride, Mrs. G. Forbes, to dinner, and I went down with Mr. Warden. The Governor thought proper not to allot any Lady to Edward, though the First Person in the room, and it was so unusual that before he had time to look round all the Ladies were gone, and he left to walk downstairs among the Cadets; and when he reached the dining-room he was obliged to ask General Wilson and Mr. Burrowes[1] to allow his Servant to place a chair between them. Edward wished to have come away quietly as soon as the gentlemen came up into the Drawing room and to avoid Mr. Elphinstone, who stopped him at the head of the

[1] See p. 232.

stairs and said something about a slight mistake. Edward of course asked for an explanation, this not being the first or the 10th time Mr. Elphinstone has behaved with rudeness at his house. Of course, we then came away, expecting to receive some apology next morning for such extraordinary conduct. This morning, whilst Edward was walking on the esplanade a note was brought from Colonel Macdonald[1] to beg for a few moments' conversation alone. He soon rode up, and with not much Courtesy actually challenged Edward unless he made an apology for what he said the night before; certainly rather reversing the Tables, as of course Edward [illegible] an apology from him; and as to going out, as Edward told Colonel Macdonald, he was amazed both at Mr. Elphinstone's sending, and his bringing such a Message. He could only consider it as a Taunt; and then to get out of it, Edward's word the night before of "explanation," was tortured into "*satisfaction.*" Edward, of course, wrote to Mr. Elphinstone his astonishment at the mistaken words, and if he fancied Edward challenged him, why did he send a friend to appoint time and place.

I fear this must end in an open breach, which I shall regret, as Edward has put up with so much for the last 3 years. Capt. Tucker dined here in the Eveng. Edward had an answer from Mr. E., shuffling of course as he always does. Edward has been writing again to Mr. Elphinstone.

The following letters of Sir Edward West are copies in Lady West's handwriting. The letter from Elphinstone is in his own handwriting.

BOMBAY, *Jany.* 6, 1826.

SIR,—I was much surprised at receiving this morning a Message from you through Col. Macdonald, conveying to me a Challenge.

After expressing my astonishment at this to Col. Macdonald, he stated that you had understood me last night to say that I would waive my situation, and that I said something about satisfaction—I gave him my honor that I had

[1] Colonel Macdonald, a relation probably of Captain Macdonald who had married Miss Elphinstone. Chapter ix.

never used those words, or any which would bear such construction, and utterly disclaimed any intention of using terms which could convey such meaning. Col. Macdonald in answer said that you had not asserted that I had used those terms, but that the impression upon your mind was that such was my meaning.

I again disclaimed such intention, and repeated the words which I did really use, which were that I expected an explanation of what occurred last night. Col. Macdonald, however, did not think proper, even upon this disclaimer and explanation, to make any apology for his extraordinary message to me, but stated again and again that he was requested to convey to me the challenge, and that he was desired by you to make no concession; the explanation which I expected was certainly an explanation by you of what occurred at your House yesterday. You must be quite aware that it is absolutely impossible for me in my situation as a judge to accept a challenge.—I have the honor to be, Sir, your Obedient humble servant,

EDWARD WEST.

P.S.—I send this by my Nephew to insure its reaching you.

From the HON. MOUNTSTUART ELPHINSTONE *to* SIR E. WEST.

SIR,—I have had the honor of receiving your letter by this Post.

To challenge a Chief Justice is one of the last things that could have entered into my imagination. I understood you to have almost in plain terms challenged me, and when I sent a friend to you this morning it was not without a hope that on reflection you would have expressed your regret at the proceeding you had adopted. With regard to explanation, I can have none to offer beyond that with which the conversation of last night commenced; and I can make no apology when I am conscious of having been guilty of no aggression.—I have the honor to be, Sir, your most obedient humble servant, M. ELPHINSTONE.

Jany 6th.

SIR E. WEST *to* HON. M. ELPHINSTONE.

SIR,—I had the honor of receiving yesterday your letter.

You say that to challenge a Chief Justice is one of the last things that could have entered your imagination. What directions you may have given to your friend Col. Macdonald I cannot know but from what he said. He delivered to me, as from you, a direct Challenge in plain terms, and the word Challenge was used both by him and by me, during a conversation of more than an hour, thirty or forty times at least, as the whole of our conversation turned upon the Propriety of the Governor sending a Challenge to the Chief Justice.

I was walking upon the Esplanade at Seven o'clock in the morning when the following note was delivered to me:—

> "MY DEAR SIR,—Will you allow me to speak with you alone for a few moments.—Yours very faithfully, J. MACDONALD.
>
> *Friday Morning.*

The Servant who delivered the note pointed to the Beach; I followed him for more than half a mile, when not seeing Col. Macdonald I returned. Soon after Colonel Macdonald overtook me on horseback, and when he came up to me, dismounted, and addressed me with certainly very little courtesy, with none of those demonstrations of respect which are usual even as between equals. He immediately stated that you had desired him to call upon me to request, or demand, an Apology for what he stated I had said the night before; I expressed my astonishment, and said that I had certainly expected an Apology from you for the treatment I had received. He again desired an Apology, and said that you had desired him to make no concession. I said it was out of the question, and that you ought to apologise for the whole of your conduct for the last two years and an half. He said that if that was the case he was desired by you to demand or request a Meeting, or some such words, for I do not remember them precisely. My answer was in these words: "Colonel Macdonald, it is utterly impossible for me to go out with Mr. Elphinstone, it would not only be a loss of my situation as Chief Justice but it would be an utter loss of Character." Col. M. replied, "Mr. Elphinstone understood you last night to have waived your situation." I then, as stated in my first letter to you, disclaimed having used those words or any which would bear such construction.

During our conversation I said to Colonel Macdonald at least eight or ten times, stopping and turning towards him face to face, "So really, Col. Macdonald, Mr. Elphinstone has thought proper to send, and you have thought proper to bring a challenge to a Person who you both know cannot accept it. I am astonished at both Mr. Elphinstone's conduct and yours, and can consider it only intended as a Taunt." The only answer which Colonel Macdonald thought proper to make was, "Mr. Elphinstone understood you to have waived your situation."

In the course of conversation I detailed your conduct to Lady West and myself for the last two years and an half, both public and private—Your laudatory address to a man who had been dismissed from his situation as an officer of the Court for fraud—at his own request, too, instead of undergoing a Trial; and the consequences of this act, the insults to and defiance of the Court. The libel on the Court which you thought proper to publish by sending it to me, to the Aldermen, and the Court of Directors,—I being amenable, thank God, neither to you nor to the Court of Directors—Your sanction of Mr. Crawford's Dinner; a dinner notoriously got up for Party purposes, and of the inflammatory toasts there given—among others "Sir Ralph Rice [1] and the Supreme Court"—I mention this Toast in particular because nearly the same course of conduct had been pursued by you but a few days before that Dinner—You thought proper at a Dinner given at your own house to give Sir Ralph Rice the precedence before me.—It cannot be said that this Courtesy was paid to Sir R., as being a stranger, as the same Courtesy was never shown to me or to Sir Charles Chambers, nor to any other person since I have been here, but the Bishop—at that same Dinner you placed, or allowed to be placed, on one side of Lady West,—you yourself sitting on the other side,—Mr. Norton,[2] who was,

[1] The newly arrived puisne judge, inclined to be subservient to the local Government. Chapter xiii.

[2] "Party feeling ran so high that a mob of people used to follow the Advocate-General" (Norton) "into Court to witness and encourage his insults" (to Sir E. West).—*Oriental Herald*, vol. xvi. p. 576.

as was notorious to the whole Society, seeking every opportunity of annoying and insulting both Lady West and myself.

On that very day, as soon as he perceived me advancing towards Mrs. Jenkins, whom you had requested me to take to dinner, he offered her his arm, and was leading her towards the Door when she very properly relinquished his arm, upon my telling her that you had requested me to hand her to Dinner. I need not say a word more upon the treatment at that time of Lady West, a delicate and timid Woman. Some time before this, you had thought proper upon rising from Table at your House to join the Ladies, to walk from the Dining Room, upstairs into the Drawing Room, where half or more of Bombay were formally assembled, with Mr. Norton, leaving me, the first person in rank in your house to follow in the Crowd.

Upon another occasion you asked two Ladies of notorious character, and who were visited by no one here, to meet Lady West. Upon that occasion Sir Charles and Lady Chambers, on seeing one of these Ladies, very properly quitted your House—the next day I requested Lady West to write to you upon the subject. I adopted this mode of proceeding from motives of delicacy, thinking that you must in common courtesy make an apology for the grossest insult (even if unintentional) that a Lady can receive, and that it would be much less unpleasant for you to make such Apology to a Lady than to me. Not a word of Apology, however, was ever made, though you stated to Lady West afterwards that you had found out that these persons were of notoriously bad characters, and that you should not ask them again.

I pass by your neglect to return my visits. Some time since I determined from a sense of public duty to overlook what had passed, and accordingly called upon you several times at Malabar Point; my visits were never returned, and I was obliged to abandon the attempt at a better understanding between the Heads of the executive and judicial departments. When you returned from Candalla, I immediately, as the courtesy is, called upon you. On neither of my returns to the Presidency have you repaid to me this courtesy. Again and again have I deliberated whether, after such marked treatment, a treatment of course observed by a great part of the Community, and matter of absurd and petty triumph to many, I should continue to visit you, but I was induced to do so from a sense of public duty.

The day before yesterday when I dined with you, you took Mrs. Foster to dinner, you assigned Lady West to Mr. Warden, and, contrary to the practice which has prevailed here invariably since I have been here, assigned no Lady to me, nor said a single word to me, but left me to follow in the Crowd of young Men. When I got downstairs I expected to obtain a seat opposite to you next to Colonel Bellasis. The seats were, however, all full, and I was obliged to request a gentleman and Lady half way down the Table to allow my Servant to put a chair for me between them.

You must remember that in your House I am the first guest in Rank, as you are in mine; and let me ask you what you would have thought of my conduct, had I treated you precisely in the same manner. Had you even told me to take any Lady I pleased, or that you did not intend to assign any lady to me, and that you wished I would take my seat near you, your conduct would not have been so marked, but I waited till the last moment, expecting you according to your invariable custom to name some lady. You named none nor said a word to me upon the subject. Could you expect me to push my way downstairs by myself before the Ladies?

After detailing this conduct to Col. Macdonald, I observed to him that you must well know that I cannot give or accept a challenge, and again added that I could only consider the challenge sent by you as a Taunt.

My feelings have not been hurt in the slightest degree by these proceedings, my only doubt has been whether I was lowering my situation by continuing to visit you after them. I have long since learnt to disregard the opinion of the Society here, and to consider merely the approbation of the Authorities at home.—I have the honor to be, Sir, your obedient humble servant, EDWARD WEST.

BOMBAY, *Jan. 7th*, 1826.

Lady West says:—

Jan. 8. When we came home we found a letter of 9 sheets from Mr. Elphinstone. He admits more than I expected, but I think Col. Macdonald has behaved most dirtily, trying to put words into Edward's mouth which he never uttered.[1]

Jan. 9. Edward is now answering Mr. Elphinstone's letter. I am glad that it does not annoy dear Edward, and I hope that it will not. I confess that it makes me a little anxious.

Jan. 10. A long letter last evening from Mr. Elphinstone, which Edward has answered this morning.

Jan. 11. Edward had a very gentlemanlike and proper letter from Mr. Elphinstone.

Jan. 12. We have been to call on Mrs. James. Edward has written a very handsome letter to Mr. Elphinstone. A long letter from Lady Chambers full of disasters and fancies, poor soul!

Jan. 14. After another handsome letter or two passing between Edward and the Governor, he offered to call upon him this morning, and of course was received very cordially.

It would be interesting to learn how the diplomatic Governor managed to convince the Chief Justice of his good intentions. Two things are clear—that there was much to be explained away, or apologised for, and that Elphinstone succeeded in this task, even to the satisfaction of Lady West.

Meantime the pathetic life of the place went on, and members of "Bombay society," made irritable by stifling heat, by their northern customs of eating and drinking, by ill-assorted companionship, continued to feast—to quarrel—and to die!

FROM LADY WEST'S JOURNAL

Jan. 24, 1826. Last night I received a most distressing letter from Capt. Bradford, from Panwell, with such an account of poor Col. Baker that I fear there is hardly a

[1] The rest of this correspondence is unfortunately missing.

chance of reaching Bombay alive. Edward instantly wrote to offer our House to them when they land, which we expected they would do by this morning's tide.

Jan. 30. Sir Ralph Rice acted so irregularly, improperly and unjudge-like to-day in Court, that after Edward had addressed the Jury, Edward very coolly put a stop to his violent and intemperate remarks, and adjourned the Court for 3 hours. I understand Edward did not change colour or countenance, but was as cool and collected as possible. When they met again Edward went on with the Trials, and requested the Grand Jury to attend next Saturday, which prevented any further impertinence from Sir Ralph Rice. We heard last night of the death of Mr. Malcolm.

Jan. 31. Edward in Court till 6. The assault of Mr. Graham on Mr. Irwin. The Court overflowing, and half Bombay examined and cross-examined, amongst others the great Mr. Warden in the Witness-box. I fancy from Edward's account it was most amusing; he did not give judgment, as the libel will be brought forward to-morrow.

Feb. 1. The Chambers arrived, Bag and Baggage, to breakfast after Edward was gone to Court. Poor Col. Baker died at 2 o'clock. I sent the carriage for his poor agonised Wife,[1] and here she is; we hope to comfort her; they were so happy and so attached to each other. Edward did not come home to dinner till 9 (Mr. Graham's Libel), and returned at 10 to receive the verdict of the Jury—"Guilty." He had also a most extraordinary note from Colonel Stannus requesting five minutes' private conversation. We can only suppose it alludes to Edward's returning a Note unanswered to Mr. Warden. His last was so insolent a one, he could not open a second. The weather quite cool.

Feb. 2. Three years to-day since we landed; how thankful do we feel to have passed them in such good health and happiness, though they have been very turbulent in Court. Edward pronounced judgment on Mr. Graham, 150 rupees for assault and libel. Edward left Sir Ralph to try the Causes, wishing to attend poor Col. Baker's funeral, which took place at 5. He was buried in the Church with military honour, Edward was Chief Mourner, and says there was an immense attendance. No man ought to have been more beloved or respected, and so he was by all Classes. Poor Mrs. Baker wished to have attended, and it seemed

[1] Mrs. Baker had sailed from England with the Wests.

almost cruel to prevent her; but it was thought best, and I read the Service to her when I heard the Bell toll, and the volleys fired. It was a trying and a dreadful scene, but she has a strong mind and a high sense of Religion that will, I hope, carry her through so heavy a calamity.

Colonel Stannus called on Edward this Morning on the part of Mr. Warden for an explanation, which Edward did not choose to give, and requested the tipstaffs to show him downstairs. Mr. Fenwick was present. Can there be such another place on the face of the earth for odd, and I might say blackguard People and things as Bombay?

From a MS. memorandum by Sir E. West it appears that in June, during a sitting of the King's Court, Mr. Warden had handed to the judges and others a printed letter, signed by himself, insinuating that the judges had furnished the *Oriental Herald* with a statement that he had unfairly used his power as a newspaper proprietor. In this letter Mr. Warden acknowledged his proprietorship of the paper, but denied any bias against the King's Court.[1] Sir E. West, after pointing out the impropriety of the letter, the groundlessness of the insinuation, and the continued misrepresentations appearing in Mr. Warden's paper, goes on to say: "Mr. Warden as proprietor is answerable both civilly and criminally for the contents of the paper, but by

[1] In a letter to a friend, written at the time, giving his account of differences with the Chief Justice, and published in Colebrooke's "Life," vol. ii. p. 179, Elphinstone says: "As this connection between the Government and the newspapers had been a private doctrine of his" (Sir E. West's), "I thought it proper to deny it officially." Elphinstone must have known privately, if not officially, that his friend Mr. Warden, member of Council, was a proprietor of both Bombay newspapers.

the charter he is exempt from all criminal responsibility in the Courts of India, and this fact alone shows the extreme impropriety that a Member in Council should be Proprietor of a Paper, as Mr. Warden was of the *Gazette*, and as it appears by the affidavit filed under the new Regulations in the Secretary's office, he still is of the *Courier*.

"Mr. Warden's narrative has rendered it necessary to advert to two Prosecutions at the Criminal Sessions held in January last, in which Mr. Warden appeared as a witness. The first was a prosecution by a Barrister against the Coroner for an assault, and Mr. Warden proved the assault to have been committed whilst he was playing Billiards with the Prosecutor in a place called the Racket Court. The second Prosecution was for a libel—and in this case Mr. Warden proved that he himself had drawn out a paper in his own handwriting containing gross reflections upon the Defendant's character, had read it publicly at two different meetings at the Racket Court, in the absence, and without the knowledge, of the Defendant, and had on each occasion made an address also reflecting upon the Defendant's character, and which proceedings, with another libel on the Defendant read at the same meetings, were the occasion of the libel in question.

"During the Progress of the second trial a letter was handed to me upon the Bench from

Mr. Warden, which, in consequence of his former letter (received by me also upon the Bench), as well as of his general conduct, I thought it probable might be of an offensive nature, and of which I should have been under the necessity of taking immediate notice in Court; and therefore returned it unopened.

"The same Evening at about half-past eight o'clock the following note was delivered to me:—

GOVERNMENT HOUSE, ½ *past five p.m.*

Lieut.-Col. Stannus presents his compliments to Sir Edward West, and will feel honoured by his being admitted to a private conversation for five minutes. Lieut.-Col. Stannus trusts that Sir Edward will find it convenient to grant him a conference in the course of this evening, but if not he will wait on Sir Edward at any hour he may appoint to-morrow.

"The language of part of this note struck me as very extraordinary, particularly as Colonel Stannus was almost a stranger to me. However, I sent the following answer:—

Sir Edward West presents his compliments to Lieut.-Col. Stannus, and is sorry that he has not been able to answer his note before, not having received it, though dated half-past five, till half-past eight this Evening, and having been obliged soon after he received it to return to the Court to receive the verdict of the Jury. As poor Mrs. Baker is now with Lady West at Sir Edward's House, and it is necessary that she should be kept quite quiet,[1] Sir E. cannot have the pleasure of seeing Col. Stannus at his house, but will be happy to see him at the Court House at nine o'clock to-morrow morning. Sir E. will be obliged to be in Court at ten.

WEDNESDAY, *Feb. 1st, half-past ten p.m.*

[1] Colonel Baker's funeral took place the next day.

"At about a quarter before ten the next morning Lieut.-Colonel Stannus was announced to me in Chambers, the Master in Equity being with me. Col. Stannus began by requesting him to retire, as he wished to have a private conversation with me. I told him that the Master was an officer of High Rank in the Court and that I had no objection to his hearing anything that he (Col. Stannus) had to say—Col. Stannus then said that Mr. Warden had requested him to call upon me for having returned a letter of his unopened, and to ask for an explanation. I immediately observed, 'You come then as a friend of Mr. Warden's?' He answered, 'Yes.' 'You are a military man, and very little known to me.'—'Yes.' I then called my Tipstaff and desired him to see that Gentleman (Col. Stannus) downstairs."

Col. Stannus afterwards wrote to the Press to say that the object of his call on the Chief Justice was to demand "an explanation," not to convey a challenge.

CHAPTER XIII

Mr. Elphinstone complains to the Directors of the conduct of the Chief Justice—Sir Edward West's Report to the Board of Control—The Directors forbid servants of the Company to own newspapers—Calcutta Press Regulation rejected at Bombay; Silk Buckingham's comments—Sir Edward West consults natives, and adapts the new Jury Act to Bombay.

Lady West's Journal (March-Dec. 1826):—Death of Hormajee Bomanjee; death of Bishop Heber; mournful cargo of widows returning; arrival of Sir T. Bradford; birth of Lady West's daughter; Sir Hudson Lowe at Bombay; the Deccan case; flogging at Surat; death of Amerchund.

FROM LADY WEST'S JOURNAL

Feb. 14, 1826. I went at 10 o'clock to the Schools for the examination of the Children, and with the usual good manners of this place none of the ladies came till 11. We divided and examined the classes and I got home tired at 1. St. Valentine's Day, Lynn Mart proclaimed.

Feb. 18. Edward had another curious letter to-day from Government here, informing him that Mr. Warden had sent them a Charge against Edward which they were going to forward to the authorities[1] at home, and thought it right to inform him of it in case he wished to have a copy of it. How mad and ignorant they seem in all their proceedings.

Feb. 21. Edward drove this afternoon to Parell to speak to the Governor, as a friend, on the impropriety of the statement the Government had sent to him making themselves parties in Mr. Warden's complaint of Edward to authorities at Home, to which he was not amenable. Mr. Elphinstone would not hear reason, and said nothing should make him retract. I fancy both of them were very angry

[1] The Directors of the East India Company.

and told each other severe things that the visit was of no use. Of course Edward now has to send home official accounts to Mr. Wynn.[1]

Thus Elphinstone threw in his lot with Mr. Warden, and with him sent to the Directors a joint complaint against the Chief Justice; while Sir E. West forwarded to the President of the Board of Control a Report on the "Interference of the Bombay Government with His Majesty's Court and Judges." In this Report, of which a copy has been preserved, Sir E. West says:—

. . . "I understand that the purport of it" (Mr. Warden's statement) "is that he was not invited by the Court to the Bench when he gave his evidence.

"Mr. Warden certainly was not invited to the Bench, nor (though it now appears from a Paragraph of one of the letters of the Government that such distinction is claimed as a Right) did he ever request that distinction. Had it been requested, it would have been matter of consideration with me, as one of the Court, whether I should have accorded it or not. I should first have enquired into the practice at the other Presidencies, and certainly should not have accorded it, unless I had found it to be the established Practice, particularly as in the only instance I have heard of a Member of Government being examined in Court here, that

[1] President of the Board of Control. See p. 82.

of Mr. Duncan,[1] the Governor, he was not invited to the Bench. I should also have taken into consideration the general tenor of Mr. Warden's Conduct and the nature of the cases and of his evidence; and in particular whether it would have been right to have admitted to the Bench a Gentleman, who had committed repeated public Contempts of Court, both by the misrepresentations of the Court's Proceedings in the *Gazette* Newspaper, of which Mr. Warden was, and was universally known to be, Proprietor, and also by the handing to me, whilst sitting on the Bench, a printed Paper, signed by himself, in which he charged in a manner too clear to be misunderstood that I was the Author of the insinuations in the *Oriental Herald* calculated to 'undermine his official Reputation,' and 'the calumnious attack upon his character.'

"The distinction of giving evidence from the Bench cannot be claimed as of Right, it can only be matter of courtesy, and must rest in the discretion of the Court; and I still am of opinion that under all the circumstances above mentioned the Court were right in not offering such distinction to Mr. Warden.

"But a charge is brought against me by the Government in the course of the correspondence that 'a Member of the Government had been

[1] Jonathan Duncan was a well-intentioned, laborious Governor of Bombay in the time of Sir James Mackintosh.

treated with marked and public indignity, in consequence of his claiming a distinction common to him and to the whole of his colleagues.'

"I suppose that this passage alludes to my having returned unopened a letter handed to me upon the Bench, and it will be seen from the following facts how far the Government are justified in calling this a Public indignity.

"During the second day's trial a letter was brought to me by a native attendant of the Court, through a door which opens behind the Bench into another room. The writing appeared to be Mr. Warden's, and I asked whether it came from him. The attendant answering in the affirmative, I immediately wrote upon the cover as nearly as I can remember the following words: 'After the letter which I received from Mr. Warden upon a former occasion, it is impossible that I can open a second,' and returned it to the person who brought it, to give it to Mr. Warden. This I conclude is the *public* indignity of which the Government complains, and with which they have thought proper to charge me, the Chief Justice of His Majesty's Court. The Reasons for my returning the letter unopened have been stated, and I shall merely add that even without such reasons I should certainly have refused to read a letter from any person attending the Court as a Witness."

Elphinstone, with his usual "finesse," had denied

"officially" that there was any connection between the Bombay Government and the Bombay newspapers, and had asserted[1] that such a belief was a "private doctrine" of Sir E. West; and so no doubt made easier the unexpected answer from the Directors ordering that in future no Company's servant shall be proprietor of a newspaper. The order must have been extremely inconvenient; for the law of England, that the names of proprietors, editors, and printers of newspapers should be registered as a protection to the public had just been accepted, though with reluctance, by the Bombay Government.

"The Bombay Government," Silk Buckingham says,[2] "waited for six months before they carried this moderate suggestion of the Court into effect, in order to give time to Mr. Warden to dispose (at least nominally) of his property in that very newspaper whose misrepresentations of the Court's proceedings had occasioned such a measure. . . . The Government adopted it reluctantly, because when carried into effect the registry of the real names of the newspaper proprietors at Bombay would necessarily expose the system of duplicity which they had carried on so long. It must expose the hollowness of Mr. Elphinstone's enfranchisement of the Press; the newspapers of his Presidency being the property entirely of

[1] See letter in "Life of Elphinstone."
[2] *Oriental Herald*, vol. xii. p. 207.

his personal friends, who were all in places of emolument under his Government, and therefore subject to his wishes. Next to this, it must expose the facility with which they might have restrained the abuse of the Court without banishing Mr. Fair.[1]

"Thirdly, it would expose all the flattery of Mr. Elphinstone and Mr. Warden as emanating from their own immediate creatures. On these as well as on other grounds anything approaching to the English freedom of the Press the Government were most reluctant to consent to."[2]

The registration of the names of newspapers, editors, and proprietors had, however, been effected. And then followed the order from the Directors that servants of the Company shall not own newspapers—an unlooked-for answer to the Warden and Elphinstone manifesto. The command was, however, only partly obeyed. Warden transferred his shares in the *Bombay Gazette* to a former clerk, but retained a share in the *Bombay Courier*.[3]

The Government of Bombay then presented to the King's Court for their sanction a proposed law prohibiting the publication of any newspaper, except by persons holding a licence, revocable at will, from the Governor.[4]

The proposed Regulation was carefully con-

[1] See case of Fair on p. 145.
[2] *Oriental Herald*, vol. xii. p. 207. [3] Ibid., vol. xi. p. 363.
[4] A similar rule had been introduced into Calcutta by Mr. Adam and Lord Amherst.

sidered by the King's Court. Sir E. West decided that there was nothing in the state of Bombay society to justify such a restriction on the liberty of the subject, and gave his opinion against the Regulation. Sir R. Rice thought the Regulation inconsistent with British law, but would defer to the Council. Sir Charles Chambers supported the opinion of the Chief Justice, and believed that to introduce such a rule at a "time of perfect tranquillity . . . would be imposing new shackles to restrain no evil, and, by leading to by-paths of favour and influence to create perhaps a greater evil than it could obviate." The Court then gave a judgment against the proposed Regulation,[1] to the relief of all honest journalism, and to the indignation of the Bombay Government.

On news of the rejection of the proposed Press Regulation reaching England, Silk Buckingham, who had hardly forgiven the King's Judges their supposed share in Fair's banishment, expressed no half-hearted approval of their action.

"Of all remedies," he wrote, "proposed for checking evils inseparable from authority exercising almost absolute power, there is none that can be compared with a free Press . . . when men know the eyes of the world to be upon them, and that their conduct will be scrutinised by their enemies as well as friends, they are more careful

[1] See "Diary," July 11, p. 256.

to act justly than when they know their deeds will neither be seen nor questioned.

"But because it is more agreeable to all men to act without control, than to submit to the censure of others, whoever has the power to render himself irresponsible to his fellow-men, will be sure to do so. It is the province of law to set limits to the exercise of this power. And therefore all men in authority, especially those who are despotically inclined, and who are conscious that their conduct will not stand the test of free discussion, hate this part of the operation of the law, and hate also its upright administrators.

"Even British Judges—the most upright of all public functionaries—betray a leaning towards the side of power.[1] But if this tendency to strengthen the hands of authority be manifest in those who sit upon the bench in England, what may be expected to be the state of feeling and conduct among judges in distant dependencies?

"There, in the narrow circle in which they move—the constant personal intercourse with governors and their favourites—the absence of a free Press, or a scrutinising public, the power of governors to make their lives uncomfortable by a thousand nameless means, the love of ease in enervating climates, and the desire so to please the persons in immediate authority, as not to endanger their present gains, and to establish a

[1] Written in 1827.

strong claim to future consideration; there, where all these powerful agents are in continual operation to tempt the judges from their duty, and turn them into mere instruments of those who hold the reins of government, what may be expected of their conduct?

"Why, precisely what it generally is; namely, a just administration of the law in all cases that occur between individual and individual, where there is no reason to believe that the decision will excite the disapprobation of the ruling power; but a complete subserviency to this power in all cases that occur between it and those subject to its sway. This is the general rule. Whenever the reverse happens it is a fortunate, as well as an honourable exception; and wherever that exception occurs it is the duty of those who honour virtue and integrity to proclaim it aloud; for the sake of imprinting, by every possible means, this precept on the minds of men—that whenever an individual with a superior head and heart is found; with an understanding large enough to know, and a courage undaunted enough to perform, his duty to his fellow-creatures; it behoves every man who honours virtue to rally round him, to shield him wherever possible from his enemies, and to cheer him with admiration, sympathy, and regard. Such a man is Sir Edward West, and such a man should every lover of his country delight to honour."

Among events in 1826, mentioned in Lady West's diary, are the birth of her only child Fanny Anna, afterwards Mrs. Wale; the arrival of Sir Thomas Bradford, the new Commander-in-Chief of the King's troops, and of Sir Hudson Lowe on his way to Ceylon; the suit of Narroba the Peishwa's banker; the deaths of Heber, and of Hormajee Bomanjee, the philanthropic Parsee; and Sir E. West's first conference with natives on Wynn's Jury Act.

Great care was taken by Sir E. West to ascertain the feeling of the native population before framing regulations for the Court under Wynn's new Jury Act, which, as it had passed Parliament, admitted to the Grand Jury those natives only who happened to be Christians. In Bombay these were chiefly the descendants of half-caste Portuguese; the Island in the early part of the seventeenth century having been a Portuguese settlement. All other natives, whatever their social position, were to serve only on Petit Juries; and not even on Petit Juries during the trial of Christian natives.

Thus an Act destined to be the first instalment of wiser measures began as an undeserved slight on Mahometans, Hindoos, and Parsees, who were inclined to look upon it as a bribe to forsake the religion of their fathers. A petition, signed by all the chief natives, praying that native gentlemen might be admitted to the Grand Jury, was presented to Parliament by Sir Charles Forbes and Joseph Hume; and a like request was sent home from Calcutta and Madras.

Sir E. West and Sir C. Chambers in the meantime began with prudent deliberation the not very easy task of adapting the Act to Bombay; and they showed both wisdom and consideration in making the service on juries as little of a burden as possible. The principal natives of each caste were consulted personally; British jury laws were expounded to them; and the heads of each caste were invited to present to the judges in writing such suggestions as occurred to them, as a guide to the King's Court in adapting regulations suited to their different religions, habits, and circumstances. All the heads of the various castes to whom Sir E. West applied willingly co-operated with the judges, in spite of disappointment at the restrictions of the Act.

The answer of the Hindoos to the first invitation to become jurymen was quoted by Sir Charles Chambers in his address to the Grand Jury as a type of all the replies, and was published in the local papers:—

To the Honble. Sir EDWARD WEST, *the* Hon. Sir CHARLES CHAMBERS, *the* Hon. Sir R. RICE.

Agreeably to the intimation received from your Lordships, We the undersigned Hindoos have the honour to submit to your Lordships' consideration certain matters on which we, from a regard to our religion and customs, request that the Supreme Court of Judicature at Bombay will be pleased to frame regulations in relation to our service on Juries.

We request that we may be exempted from all service on Coroner's Inquests; the inspection of a dead body being considered a pollution by us, and requiring to be removed by purification before we can attend to any business, domestic or public.

We request that we may be exempted from all Juries when a Brahmin is tried for a capital crime; it being our religious duty not to contribute to the death of any Brahmin.

We request that Hindoos of the Jain[1] caste may be exempted from all juries for the Trial of Capital Crimes; it being contrary to the Jain caste to contribute to the death of any animal.

We request that for the present on all Juries on which Hindoos may be required to sit there may be associated with them six of His Majesty's British subjects; it appearing to us that Hindoos are not as yet sufficiently conversant in all the duties of Jurors; but that such association be only temporary.

To enable Petit Jurors to converse with each other, we request that one juror who has a competent knowledge of the English language, and of any language in ordinary use among the natives of Bombay, be always on the Petit Jury.

We request that Hindoo Jurors may be selected only from the following castes, the persons of those castes being best qualified to act as Jurors, viz., Brahmins, Senoys, Purvoes, Goldsmiths, Banians, Bhatias.

As the Heads of those castes of Hindoos are most capable of judging of the qualifications of the Hindoos to serve on Juries, and as the two Hindoos whose names are first among the undersigned are considered to be the principals of the natives of Bombay, we request that the Head of each of their Castes may in conjunction with them be authorised to return to the Court the names of the Hindoos of those castes who are best qualified to serve on Petit Juries, and that the Sheriff be directed only to summon as Jurors such Hindoos.

[1] Jains form a sect of Hinduism. "Jainism like Quakerism found its chief supporters among the rich middle class."—Forrest's "Cities of India."

We request that Hindoos may be exempted from service on Juries on the following days and occasions, their abstaining at those times from the business of the Court being enjoined by their religion and customs, viz.:—

We request that Hindoos may be exempted from all Juries before the age of 21 years, and after the age of 60 years.

We request that as far as is practicable and consistent with law the service of Hindoos on Juries may be limited to between 11 and 5 o'clock.

We request that Hindoos may be exempted when afflicted with sickness—or when any of their family is dangerously sick.

We request that a certificate of such cause signed by the head of the caste may be deemed sufficient proof of the truth.

We request that only respectable Christians may be selected to serve on Juries with Hindoos.

We request your Lordships' acceptance of our thanks for the very conciliatory manner in which your Lordships communicated your wishes that the Hindoos should explain the points on which they were desirous the Court should make regulations respecting their service on Juries, and although some difficulties may occur at the commencement, yet in the patience and moderation of the Judges of the Supreme Court, we anticipate an effectual remedy to those difficulties.

(Signed) Davidass Hurjeevandass (and Others).

The answers of the natives showed good sense and friendliness to the King's Court. Some of the suggestions could not be embodied in the regulations, as they were inconsistent with English jury law, but Sir E. West drew up an outline of rules regarding the service of Mahometans, Hindoos, and Parsees, with which Sir C. Chambers agreed.

He explained that it was difficult to draw the line between the different classes of natives; but that the heads of castes would be asked to furnish native Petit Jury lists; that the jurors would be drawn from the middle classes, not from the heads, nor from the inferior men of a caste; that no one would be required to serve who did not understand English; that in each Petit Jury there would be six or eight Europeans; that on the religious holidays of each caste, the jurymen of that caste would always be exempted; that there would also be exemption on the occasion of a funeral of a near relation.

Sir Charles Chambers in his address pointed out that considerable proficiency in the English language would be necessary, as there were no ideas derived from the manners and customs of the natives which would assist the judges in explaining the principles of English criminal law; but that the burden which the new statute would impose on the judges would be cheerfully borne, and that though progress would be slow during the first few sessions, good would come of the measure. The natives would be ambitious to learn our language, ignorance of which was the chief cause of the misapprehension and distrust that prevailed on both sides.

The pains taken by Sir E. West to explain their duties to the new jurymen, and to make service on Petit Juries as little irksome as possible, were warmly appreciated by the whole native population.

FROM LADY WEST'S JOURNAL

Jan. 22, 1826. Mr. Elphinstone sent an excuse not to dine with us on the 26th, when he was engaged to us. We went this morning at 10 o'clock to the annual Meeting and Distribution of the Prizes to the children of the school. I gave them to the girls, and Mr. Elphinstone to the boys; we all bowed coolly, but did not speak. The Chambers' were there. I was quite tired by it.

Feb. 2. Edward had a holiday to-day from Court. We drove to pay our Compliments to the Hawtaynes and found them at home, and were much pleased with their manners and their appearance; they looked genteel, quiet, and not Indian in their address, and I hope will be an addition to our Society.

Feb. 3. There are curious reports afloat that Sir Lionel Smith has been fighting a Duel with his brother-in-law, Mr. Pottinger, and that Mr. Warden is to give up Council and be appointed Commissioner at Poona, as Mr. Chaplin [1] is going Home. I wish it may be true.

Feb. 7. Captain Smith called and explained to me all about the report of Sir Lionel Smith. He seems to have behaved in a very gentlemanlike and proper manner. I am happy to find by the interference of Col. Lodwick that it has all been amicably settled.

Feb. 8. We have just heard of poor Hormajee Bomanjee's [2] death. He will be much regretted by all the Parsees, and indeed I believe by most of the natives, as he was a very kind and good man. It is said that we have put 50 lacs of Rupees into the 5% loan from Bhurtpoor.[3] This is the Indian way of protecting a poor boy from a Usurper, to pillage him!

Feb. 9. Edward went at 5 o'clock to poor Hormajee Bomanjee's House to sit half-an-hour with the Family, which they consider as a very great compliment, and the sons gave Edward a letter, written just before his death, of

[1] Commissioner in the Deccan.

[2] One of the most worthy and intelligent Parsee merchants, whose family had been distinguished for talents and integrity, as well as for wealth.

[3] An enormous amount of treasure was taken out of Bhurtpoor. Lord Combermere's share alone was about £50,000.

thanks, and hopes that Edward would still be kind to his Family, and full of gratitude to Sir Charles Forbes.

Feb. 13. Sir Roger de Taria called with a message from the poor Vice-royess of Goa, who has sailed in a Frigate to Lisbon, and who is to write to me from thence. The Archdeacon called, and Lady Chambers' cousin, Mr. Grant; certainly the finest young man I have seen, and something so open, so manly, and fine about him, talking with horror of the dreadful system of flogging, and mentioning some horrible instances of a Mr. S. sending all his hammauls to Mr. G. to be flogged because he could not make them understand his language, and of a Mr. M. he was travelling with hitting a servant 20 times on the face and knocking him down because he had not provided milk, which he had no directions or business to get, which so disgusted Mr. Grant he left the tent and said he never felt so inclined to assist a poor creature; and another story of a Mr. H. at Surat knocking his servant down by blows in the face and then stamping on him and kicking him in the face with his iron heels; and to conclude taking off the stirrup and beating him with the iron part; and Mr. M. the same day knocking down a Guide with the brass end of his whip, and struck him in the face because the man said he was out of breath and could run no further; what a horror the Natives must have of us and what a blessing Edward has been to this place. Here I believe it is almost entirely given up, the poor creatures know they can petition him, and he will see into the Case.

March 22. We heard with regret to-day of the death of poor Mr. Lavie at Cutch; what a dreadful thing for his poor wife and all his Family; he has only been arrived in India 3 months, they seemed so happy and pleasing. Poor Mrs. Baker in sad spirits; her Sale is now going on.

March 31. Attended the Monthly Meeting at the Girls' School, and at last carried the point of the children having better bread, and being made more useful.

April 1. Term began to-day. There seems to be no end of business for poor Edward, but he is indefatigable in doing good, and, thank God, in excellent health. Lord Amherst[1] positively going Home.

[1] Lord Amherst, Governor-General of Bengal 1823-1828. This report, dated April 1st, may have been a hoax. Lord Amherst did not resign until 1828. With the best intentions he had not succeeded

April 6. A dreadful fire broke out yesterday at 2, and is still burning, there is so much wind. About 500 houses have been burnt down, and I am afraid there will be great distress.

April 7. Edward answered the letter from the Government about Mr. Warden's statement, and yesterday received a very improper and impertinent answer. He is obliged to send copies of it all to Mr. Wynn, as they have sent it to the Court of Directors.

April 9. The *Lady East* sailed away at 2 o'clock for dear England, a mournful cargo of widows.

April 13. Edward has just received another answer from Government full of fibs.

April 16. We were dreadfully shocked to hear of the death of Bishop Heber on the 3rd April. I always feared that he would fall a martyr to these visitations. I have such a horror of travelling in this country. His poor wretched wife, how she will regret not having accompanied him, and staying at Calcutta with the children. Separations are awful things in this climate. It makes one tremble, so many sad events amongst our friends since we arrived. May God preserve my good husband to me.

April 17. This morning the minute-guns began to fire for the poor Bishop. It was an awful and sad sound. Captain Robinson of the Marines died last night of cholera in 6 hours—these things rather alarm one.

April 21. We had a small select party at dinner yesterday for Sir Lionel Smith.

April 23. The account of Peace with the Burmese arrived by land, and we have had a salute on the occasion. Edward says they had an interesting Prize Cause in Court, a matter of great interest to all the Military. Sir Lionel Smith is here to see about it, and Mr. Norton of course trying to be impudent to the Court.

April 29. There has been a Signal all day, and at 6 this evening the *Exmouth* came in, bringing Sir Thomas

as a Governor-General. Though helped by the invaluable advice of Sir Thomas Munro, Governor of Madras, he had not been able to hold his own against the Council at Calcutta. Even Sir Charles Forbes had publicly expressed an opinion that Lord Amherst was not the man to govern India. A long and interesting debate on Lord Amherst took place at the India House on December 13, 1826, and was published at the time.

and Lady Bradford, and an immense quantity of passengers.

May 1. Edward has been to Malabar Point to call upon Sir Thomas Bradford, he seems pleased with his unaffected manners.

May 3. We have had a visit from Sir Thomas Bradford and his military Secretary, Col. Renny. I know not when I have been so much pleased. Sir Thomas is certainly handsome and young looking, and with such very pleasing *English* address and manner.

May 5. Edward, I hear, gave an excellent judgment to-day. Sir Charles and he agreed, but Sir Ralph appealed to the audience! Edward had a letter from the Duke of Buckingham.[1]

May 22. I had the pleasure of Edward's society to-day. No Court. We have just heard with great regret of the death of poor Mr. Hopkins, the Solicitor; he was such an honest and upright man, and there are so few now here I hardly know how business can be carried on.

June 19. At 10 o'clock Mr. Davis was appointed at the Church to name our dear little girl Fanny Anna. Lady Chambers was one of the sponsors, and Edward and I were proxies for dear ffolkes and Anna Martina. The little darling was very good.

June 30. We heard of the awful death of Capt. Palin to-day. He has left a widow and 3 children.

July 11. Yesterday registering the Regulations was negatived. Edward and Sir Charles gave a written and good judgment against their expediency. Sir Ralph said more against them than either, yet was for having them registered; very consistent, as all his conduct is both in and out of Court![2]

July 12. The *Columbine* arrived from Portsmouth; it has brought me a letter from Anna, which brought me such a wretched bad account of dear Edward[3] that it has made me quite wretched, and quite haunts Edward to think of the lovely boy we brought out with us and the wreck he went home, I fear with little hope of recovery. What a horrid place India is for health, morals, good feeling and everything, especially among the old Indians.

[1] Mentioned in England as a possible successor to Lord Amherst.
[2] See p. 244.
[3] Edward Stamp West, nephew of Sir E. West.

July 15. The Judges hearing Kinnersley and Prendergast case every day. Many robberies, amongst other Sir Ralph Rice. The people say "no wonder." . . . We hear that many Ladies will be examined at the Police Court for reading a libel on poor Mr. ——. Whatever may happen I shall not pity them, as what business have people to read and circulate slanderous stories against their neighbours.

July 21. Mr. Carr tells me that 3 of the children died of cholera at the School last night; 3 more were ill. To-morrow a meeting is called to know what is best to be done.

July 22. I attended the meeting this morning; 5 other Ladies were there; 5 poor children died yesterday; 25 more are ill.

July 24. The Sessions commenced to-day, and Edward is to charge the Jury, chiefly as to the bad state of the Gaol as to security and classification, which has been continually named for the last 5 years by the Grand Jury, and named to the Government by the Recorders, but has been unheeded.[1]

July 25. I hear the Charge was considered very good, but it will not please the local Government.

July 27. We heard this morning with awe and horror of the death of poor Mrs. Wilson, only 32, a most amiable excellent Woman; she was only unwell a few days, and ill only 36 hours. These frequent sudden deaths make one tremble. The last year they have been quite awful.

July 29. Sir Hudson Lowe landed this morning under a Salute of 13 guns.

Aug. 2. Yesterday we had a dinner to Sir Hudson Lowe. He took me to dinner, and is, I think, a stupid man; looks sheepish, very silent and anything but pleasing.[2] Sir

[1] See p. 59.

[2] Napoleon had died in 1821. Sir Hudson Lowe, his custodian, must have been at this time on the way to Ceylon, the Governorship of which he had been promised. This he failed to obtain owing to the fall of the Wellington Ministry. Much controversy, as is well known, has been waged round Lowe's treatment of the captive—from every point of view the choice of Lowe seems to have been an unwise one. Lord Holland, in the "Memoirs of the Whig Party," recently edited by Lord Ilchester (p. 218), says that even Wellington "censured privately" Lowe's appointment; but that the Prince Regent agreed to it, and subsequently showed himself "full of rancour to the very memory of a man who had eclipsed the glory, and assumed . . . all the functions of Royalty."

Ralph Rice sailed to-day for Singapore, and will I suppose be absent 5 months. 11 poor children have died in a month.

Aug. 14. We dined yesterday with the Chambers to meet Sir Hudson Lowe, who I certainly think one of the most unprepossessing persons I ever saw. He seems indifferent even to civility and attention.

Sept. 6. We were at home this morning at a quarter to one o'clock from a Ball and Supper given by Limjee Cowasjee, where there were 3 sets of Nautching Girls. I always think the dancing too slow, the singing too monotonous, the music bad; but altogether it was a pretty and amusing sight—so many Natives, a beautiful House, well lighted, and most excellent Supper for 300 People. We were, of course, the Grandees. Sir Charles took me to supper, and Edward Mrs. Sparrow. Edward gave the Host's health, and christened the house "Claremont," and gave the Governor's health. It appeared to go off uncommonly well, everyone extremely amused, and the Natives always polite and really well bred.

Sept. 18. The *Boyne* from England, 18th May, brought Edward a very gratifying Letter from Mr. Wynn, approving of the rules he had passed for the Supreme Court, and also his Charge. The new Barrister, Mr. Mill, has called. He recollected Edward on the Oxford Circuit. Lady Bridport has a son.

Oct. 1. The Judge still engaged in a long Cause.[1] They seem quite knocked up, the weather is so hot. The poor nurse's husband died to-day.

Oct. 14 (*Saturday*). Yesterday we had one of our Dinner Parties. Colonel and Mrs. Hardy, Captain and Mrs. Jervis, Mr. and Mrs. Morley, Miss Mckintosh, Mr. Mill, Mr. Lyall, Mr. Inglis, Mr. Montgomery, and others.

Oct. 17. Edward had the painful duty yesterday of sentencing a man to death for murder, due it is said to revenge.

Oct. 19. Sessions finished yesterday, and the Grand Jury made an impertinent presentment, and Sir Charles gave them a trimming; I think it will not end here.

Oct. 20. To-day the Deccan Cause begins again; it will consume, I fear, all the long vacation. It is hard to have no holiday.

[1] The case of Narroba. See chapter vii. p. 129.

Oct. 21. Sir Lionel Smith arrived to-day to give evidence in Court, and returned to the Deccan that evening. The King of Johanna also arrived, and had only a salute of 9 guns.

Oct. 23. The poor man was hung this morning.

This is the worst part of a Judge's duty. The long Cause still going on.

Oct. 26. Small Cause Court again to-day, no rest for poor Edward.

Oct. 28. Poor Mrs. Ducat[1] died yesterday morning, and was buried, her death, I have no doubt, hastened by the loss of 3 of her children in the last 10 months. She is the first who has died of the party who came out in the *Milford*.

Nov. 15. Last night poor Mrs. Wilson died, and has left 3 infant children. Mr. Bacon, a civilian, is just arrived from Surat, and has astonished Martin with a dreadful account of the floggings which now take place under the orders and superintendence of Mr. J——, the Chief Judge[2] there. Mr. Bacon mentioned one instance in particular. Mr. J—— ordered a Man to have 3 dozen strokes, and saw it done, and said it was not inflicted severely enough. He took the rattan *Himself* and beat the Man, and then knocked him down with his fist. To know that such horrors exist and not to be able to correct them is dreadful; and even if it were named to the Governor, . . . I am sure he would not try to prevent it—and this is a common thing. Mr. Bacon says he did once send a servant with a complaint to Mr. J——, and the man was so severely treated he shall never do it again. People talk with horror of flogging in the *West Indies;* can anything be much worse than this? Sir Lionel Smith called.

Nov. 29. Yesterday we had a large and formal dinner to the Commander-in-chief, and we asked all the chief of the military; Major and Mrs. Bellasis, Major Morse, Capt. and Mrs. Seton, Mr. Knox, A.D.C. to Sir Thomas; Mr. Fenwick, Mr. Mill, and others. I think Sir Thomas Bradford a particularly pleasing and gentlemanlike man; but I fear he will not be liked. He is so devoted in his attendance upon Lady Bradford, and cannot receive any

[1] The wife of Dr. Ducat, a fellow-passenger of the Wests in 1821.

[2] Judge in a provincial Court.

company, nor does he go out. This is considered a great compliment to us.[1]

Nov. 30. I have forgotten to mention a most interesting judgment given by Edward and Sir Charles Chambers last Tuesday; a Native against Mr. Elphinstone and Capt. Robertson for taking away his Property, imprisoning him, &c., and committing all sorts of illegal things at Poona. The sum is no less, I fancy, than £200,000. Edward's judgment in my opinion was very moderate and good, stating the plain facts and quoting authorities. Edward says that Sir Charles' was very good, but much stronger than his against Mr. Elphinstone. Edward felt it more delicate not being on good terms with him.

Dec. 10 (*Sunday*). Mrs. Baker wrote to me early this morning to tell me that poor Mrs. Ogilvy died last night, most perfectly sensible, having her child baptized, and taking leave of them all. I wish she had seen her uncle, Major Kinnersley. I think it would have been a comfort to both. Singular that, after 6 years, judgment should have been given yesterday, when one of the nieces was dying.

Dec. 18. Edward had a great Parsee and a great Hindoo call on him to-day, and I overheard them both say that "He was a good Judge and did justice to poor Native, and they pray God every day for Lordship's long life." This is very gratifying to me to know that they feel his independence and the good he is always trying to do and does do. His has been nearly 4 years' incessant labor to effect Reform, and he has, I believe, nearly succeeded in most things.

Dec. 19. Poor Amerchund [2] is dead, who only gained his Cause on the 28th.

Dec. 20. Edward had a Meeting yesterday of all the great Parsees to talk to them about sitting on Juries; they have some objections, but for *their own* sakes I hope they will accept of the offer Ministers have given them. Sir Charles forgot the Meeting, and was too late for it.

[1] "The commander-in-chief was Sir Thomas Bradford, celebrated for his admirable management of the commissariat during the Peninsular War; a very gentlemanly person, liked by those he took a fancy to, a despot in his family, and ruled in turn by his wife, a confirmed invalid."—"Memoirs of a Highland Lady," p. 424.

[2] Narroba's heir. By his will he paid the debts of all native debtors in Bombay jails. See p. 134.

Dec. 22. Edward and Sir Charles have to-day the Meeting of the principal Hindoos about sitting on Juries. I expect they will have more objections than the Parsees.

Dec. 23. Edward has to-day had a meeting of the Mussulmen about the Jury Bill, and from what he says I think there will be more difficulties with them than the other castes.

Dec. 25 (*Christmas Day*). All the Natives and Servants making salaams, the latter expecting little presents, it being one of our great religious festivals. How different to those I used to pass at Hillington; so noisy, and numbers assembled at the dear old Hall. I hope it may please God for us to spend some there again.

CHAPTER XIV

Lady West's Journal (January-October 1827) :—Frequent deaths; new house at Poona; Sir R. Rice; a nautch; mutiny trial; illness of Lady West; death of Sir T. Munro; the *Courier* attacks the King's Court; newspaper war; arrival of Sir John Malcolm; death of Col. Chambers.

Sir John Malcolm, his career and character; appointed Governor of Bombay; his attack on the King's Court.

Lady West's Journal (October 1827-February 1828) :—Appeal on the Deccan case received by Privy Council; eclipse of moon; departure of Mr. Elphinstone; farewell entertainments; Sir J. Malcolm as host; his personal courtesy to the Wests; arrival of Sir John Peter Grant.

FROM LADY WEST'S JOURNAL

Jan. 2, 1827. Poor Mrs. Baker arrived here last Eveng in a sad state, having just visited her Husband's grave. We and Mrs. and Major Barr accompanied her and sat with her an hour in her Cabin, which looked as comfortable as it can do. Poor soul, I felt much for her and a great deal for myself, as she is our oldest Indian acquaintance and sincerely attached to us, and in this place the loss of such a friend is a serious loss. They were to sail this morning.

Jan. 4. We went to look at the improvements that are making at our new house. Edward deeply engaged making rules and thinking how most effectually to arrange the matter of the different Natives sitting on the Jury.[1]

Feb. 5. Edward had a long and friendly letter from Sir John Claridge, from Penang, to ask his opinion on many points of law, &c.

Feb. 10 (*Sunday*). Poor Kempt, the shopkeeper, died yesterday; one of the most respectable men here in every respect. There was a most extraordinary attendance of Natives at his funeral as well as Europeans.

[1] See chapter xiii. p. 249.

Feb. 11. Mrs. Grant, the Solicitor's wife, died yesterday; these frequent deaths are very awful. Thank God our Child is quite well.

Feb. 21. Sir Ralph Rice arrived to-day and just peeped in upon the Judges while they were sitting in Court.

March 1. Dear Edward's birthday. I hope it will please God to give him a long, healthy, and happy life.

March 16. Signals every day, but nothing but Brigs seem to come this year; it is sad how little news from England.

March 30. Edward started this morning at ¼ to 8 for the party at Elephanta. I am better, but I would not venture, not feeling well enough to be sure I should not be troublesome; having once seen the Caves I am not sorry for the excuse to stay at home with the dear Baby, though I doubt not I should have enjoyed it.

March 31. We drank tea last night with the Chambers. Yesterday as usual Sir Ralph Rice was insolent to a degree to Edward. The three Judges began upon the Jury Rules, but Sir Ralph Rice cavilled so much and made so many objections that they could not get through them. They were adjourned *sine die*.

April 3. Term began yesterday and Sir Ralph Rice behaved very well. The Regulations[1] were read.

April 26. Edward had a full Court yesterday, but no Judge.

April 27. He was so feverish and unwell all last night that he could not attend Court this morning; we had a great deal of thunder and hard rain, thermometer 90°. We have just heard of poor C. Brisbane's death, another victim, I fancy, to Rangoon,[2] for which these people, Lord Amherst and Combermere, get a step in the Peerage.

April 30. We hear a report that Edward's friend, Mr. Ryan,[3] is to replace Sir Anthony Buller at Calcutta; that is pleasant, but I wish he had succeeded Sir Ralph Rice here. Edward is gone to try an important case, the Sailors on board Capt. Tucker's ship for Mutiny; Sir Charles Chambers

[1] The regulations for admitting natives to juries. See chapter xiii.

[2] The Burmese war cost thirteen millions sterling and the lives of nearly 5000 men.

[3] Sir E. Ryan of Trin. Coll., Camb., a friend of Sir John Herschel, became Chief Justice of Bengal in 1833, and on his return to England a Privy Councillor ("Dictionary of National Biography").

cannot attend as his cousin, Mr. Chambers, a passenger, is implicated in it. They talk of the late Archdeacon here as the Bishop of Calcutta. I hope it is not true.

May 5. Edward went up for Chamber business and found it very hot. He had a letter from Mr. Whalley, flattering and satisfactory, about his official conduct here; he says it is highly approved by everyone whose opinion is worth having in England.

May 6. The Heat worse than ever; Therm. 92°; there is no sleeping at all. Edward, I am sorry to say, has gone up to Court. We hear of the death of the Duke of York.

May 17. The Natives are so anxious to have Edward fix a day to go and see the grand Nautch that he has been obliged to fix to-morrow night. I dislike them, and think it very dull and uninteresting entertainment.

May 19. We attended the Nautch last night. I passed a pleasant evening meeting the Chambers, &c. The music, dancing, and singing were much as usual; the wedding arbour brilliantly lighted and the ceiling intermixed with glass, foil, and tapestry had a beautiful and striking effect, and it really was not very hot. It was quite pleasing to see the manner in which they received Edward, with so much heart and grace. The Bridegroom was 16 and the Bride 12, quite an old Couple; the dress of the former was very superb gold tissue, and the precious stones and pearls very beautiful in his turban, the latter alone they say are worth 2 lacs of Rupees. A fine wind to-day but thermometer 90°; the Natives say there has not been so hot a season since 1780; visitors without end, which is very fatiguing.

May 21. This hateful Trial still going on; I think every day Edward feels the heat more.

May 25. The Trial is over to-morrow, and I hope Edward will have no more to do before we go to Poona, for he is almost knocked up.

May 26. Edward had 700 Pages of Evidence to read over to-day which with remarks took him 6 hours. The Jury were locked up, and he came home thinking they would be all night disputing, but in half an hour he was sent for, and I am sorry to say received the verdict of Guilty against all but one sailor; Party spirit pervades all ranks here and of course the Merchants and Captains have made a party against these poor creatures. Fortunately for them Edward will see that no injustice is done, and he will pronounce the sentence. The Court is adjourned till Tuesday, when Sir Ralph will sit alone, as Sir Charles Chambers' cousin is implicated.

June 3. We are very much pleased with our house at Poona; neat, clean, and apparently comfortable, though we must add a room immediately for some of our Servants. We have a larger garden than I expected, and it looks quite like an English Parsonage. Sir Edward and Lady Ryan have just arrived at Calcutta.

June 8. We have shut up our rooms according to the Deccan custom, which I think quite unbearable; such a close feel; even the scorching wind I like better. Colonel Fitzgerald sent us a guard, a very inadequate one of 6 men, and after 2 days told Edward he must withdraw it as he had not men enough. Yesterday we had another thunderstorm and large hailstones fell, to the astonishment of the Bombay servants, who had never seen such things before. Therm. 94°.

June 12. Continual violent thunderstorms. Edward has had a visit from a Rajah from the City of Poona. His set out very miserable.[1]

June 15. Edward has had a letter from dear ffolkes, and a most interesting and gratifying one from Mr. Stewart relative to all his Court concerns, the rejection of the Press Regulations generally approved and nothing! he has done disapproved. I trust with the new Governor [2] we shall go on smoothly and agreeably.

June 16. The *Atlas*, Indiaman, came in. Edward had a letter to introduce Mr. Dewar,[3] the new barrister

June 24. We went to Church and heard Mr. Ward preach; short and well enough. I took a long walk in the evening over ground somewhat like the Downs at Brighton; have written to Caroline Dunraven.

June 27. I went out in the carriage this morning at half-past 5, but I feel so tired that I shall not repeat it.

Aug. 6. I am up to-day having been 6 weeks in bed. Thank God, I hope soon to be as well as ever. I feel the freshness and pleasantness of this climate, of which I cannot say enough in praise; and there is no damp; the days are

[1] See Elphinstone's Report on the Deccan, p. 125.
[2] Sir John Malcolm.
[3] Afterwards Chief Justice of Bombay.

like Spring and the nights like Autumn. We have delightful English flowers in the garden, and green peas almost as good as in England. I have written twice from my bed, but I did not name my illness. I fear it has been sadly dull for poor Edward. We have heard of the death of poor Sir Thomas Munro on a land journey (my perfect horror in India). I suppose no man could be more regretted in India or by the Court of Directors in England.[1] He is another of the melancholy sacrifices to the Rangoon business. Mr. Parry, the Barrister, has been behaving in a very ungentlemanlike way to Mr. Graham, and he received a severe rebuke in Court from Sir Ralph Rice, seconded by Sir Charles Chambers, which so annoyed the gentleman that he took his passage in the *Triumph* and sailed for England on the 1st of August. It is very lucky for the new set, as they will probably divide his business and get places under the Court, which will give them a fair income to begin with. During my illness 9 carpet snakes were killed in the garden close to the house; they are small, green spotted creatures with flat heads; the Natives say they are very venomous—"if bite man, man dies 5 minutes," they tell you. Edward still busy on his Political Economy. Our absence from Bombay has, I think, been most fortunate, as we have escaped all the numerous arrivals who have been introduced to us, and this place is so much healthier than Bombay I am thankful to be here.

Sept. 12. Another wet day, but Edward got his drive in the evening. We hear that all the troops are marching against the Rajah of Kolapore; why or wherefore I know not. I suppose Mr. Elphinstone wants to carry home money, or the account of having gained more Territory to the Directors; what a Country this is! Col. Chambers of the 41st and his wife have died near Bangalore.

Sept. 14. Edward has sent off 2 letters to John Macbride[2] and Mr. Long about the publication of his Book on Political Economy.[3]

[1] Sir Thomas Munro was a wise and liberal-minded "collector," and afterwards Governor of Madras. He had served in the Mahratta war as Brigadier-General. Though opposed by the Council at Calcutta, his firm, just, and benevolent rule helped to raise the reputation of the Company. His death was mourned as a public calamity.

[2] Principal of Magdalen Hall, Oxford, son of Admiral Macbride, uncle of Lady West.

[3] The book is still in manuscript.

Sept. 22. Mr. Grant[1] is appointed our puisne Judge; we shall have to receive him, his wife, and 2 daughters. That is rather a bore; ladies are very troublesome. Sir John Malcolm is coming, but not Lady Malcolm.

Sept. 24. Edward has gone to return Sir Lionel Smith's visit. At excellent article in the *Bombay Gazette* on Wednesday about the ex-Sheriff and Mr. Warden, signed "Giovanni"; I cannot think who wrote it; it is very good, so temperate and true, and will I fancy not be answered, or rather cannot. Edward has found out illegal regulations passing by the Government; no more notice taken of the Court than if it did not exist, just after all the fuss at Calcutta about the Stamp Act[2] which has been referred home; they must be wilfully silly and ignorant.

Sept. 29. The Government *Courier* has 2 letters, most violent libels against Edward and the Court, and raking up Mr. Erskine again;[3] also some illegal regulations which the Government will try to smuggle into effect without being registered in the Supreme Court.

Oct. 4. Poor Edward is very unwell. He has, I think, fagged too much at Political Economy.

Oct. 10. The nights are so cool, the mignonette and all the flowers so sweet, I can almost fancy myself near the Garden at Hillington. All the invalids better. I went out last evening in the Palankeen after 16 weeks' confinement, and was not at all the worse. Sir Lionel Smith has called. He tells us that the Kolapore business is concluded, the Rajah having surrendered.

Oct. 17. A most violent rain with high wind, which has "tousled" our roof, as poor old Harrison would have said. Sometimes all the thatch comes off.

Oct. 21. An article in the *Bombay Gazette* by "Giovanni," in answer to "Vindex," telling a few truths relative to Mr. Erskine. How angry his friends must be to have brought

[1] The first notice of Sir John Peter Grant, well known to all readers of Lady Strachey's "Memoirs of a Highland Lady."

[2] An attempt to impose the stamp tax, already existing in the provinces, on Calcutta led to much opposition, and a petition against it was sent to England. "The (Calcutta) Government not only forbade a meeting of merchants to discuss the stamp tax in the Calcutta Exchange, but threatened to fire on them."—*Sphinx*, Dec. 1, 1827. The *Sphinx* was incorporated with the *Spectator* in 1829.

[3] This opened the newspaper battle on the Erskine case in the *Bombay Gazette*. See chapter iv.

all this upon themselves by their base attack again upon Edward.

Oct. 26. Col. and Mrs. Williams called and I saw them; and the Rajah came again; they all seem to like the thoughts of Sir John Malcolm as Governor, and dislike Mr. Elphinstone.

Oct. 28. A letter from Martin to tell us of the arrival of the *Neptune*, which has brought Sir John Malcolm and his daughter Lady Campbell and a ship full of people, at least a fortnight earlier than was expected.

The history of the King's Court of Bombay now becomes the history of its siege by the Governor.

Sir John Malcolm, Governor of Bombay, one of Britain's Indian Empire-builders, had gone almost as a child from a hillside in Dumfriesshire into the Company's army, and had fought the Company's battles in diplomacy and war for more than forty years.

A genial manner, high spirits, rude health, untiring ambition, and fearless self-assertion insured a career in India in those days, and Malcolm had been given an active and important part not only in the Mahratta and Pindaree wars, but in almost every important event of his time in the East.

Unhampered by shyness or reserve, he had been popular, too, with the natives: villagers, with whom he would sit on the grass and chat; Bheel robbers, with whom he would exchange banter; petty rajahs, indebted to him for Government pensions.

Still, Malcolm was an Anglo-Indian of the old

school, and when in 1805 Lord Cornwallis nobly sacrificed what remained of his old age by going to India to restrain the growing love of annexation, Malcolm protested—to his friends.—"Every day," he wrote, "confirms me in the opinion that it is only by the most spirited and decided policy that we can hope to preserve the vast advantages we have gained." But Malcolm did not quarrel with Governor-Generals; and when Lord Cornwallis, explaining his policy, wrote: "I deprecate the effects of the almost universal frenzy which has seized some heads (which I thought the soundest) for conquest and victory, as opposed to the interests as to the laws of the country," Malcolm bowed low: "I feel infinitely obliged," he said, "by your Lordship's condescending to explain to me. . . . However inferior I may be found to others in knowledge and ability, I shall be surpassed by none in zeal and obedience, and it will add greatly to the happiness of my life if my exertions should ever be judged to merit the distinction of your Lordship's notice and approbation."[1]

In 1808, when Napoleon, with Russia as an ally, planned a descent on India, a mission to Persia was determined on in England. Malcolm was recommended. But the directors at the India House had found him on a previous mission "unsafe" and "extravagant," and refused to support his claim. Sir Harford Jones, a Bombay

[1] Kaye's "Life," vol. i. p. 328.

civilian who had lived in Persia, was appointed King's Ambassador. In India, meanwhile, the Governor-General (Lord Moira) and Council, seeing that the Company had lost, and was still losing, prestige, hastily gazetted Malcolm Brigadier-General, and despatched him on a rival mission, discredit meantime being thrown on the proceedings of the King's envoy, whose bills were dishonoured by the Company's agents.

Malcolm's mission failed. His manner was too dictatorial. The Shah refused to meet him.

The following year another attempt was made to restore the influence of the Company in Persia, where the envoy of the King of England was engaged in making a treaty without reference to the Company. Malcolm was again despatched, and efforts were made to render the Company's mission more imposing than the King's. The Shah, delighted with rival missions bringing rival presents, welcomed Malcolm ; but negotiations on behalf of the Crown were carried on through Sir Harford Jones and his successor, and although Malcolm had the satisfaction of being able to embarrass the King's mission, these attempts to restore the fallen majesty of the East India Company could hardly have been worth the vast sums spent on them.

Malcolm after this seems to have been out of favour in England, especially with the King's ministers. Though a voluminous writer, not backward in urging his claims, and though supported good-naturedly by the Duke of Wellington, he was passed over for Bombay. Mountstuart Elphinstone, his junior, was appointed Governor. This Malcolm considered a direct and unmerited injury. He attributed it to the influence of Elphinstone's uncle, a Director. "Juggled and ousted," said he, "from the succession to Bombay as I have been, I shall not stay in India unless as Lieutenant-Governor of the Central Provinces."[1] The Central Provinces were not given him. In 1820 the Governorship of Madras fell to Sir Thomas Munro, one of India's greatest men, and Malcolm was again indignant.

In 1824 the Governorship of Madras once more became vacant. The Board of Control decided that Bombay and Madras must not both be governed by Company's servants, and chose Stephen Lushington,[2] secretary of the Treasury. Malcolm, disregarding the advice of both Canning and the Duke of Wellington, and depending on the latent hostility between King and Company, canvassed with his usual vigour. To the Duke he wrote sheets, and provoked the well-deserved reply: "*3rd April* 1824.—You are become popular in Leadenhall Street, not because you deserve to be so, but because you happen to be the fittest instrument at the moment to be

[1] The native States of Central India.
[2] Stephen Lushington had resigned the Madras Civil Service in 1807.

thrown in the face of the Government, and to oppose to them. . . . I told you before, and I repeat it, that you cannot succeed if Lord Liverpool does his duty firmly, as he ought."[1] Malcolm, however, persisted until the King put a veto on his election.

And now at last Elphinstone had resigned, and Malcolm found himself Governor of Bombay, smarting under previous defeats, mortified that the Lieutenant-Governorship of the Central Provinces had not fallen, and could not in the future fall, to his share, and that there was not the smallest chance of obtaining, even temporarily, the Governor-Generalship.

He had been sent, too, to Bombay, as Bentinck to Bengal, with orders to reduce expenditure and check extravagance, a commission not to his liking.

A writer in the *Oriental Herald*[2] of the time shows the nature of the task he had undertaken :—

"Our new Governor, Sir John Malcolm, is a man of great urbanity of manner. He is also friendly to the natives, and disposed to do justice; but he will be unpopular with many, more particularly so with gentlemen of the Civil Service, as upon him has devolved the invidious task of curtailing some of the enormous allowances which were added to the salaries of civilians by his predecessor; and to which Mr. Elphinstone was

[1] Kaye, vol. ii. p. 467. [2] Vol. xx. p. 175.

indebted for his popularity with that branch of the service. It, however, has done them no good; for whilst he increased their income, he set an example of such waste and extravagance that the additional allowances, great as they were, did not enable the civilians to keep pace with the expenses they incurred in imitating the example set them at Government House, where unlimited profusion and expense were the order of the day. Thus a serious injury has been entailed upon the service; many members being irrecoverably involved in debt, after enjoying incomes of from three to five thousand pounds."

This was unpromising material, and Malcolm was not the best workman. Though often generous to natives, friendly with many rajahs, and with his own following of sepoys, he was at heart opposed to reform of the Company methods; and now smarting under wounded pride and thwarted ambition, he had little inclination for serious retrenchment.

But his office happened to give him an opportunity of attacking an institution he hated—the King's Court. His disappointed ambitions, and antagonism to the Crown, explain the eagerness with which, when the opportunity came, he "girded up his loins for the conflict," [1] and fought the battle of the Company against the King's Judges. The pity of it was that the battle was not against

[1] Kaye's "Life of Sir John Malcolm," vol. ii. p. 504.

Pindaree freebooters, but against English gentlemen of culture and refinement. And even in Malcolm's victory there is the sense of defeat.

"I have tried," he afterwards wrote, "to deal some heavy blows at these dangerous fabrics yclept supreme courts; but they are too essential . . . to feed the rising spirit of the age for me or any man to prevail against them."[1] Happily for India Malcolm's fears were well grounded.

When Malcolm left England, Wynn had impressed on him the importance of keeping on good terms with the judges, but the advent of the Duke of Wellington's ministry, and a new Board of Control with the Duke's nominee, Lord Ellenborough, as President, must have tempted him to open the attack.

Lady West's diary shows that at first all went smoothly; Malcolm was affable to every one, and especially attentive to the Wests, sending Lady West presents of fruit, and devoting himself to her at public entertainments. To the judges and their wives, poor people! accustomed to the hostility of Elphinstone and the insults of his friends, the whole social atmosphere of Bombay seemed to have changed. Letters were written to the Board of Control in praise of the new Governor; and the judges looked forward to the remainder of their term of office in India with pleasure. The Wests were almost persuaded to accept Malcolm's invi-

[1] Kaye's "Life of Sir John Malcolm," vol. ii. p. 522.

tation to stay with him at Dapooree, and arranged to be near him at Poona.

FROM LADY WEST'S JOURNAL

Oct. 31, 1827. Edward received last night a very kind letter from Sir Charles Forbes (July 4) to introduce a Mr. Money, and also one from Mr. Wynn, brought I should think by Sir John Malcolm, both hoping we shall like Sir John Malcolm and Sir J. P. Grant. Mr. Wynn says the appeal has been received by the Privy Council.[1] It does astonish me as few things do now, as no one can tell what India or Indians are, and really instead of being applauded people are scarcely safe when they do their duty honestly and uprightly, if against the Government and their satellites. However it does not annoy us.

Nov. 4. An Eclipse of the Moon last night which the Hindoos explain as laughing; and to work or to eat will occasion all sorts of calamities; so the Portuguese nurse, and my little Mussulman Protégé told me.

Nov. 5. Edward has had a very civil letter from Sir John Malcolm. He took over the Government on the 1st of this month. Mr. Lushington [2] is also arrived at Madras.

Nov. 9 (*Friday*). Edward is gone this morning to return the visit to the Rajahs, a great bore, and he says so dull. As he requested to have no nautching, they wished to amuse him by seeing some Birds fight; but that Cruelty Edward begged to decline seeing. Captain Ottery called.

Nov. 12. How fulsome have been the speeches at the Meeting at Bombay. Having allowed the C.S.'s always to do as they liked, and having immense patronage, and his whole and sole object popularity, he (Elphinstone) has succeeded amongst the Europeans. The poor Natives have no voice, or I fancy they could tell a very different story. How little he thinks of their good or advantage. It is right that the C.S.'s [3] should pay their Rupees, but shameful to squeeze so

[1] The case of the Deccan banker. See p. 131.

[2] Sir Stephen Lushington at this time was M.P. for Canterbury. He had been appointed Governor of Madras, as the Crown refused to appoint Malcolm, the nominee of the Directors.

[3] "C.S."—Civil servants.

much out of the poor ignorant Natives, who dare not say "No," and scarcely know what it is for.[1]

Nov. 15. To-day Mr. Elphinstone sails from Bombay for the Red Sea. The only regret I feel is that Dr. Wallace accompanies him, as his loss is a very great one to us all as a Medical man, and a kind friend.

Nov. 24. We all returned to Bombay safe and well. I always think the Ghauts beautiful, and more so every time I see them. Edward called on Saturday on Sir John Malcolm and found him scrupulously and pleasingly polite and attentive, and this morning he has sent me a present of 8 fine apples. A host of visitors, Sir John Malcolm, Sir Thomas Bradford, Sir Alexander Campbell, and others. Edward has appointed Mr. Dewar[2] Clerk of the Crown and Mr. Luke attorney for paupers. I drove out last evening in the Carriage. The first time for 5 months.

Dec. 1. The loss of life in the storm has been dreadful, bunder boats, and boats going to Surat, one especially laden with people going to the marriage of the High Priest; it is said that 100 have perished.

Dec. 29. Sir John Malcolm is just returned from Poona, and has sent me some grapes. He evidently wishes to be civil and attentive.

Dec. 31 (*Monday*). All days and seasons seem alike here; none of the delightful family meetings which people enjoy so much at this season of the year in dear England. I trust that it may be God's will for us all to return and meet again in health and happiness. I went another round of visits this morning, and have I believe finished them all for the present.

Jan. 2, 1828. We attended last night the Ball and Supper given by the Governor, it was the first time I had ever been at one. Sir John Malcolm was markedly polite and attentive; I went with him to supper, and Edward took Mrs.

[1] An address to Elphinstone was predicted in a letter to the *Oriental Herald* (vol. iv. p. 320), dated February 7, and signed with initials. "Mr. Elphinstone has all at once become affable to the Natives, and aims at popularity with them. . . . Government House was full of them the last New Year's Day." . . . He is "turning every stone to get an address from the Natives on leaving the Government. He will, of course, succeed; it will be drawn up by Mr. Warden, and none of the Natives will venture to refuse his signature."

[2] On Sir E. West's death appointed Chief Justice as a friend of Malcolm.

Pierce. I shall always think Sir John a much more agreeable man than Mr. Elphinstone, he has lived so much more in the World, and in good society, and knows how things ought to be, and is very amusing, though certainly with a large proportion of vanity, and self is not forgotten.[1] We were at home by half-past 12.

Jan. 3. We have a nice garden, and I am pleased to see that Edward takes an interest in improving it, and it occupies a little idle time. He now rides twice a day and looks all the better for it. I often take Batt out in the carriage of an evening, which is a great treat to her, tho she walks every evening and has frequent tea parties.

Jan. 6. Edward has had a letter from Sir Charles Chambers in a most distressed state, having just lost their English wet-nurse in a few hours of Cholera; a most healthy fine young woman. This is one of the most awful and dreadful complaints in India, and one can never feel secure from it. Pray God preserve all my family from it here.

Jan. 11. Edward has written to Mr. Wynn to tell him how comfortably we are likely to get on here, as Sir John Malcolm seems to wish to be all that is obliging and friendly, and Mr. Norton is going away to Madras. It will appear as if we were just arriving fresh from England. Sir John Malcolm has purchased a beautiful horse for the King of England, which goes in the *Cambrian* on the 6th; he very obligingly came with it this morning at 7 to show us, and certainly it struck me as one of the most beautiful animals I ever saw. We had our party to Sir John Malcolm yesterday. He was so cheerful and agreeable, the day went off most pleasantly.

Jan. 26. We dined yesterday at Parell, about 100. I fancy to most it was flat; I spent a very pleasant day. No one could be more markedly attentive than Sir John Malcolm.

Jan. 29. To-day the Sessions commence; Edward will

[1] The "Highland Lady," p. 424, says: "Sir John Malcolm, a fine soldierly-looking man, rather coarse in manners, but kind and hospitable. His wife, with whom he did not live happily, did not come out with him. His married daughter, Lady Campbell, did the honours for a time. She died within a year. Major Burrowes was an A.D.C. and private secretary, very popular and agreeable."

Charge the Jury. There are 2 murders to try. He will have almost all the business to do, as Sir Charles says he is unwell. I have just sent off letters to Anna, Caroline Adair, and Mary Cust.

Jan. 31. Edward attends the Sessions every day. He tells me he made rather a long Charge again about the Gaol. Sir Charles is nervous and unwell. To-morrow 2 murders are to be tried, and I hope he will attend. Edward came home yesterday at 3 o'clock to allow People to attend the Races, as there was a very interesting match to take place.

Feb. 1. Five years to-day since we anchored in the harbour of Bombay, and I cannot be sufficiently thankful for the good health we have all enjoyed, and the innumerable blessings we have received.

Feb. 2. The Sessions finished to-day. Sir Charles came and tried the other murder, and condemned the man to death; it was for the murder of his Mother; such terrible depravity.

Feb. 6. Edward is gone to Court, but not very well. The poor man was to be hung this morning. I wish such a punishment could be avoided; although just, life for life, still it is dreadful. Races and Reviews now twice a week, but we do not attend either. Edward comes home tired from Court, and we enjoy our quiet ride and drive together. A brig and two ships signalled, probably one is the *Mountstuart Elphinstone* bringing our new Judge, Sir John Grant and Family. I trust they will not come to us, a large party of that sort interferes so much with one's daily comfort, and early hours, and it is nothing but visiting, etc.

CHAPTER XV

Arrival of Sir J. Peter Grant of Rothiemurchus at Bombay; his strong and upright character—"Memoirs of a Highland Lady."

Lady West's Journal (February to July 1828):—Pleasant change in Bombay society; burning of the *Tyne;* Sir J. Malcolm; eclipse; murder of native policemen; Duke of Wellington premier; sudden death of Mr. Bridgeman, Advocate-General; journey to Poona in the rains; life at Poona.

Sir J. P. Grant's speech at Quarter Sessions on neglect of duty by Company's Magistrates—Sir Edward West's letter to Sir J. Malcolm on police regulations, and on the incapacity of the Magistrates—Sir J. Malcolm begins his attack on the King's Judges.

Sir R. Rice appears to have left Bombay in ill-health, and shortly afterwards to have died. In his place Sir John Peter Grant[1] of Rothiemurchus, Edinburgh advocate, and Highland laird, became junior puisne judge.

News of the appointment must have been welcome to opponents of the King's Court. "Here at last," they must have argued, "is the very judge to counteract the uncompromising morality of West and Chambers! Countryman of Elphinstone and Malcolm, he will not quarrel with their friends! In urgent need of money; with wife and children feeling the sharp pinch of poverty, he will have no quixotic scruples on questions of justice to the natives! He can be

[1] See "Diary," p. 275.

trusted to consult his own and his family's interests; to side, like a sensible man, with the stronger party, to leave the magistrates alone, and to join in shaking the boughs of the ever-fruitful pagoda tree! Let us send him invitations as soon as his ship is sighted,[1] and instruct him in the right way before he meets the Chief Justice."

They reckoned without their host. Not the smiles of the Governor; nor the prospect of wealth and advancement; neither personal ease, nor his children's interests, could make this Highland gentleman budge from the position he saw to be the right one. Though the pine forest at the foot of blue Cairngorm, where great storm-beaten firs clutched, as they still do, the granite rocks with their snake-like roots, scarce furnished income for its hospitable owner—though the laird of Rothiemurchus had looked ruin in the face, and well knew its depressing ugliness—though he was bound by family ties[2] and his children's friendships to the local government—fearlessly loyal to his convictions, he supported his colleagues during their lives; and after their death there was no more picturesque figure in India than this lonely judge standing over his dead comrades, defying that incarnation of the buccaneer spirit of the

[1] Messages and invitations reached Sir J. P. Grant before the ship came inside the Bombay Lighthouse (*Oriental Herald*), and he was warned against his fellow judges. ("Memoirs of a Highland Lady.")

[2] "Such a cousinhood at the Presidency."—"Memoirs of a Highland Lady," p. 419.

old East India Company—Sir John Malcolm; declaring that, though the letter of the Bombay Government "had killed his fellow judge,"[1] it should not kill him; and bereft of friends, and all the legal help on which he had depended, bravely administering English law to the best of his power.

Peace to his ashes!

FROM LADY WEST'S JOURNAL

Feb. 9, 1828. Edward came home from Court at one o'clock, and to my surprise brought Sir John Grant. He took some luncheon with us, and Edward has now taken him to call at Parell. I have been much pleased with his manners and what I have seen of him, and Edward with his sentiments on several subjects connected with India. I look forward to our remaining residence here almost with pleasure, Edward likes the appearance of the ladies, the Mamma in particular, also the son.[2] I shall call there on Monday.

Feb. 11. We went this morning to pay our compliments to Lady Grant, and found them all at breakfast. She is a very quiet, pleasing-looking old lady; of the young Ladies I can form no opinion, except that they look nice People; the Son, a fine young man, and Sir John very prepossessing. They fixed to dine with us on the 21st, when of course all the Big-Wigs will come to meet them. Edward is pleased with Sir John's manner in Court, quiet, and to the purpose.

The history of the Grant family was (in 1845) written by the eldest of the daughters. The whole story of their life in the Highlands, of the embar-

[1] Kaye's "Life of Malcolm," vol. ii. p. 520.
[2] Afterwards Governor of Jamaica.

rassments of the father, John Peter Grant, formerly M.P. for Tavistock, the new puisne judge of the King's Court of Bombay, is told with simplicity and directness. The history, originally printed for private circulation, was, a few years ago, edited and given to the world by Lady Strachey as "Memoirs of a Highland Lady." In it the eldest daughter thus describes her parents, who were such a welcome addition to the better part of Bombay society:—

"There was a charm in his (Sir J. P. Grant's) manner I have never known any one of any age or station capable of resisting. My mother" (Lady Grant), "though accounted such a handsome person, impresses my memory much less agreeably. A very small mouth, dark hair curling all over her head in a bush close to her eyes, white shapeless gowns, apparently bundled up near the chin without any waist visible, her form extended on the sofa, a book in her hands, and a resident nervous headache, which precluded her from enduring noise, is the early recollection that remains with me concerning her."[1]

There is a metallic ring in this description of a mother by a daughter no longer young— Heaven help us all as we pass from the age when "we live by admiration, love, and hope" to the chill age of criticism!

[1] "Memoirs of a Highland Lady," p. 7. London, 1898.

FROM LADY WEST'S JOURNAL

Feb. 12. Edward is still indifferent, but does not like to absent himself from Court.

Feb. 14. Edward returned home yesterday so flushed and heated, and so unwell; I sent for Dr. Eckford[1] and am thankful I did, as he said his pulse was galloping, and it was a determination of blood to the head. He bled him profusely, which seemed to relieve him very soon, but he passed a wretched night. He is in all respects better to-day, and I hope it will not be necessary to bleed him any more; but he must not think of Court for the present. The doctor is very urgent that they should leave off their wigs in Court, and I hope they will do so.

Feb. 19, 1828. The annual meeting of the Schools was held this morning to distribute the prizes, and as Edward was better he wished me to go. Martin went up with me, and I found Sir John Malcolm there, who immediately devoted himself to me. The Grant family came in for a short time. How different is Sir John Malcolm's conduct to Mr. Elphinstone's, to me and to the Court in general. I really anticipate pleasure in our future residence here.

Feb. 24. Sir John Grant arrived at 10 o'clock and stayed till one, talking to Edward on business, and every time Edward seems more pleased with his apparent independence, and the wish of doing his duty, and he told Edward how much people in England were pleased with his judgments and his exertions, which is very gratifying. His only enemies are the Court of Directors.

Feb. 25. This being the last day of the term, Edward was very anxious to go up to Court, and I hope he will not suffer from it. We shall send an excuse to Parell for dinner; the two goings out would not be prudent.

March 1 (*Saturday*). To-day has been the hottest day we have had for some months. Edward wrote to Mr. Stewart about the unheeded enormities committed by the Company's Servants in India.

[1] It will be remembered by readers of "Memoirs of a Highland Lady," that their author married Colonel Smith of Baltiboys, an officer in the Bombay Army, and that her sister married Mr. Gardiner, who had a post under Malcolm, and that Dr. Eckford shared a house with Colonel Smith, and acted as "Cupid's messenger."

March 4. We dined yesterday at the Sullivans, and had a very cheerful, pleasant party. Bradfords, Grants, etc., and we had a quadrille in the evening. The Sullivans are a very pleasing, nice family, and so are the Grants. It is quite extraordinary the agreeable change which has this morning taken place in the Society. Mr. Norton left Bombay for Madras, and last evening Mr. and Miss Bridgeman are arrived from thence; Mr. Bridgeman called this morning. He appears a pleasing, gentlemanlike man.[1]

March 7 (*Friday*). We called last evening upon Miss Bridgeman, a plain young woman, but she looks good-natured. Miss Mary Grant was married yesterday to Mr. Gardiner; Martin and Miss West received some Bride's cake.

March 9 (*Sunday*). We went to a Nautch last evening given by a Parsee, and saw the bride of about 10 years old covered with pearls and emeralds said to be worth £5000, and the bridegroom of 15, a fat, stupid-looking youth. All the grandees were there except Sir John Malcolm, and the dancing was as little pleasing, the singing as little harmonious, and the music as little agreeable, as usual. We had wines of all sorts, and a very pleasant evening, but hot. We only stayed one hour. The Sullivans were much pleased with the novelty of the whole thing.

March 11. We gave our first dinner yesterday to Sir John Grant, and increased our tables to hold 48, and expected that number, but we had many excuses just before dinner, so that we numbered but 40. We had the garrison band, and in the evening we danced two quadrilles of 12, and I guess[2] that the party was thought to have gone off cheerfully and well.

March 20. Yesterday the *Tyne* was burnt down to the water's edge, and the King's ships boats were firing at her

[1] The "Highland Lady," p. 425, says: "James Dewar, though no great lawyer, was very much to be liked; as was the Advocate-General, Mr. Bridgeman, whose Christian name Orlando was an unfailing source of amusement." The name could not have been altogether unfamiliar. Sir Orlando Bridgeman—Lord Keeper—was a distinguished lawyer in the time of Charles I., Cromwell, and Charles II.

[2] This and other "Americanisms" were probably heard in Norfolk long before the existence of the United States.

to try and sink her, for fear of other ships in the Harbour. All her cargo, I fancy, is lost. Luckily, all the Passengers and their effects were landed.

March 27. Poor Edward gone up to hold a Small Cause Court; thermometer 91°, and a hot wind.

April 2 (*Wednesday*). One of the hottest days I have ever felt. Edward came home most unwell, and his head aching. I attended the monthly meeting at the girls' school and came home tired. I hope, however, I did some good in getting an asylum for one of the girls. Many people knocked up with the heat and dinners.

April 5. Edward had a note from Sir John Grant to say he was not very well and would wish to stay at home to-day if perfectly convenient. He, as usual, never thought of himself and has gone.

April 9. We dined yesterday at the Chambers' to meet the Admiral and Naval captains; Sir John Malcolm did not go; it was better than usual, having King's officers to talk to; but their Parties are too small.

April 11 (*Friday*). Two gentlemen from China called upon us—Mr. Marjoribanks[1] and Mr. Ravenshaw; this will compel us to have another dinner this month, which we had almost made a vow we would not.

April 14. An Eclipse, and a general holiday for all castes, and they cannot show their faces. Sir John Grant pleased Edward much in the sentiments he expressed to-day from the Bench about the Court of Requests. My Journal will fortunately never be looked into, or I should be ashamed of its dulness.

April 21. To-day, I am happy to say, finished the term. Edward came home delighted with Sir John Grant. I am happy to say that the hour of meeting is now 10, and the Judges hope to get it to 9.

April 23. The King's Birthday. We mean for the first time to go to the Fête, as a compliment to Sir John Malcolm.

May 14. There has been a horrid murder of some Police in the Bazaar; by whom, no one knows. I hope Government will institute some inquiry into it. The military lay it on the Police, and the Police on the

[1] "We had a peep at Charles Marjoribanks, who was going home for his baronetcy—too late, for he died."—"Highland Lady," p. 424.

Military. A Freetrader[1] came in yesterday from England, but we have not yet any letters.

May 31. We went and drank tea last evening with Sir John Malcolm at Malabar Point, and found it very pleasant and sociable. The Chambers' and Sullivans' met us there. He has made it a very pretty place.

June 1. The *Edinburgh* Indiaman is signalled. Anna tells us of the death of poor dear Edward Stamp[2] at last. I suppose one ought to rejoice in poor Edward's release, but recollecting him only in beauty and comparative health, this seems a sad loss. England seems in a wild state in regard to the Administration. Duke of Wellington premier.[3]

June 8. Sir John Malcolm has begged to call upon Edward to talk over the inefficiency of the Police.

June 9. Edward has been this morning to call upon Sir Charles, Mr. Malcolm, and Sir John, and to talk over the Police, and has suggested several necessary additions before the monsoon.

June 24, 1828. This has been an eventful and awful day; nine o'clock this morning, at Martin West's wedding, Edward heard of the dreadful event of the death of poor Mr Bridgeman, the Advocate-General. To his poor orphan sister it is indeed an irreparable loss, and to the public and to the Society. He was so gentlemanlike, independent, pleasing, and conducted himself so very well the 5 months he had been here. Sir John Malcolm sent a very handsome note to Edward mentioning his intention of appointing Mr. Dewar acting Advocate-General. Edward and the two Judges mean to attend the Funeral in person this evening, a necessary compliment, but a most painful duty in this country. Where people's nerves are not very strong these awful visitations make one tremble for those one loves, and I pray God to keep me from such heavy affliction. We expected a party of 46 at dinner yesterday, amongst others the poor Bridgemans, and we only heard he was a little unwell. The others came. Sir Thomas Bradford, Sir Charles and Lady Chambers, Sir John and Lady Grant, and Miss

[1] A ship with a licence to trade at an Indian port; but independent of the Company.

[2] Edward Stamp West, nephew of Sir E. West, who had been sent to England.

[3] The Duke of Wellington's rather unhappy administration lasted from 1828 to 1830.

Grant. Mr. and Mrs. Fenwick, Col. and Mrs. Sullivan, Col. Pollock. Miss Webbe and her brother and Mr. E. Pottinger and others. It seemed a cheerful party, and people stayed till ½ past eleven.

June 25. Edward says it was a large attendance at poor Mr. Bridgeman's funeral, which People seemed to feel very much; so awful. He was practising in Court 24 hours before he was lowered into his grave. Poor Dr. Williamson has died at Daporee.

June 27. The two Judges nominated Mr. Roper to-day to hold the Clerkship of the Crown which Mr. Dewar had.

Sessions thus continued to the end of June, and the Chief Justice and Lady West were compelled to make the journey to Poona at the onset of the rains.

This was Elizabeth Grant's first experience of a monsoon, and the Highland lady's description of it is so much more picturesque than that of poor Lady West, travelling through it with her child on her last journey, that it is worthy of being quoted.[1]

"We were sitting down to luncheon when a feeling of suffocation, a distant rumbling, a sudden darkness made us all sensible of some unusual change. The servants rushed to the venetians and closed one side of the hall, the side next the storm. The wind, suddenly rising, burst with a violence which overwhelmed every opposing object, and while the gust lasted we could hear nothing else, not a step nor a voice, nor a sound of any kind. It brought with it a shower, a tempest rather, of sand, so fine, so impalpable that it entered

[1] "Memoirs of a Highland Lady," p. 427.

through every crevice, covered the floor, the seats, the tables with a red dust that nearly choked us.

"This was succeeded by a lull almost awful in its intensity. Then the thunder growled at a distance; then, strengthening, it broke suddenly right over the house with a power that was overwhelming; then flash after flash of lightning; then rain, such as is known only in the tropics, poured down in flakes with the din of a cataract. On came the thunder; again and again it shook the house, rolling round in its fearful might as if the annihilation of the world were its aim.

"Neither before nor after did I feel so thoroughly appalled. It lasted two hours, after which a heavy rain set in, falling dully and equally hour upon hour until the following day, when we had a second thunderstorm. After this, heavy rain continued unceasingly for forty-eight hours, making a deafening noise, and creating darkness and a chill damp equally oppressive. The roads were like streams, the plain a lake, the tanks overflowing. No Europeans stirred out, only such natives as could not avoid going out on business, and they were dressed for the deluge in oilskin[1] coverings that enveloped the whole person, face and all, out of which they saw through two glass eyes inserted at the proper place, a hideous masquerade but absolutely necessary. The first desperate week over, the rain fell less constantly."

[1] Pitched cloth.

FROM LADY WEST'S JOURNAL

July 2, 1828. Our baggage is all gone to-day. It rains, and looks very monsoonish. Sir Thomas Bradford has been very kind in offering to send Mr. Parry to Poona, and Edward has kindly offered to pay a palankeen for him.

July 3. We started at 11 this morning from the Magazine Bunder[1] and got to Panwell at half-past one. It was very rough. Batt and I were very sick; we got to Chowk at seven. Edward had intended to ride, but it rained hard and we will now take a Palankeen up to Poona. The Monsoon appears to have set in.

July 4. Another wet day, but our beds and all went off dressed up in *pitched* cloth, and will be ready for us to-night at the top of the Ghaut.

July 5. Kandalla. We arrived at this place last evening; it rained hard all the way. The Ghauts looked anything but handsome, as there was so thick a fog in which they were enveloped, it was scarcely possible to see anything, and so chill when we got to the top. The cold fog quite frightened me for Fanny, but as usual we found all comfortable and went to bed at nine, got up at 5, and started for Karlee, where we dined. Our People have been unlucky, as it has rained incessantly ever since Wednesday. Dear Fanny looks better and grows more amusing every day.

July 6. Poona. We made a long and pleasant march to-day, 24 miles, no rain. We had to be ferried over 3 Rivers between Lonowlee and this place, which little Fanny did not quite enjoy. We dined at Lonowlee, we left at one and got home at five, our house and garden and everything looking very nice. We are delighted with the air and look of Poona.

July 8. Edward went this morning early to breakfast with Sir John Malcolm, and found him all that was civil and attentive. He wants me to go for a week to Dapooree, but I shall get off if I can. Sir John Malcolm has offered to dine with us next Wednesday at ½ past 3 o'clock.

July 9 (*Wednesday*). We have had a visit from Sir John Malcolm and many others; he tells us a Bridge is to be built over the River, which will be a wonderful improvement to this place.

[1] Pier.

July 10. Sir John Malcolm paid Edward a second visit last Evening on a little business, and wanted us to go to the Play, but we preferred a drive.

July 14. Edward enjoys his morning ride; he says he feels a different creature already.

July 16. Sir John Malcolm and Capt. Burrowes dined with us at ½ past 3 in the Evening. We went to see a large Tarboot prepared for the Mohurrum, which takes 150 men to carry it, and is 6 months making, and is at last consigned to the River.

July 18. The rain is gone off and all People beginning to croak and to foretell all sorts of evil. Edward has usually 2 messages a day from Sir John Malcolm. The last St. Helena Ship has come in and Edward has 2 letters, one from Mr. Way, the other from Dr. Macbride; the first kind, the other flattering to Edward as a Judge and a Political Economist.

July 20. Rain in the night, but only enough for vegetation, not for Tanks. Sir John Malcolm has sent us the "Life" of poor Bishop Heber, edited by his wife, to read; it is interesting and amusing—his Travels in India—but too general in his admiration of all Civilians and of those who courted him, and *her* especially. Her drawings too are quite ridiculous, they were *such things*. The Coachman has ague, and we could not go to Church. A little Rain to-day, and the tanks filling.

July 23. Very heavy rain in the night; the Tarboots are going past this morning with the Military Bands, a pretty sight; they are to be put into the River this evening at 5 o'clock.

July 28. We are much pleased to hear that Sir John Grant made a good and spirited Charge on Saturday with a Lecture to the Magistrates, the Coroner, the Community and the Government, and said that the conduct of the Petty Sessions in trying felonies, and in banishing, had been intolerable. This is quite delightful, as Sir Charles Chambers has always been timid—never daring openly to support Edward.

Sir John Malcolm in the meantime was preparing for the conflict. It was begun by sending despatches—sometimes two a day—to the Chief

Justice on the insecurity of life and property, and on the importance of increasing the police, and deporting aliens.

At the Quarter Sessions, which opened on July 26, 1828, Sir J. P. Grant boldly followed Sir E. West in exposing the culpable neglect of duty by the Company's magistrates and other officials. The speech is given at length in the *Bombay Gazette*. "The calendar," he said, "is a heavy one. Several of the crimes betoken a contempt of public justice almost incredible, and a state of morals inconsistent with any degree of public prosperity. Criminals have not only escaped, but seem never to have been placed in jeopardy. The result is a general alarm among native inhabitants.

"We are told that you are living under the law of England. The only answer is that it is impossible. What has been administered till within a few years back has not been the law of England, nor has it been administered in the spirit of the law of England, else it would have been felt in the ready and active support the people would have given to the law and to its officers; and in the confidence people would have reposed in its efficacy for their protection."

He then alluded to the robbery of a shop, from which bales of silks were carried with impunity through the streets, and to the easy escape of convicts from jail. He attributed this lawlessness chiefly to illegal convictions without a jury, illegal punishments, and private whippings by Company's magistrates. "The petition,"[1] he continued, "from the natives complains that most offenders escape without detection, and that daring crimes are committed by day without pursuit being made, or investigations set on foot. The complaint is well founded. Robberies take place in the day, known to magistrates and to the Government, and it does not appear that any inquiry has taken place; so that it has nothing to do with insufficient punishment. Criminals, when informed against, are not traced and brought to trial. No mistake can be greater than to believe that by increasing the amount of punishment you will deter men from the commission of crimes encouraged by negligence.

"Co-operation is expected by the law of England from all ranks in the detection of crime. I wish to impress upon the native inhabitants that the sovereign and parliament of England desire that the natives of India shall have the privileges of British subjects. Daring robberies are perpetrated within the walls of a fortified town by gangs—goods are conveyed to the ramparts and lowered down by ropes attached to the guns of the fort. Two policemen and another native have been murdered, apparently by a band of garrison sepoys in disguise, at eight o'clock in the

[1] A petition from the natives to the Governor.

evening, and though the band returned at once to the lines, and though a gentleman who was on the spot went at once to the adjutant and to the magistrate no attempt was made to trace the ruffians. And the coroner returns a verdict against 'persons unknown.' Unknown they must be if no inquiry is made, and neither bystanders nor officers, nor sentinels on guard are examined.[1]

"I fear the duties of a coroner are mistaken." Sir P. Grant then referred to the strong remarks on the subject made by his learned brother.

The *Bombay Courier*, still a Government paper, omitted to report that part of Sir J. P. Grant's speech which related to the murder by sepoys, and the writer of a letter in the *Bombay Gazette*[2] regrets that the *Courier* should have passed into the hands of one "who uses his office to get some snug little portion from the Governor, and converts the Press, which should support the weak and do justice into a vehicle of sordid sycophancy."

In the meantime Sir E. West, in a letter to the Governor, shows the "indolence, indifference, and incapacity" of the Company's magistrates' imperfections in the jail and corruption of jailors to be the real causes of crime.

[1] These two or three years were probably the high-water mark of crime in India. Thousands of robberies, with carefully planned assassination by strangling and poison, were taking place on all sides without the cognisance of the European magistrates.

[2] *Bombay Gazette*, May 7, 1828.

Letter from Sir E. West *to* Sir John Malcolm, *on the Police Magistrates.*

(From a copy in Lady West's handwriting.)

Poona, *August* 3, 1828.

My dear Sir John,—I have had the pleasure to receive your letter of the 30th ult., from Ahmednugger.[1] I have heard from Mr. Dewar[2] on the subject of the Police Magistrates; he has forwarded to me some amendments of the Police Regulations proposed by Mr. De Vitré,[3] upon which I can give no opinion without consulting my brother judges, particularly as many of them are mere transcripts of Regulations which have before been proposed to and rejected by the Court and of the illegality and inexpediency of which each of the judges has individually expressed a decided opinion.

Moreover it is quite clear that no new Regulations could have prevented the late outrages which have caused the complaints of the natives and the present inquiries, nor have given any facilities to the detection of their authors. The power of inflicting a greater number of stripes on offenders by the Petty Sessions would not have enabled the Magistrates to have *caught* the offenders, and if they had been caught the Supreme Court can punish sufficiently, and *do* when offenders are brought before them.

But it may be said that if the Petty Sessions had possessed the power of banishing idle and disorderly persons, the very persons who committed those offences might have been probably sent off the Island before, and therefore would not have been in a situation to have committed the offences.

But in order to estimate the justness of this reasoning let us consider who the offenders are according to all the evidence we have, and that we have not better evidence is the fault of the Magistrates who have failed to procure it.

In the first case there is every reason to believe that the persons who murdered the two Police Peons on the Parell Road were Penang Convicts who had escaped from the

[1] An important fort taken from Scindia just before Assaye.

[2] Just appointed by Malcolm Advocate-General to the local Government.

[3] A Company's magistrate.

bomb-proof, a prison not under the immediate cognisance of the Court but of that of the Government, who had entrusted it to the Senior Magistrate of Police. Could these convicts have been sent off the Island from the jail on the ground of their having no ostensible means of livelihood? or could any Regulations sanctioned by the Court have compelled the Senior Magistrate of Police to the performance of his duty of seeing that the jail was secure—a duty which on that occasion was by him most grossly neglected? Be it remembered too, by the way, that the attention of the Police Magistrate had been several times before directed to this jail. Once by myself in a charge to the Grand Jury, and on another very remarkable occasion before Sir Charles Chambers, when the Havildar who was stationed by the Police Magistrate over the jail was actually indicted before the Supreme Court for stealing property to a large amount, in league with those of the convicts over whom he was placed and who were also in the same indictment charged as accessories and all four convicted!!! All this is on Record. Permit me, my dear Sir John, to inquire whether the Senior Police Magistrate has ever received any Reprimand from the Government for this gross neglect—a neglect for which any Sheriff or jailer would in England most probably be indicted, and which I have had the honor of before bringing to your notice.

The other outrages were committed according to all the evidence by Sepoys of the 7th Regiment, and they of course would not have come within the operation of any Regulation which empowered the Petty Sessions to banish persons who cannot account for their mode of getting their livelihood. In one of these cases there is on the Coroner's Inquest the strongest evidence of gross negligence and incapacity on the part of the Magistrate and of the Coroner, and in the last case I myself sent for Mr. De Vitré three several times before I could prevail upon him to investigate the matter—at last it was done ten days or a fortnight or more after the commission of the crime, and two sepoys of the 7th Regiment were committed for trial upon the very evidence to which I had in vain repeatedly called his attention. This is not all, the first outrage was committed whilst Mr. De Vitré was down the coast on duty, a duty which certainly could not require his presence at all, much less as urgently as the peace of the Island—namely to bring up some convicts who had been landed on the Malabar Coast. Now by Regulation 11 of 1827, Art. 2, " each Magistrate shall attend at his office from ten to three every day and in case of sickness shall be bound to procure another Justice of the Peace to act in his stead.

This Regulation never contemplates the absence of a Magistrate except from sickness—and surely if he be absent for any other cause he ought equally to procure a substitute, or the Government ought to provide one. Mr. De Vitré did procure a substitute, it is true—namely, the other Police Magistrate, Mr. Gray—but Mr. Gray could not be at both offices from ten to three. The last outrage was committed when Mr. Gray was incapacitated from attending by sickness; and he in the same manner requested the third Police Magistrate, Captain Hughes, to attend—and two of the Police offices are, as you are aware, three or four miles asunder, and the third Police office seven miles from one and ten from the other.

Again by a late Regulation the Government is to fix the offices of the Magistrates and change them as it shall see occasion. Mr. Gray's office has been changed at his own convenience or caprice as many as four times, I believe, in the course of two or three years. This is a great inconvenience to the public for many reasons which it is unnecessary to explain, but which are enlarged upon in Sir James Mackintosh's letter to the Government. I do not hesitate to say that the Police Magistrates ought not to be permitted by the Government to absent themselves from the Island nor to change their offices without the most urgent occasion, and that in either case the judges should be officially informed thereof, which they have never been, and the public informed thereof and of the name of the person appointed to act, by further advertisement.

Another observation and I have done with this part of the subject. Every one, I think, of the outrages complained of by the natives in their memorial was committed in the day time within less than 200 yards of Mr. Gray's office, where there are a multitude of police sepoys and constables.

All or most of these facts have been brought to your notice, my dear Sir John, before by me in conversation when you did me the favor to request a conference on the subject of the Police—and I beg to repeat what I then stated, that the cause of these outrages in the first instance and of their subsequent non-detection has been the gross negligence and indifference of the Police Magistrates and Coroner and in particular of the Senior Magistrate of Police, and that therefore the prevention of similar outrages in future lies with the Government and the Government alone.

Now allow me, my dear Sir John, to request that you will have the goodness to inform me whether any steps have been taken or are in contemplation on the part of the Government to compel the Magistrates and Coroner by reprehension or otherwise to a better discharge of their duties. When such are in my opinion the obvious measures to rectify the evil, it would be trifling for me to be advising about new Regulations, and worse than trifling, as it would only be assisting to keep up the illusion which the Magistrates and others have endeavoured to raise, in order to conceal their own negligence and incapacity, that the inefficacy of the Police is owing to the want of power and not to their want of exertion. Beside, my dear Sir John, you must allow me to say that as you have done me the honour to request my advice on these subjects (on which, connected as they are with the administration of justice, my brethren and myself must be presumed to be the best judges and our advice ought to have the greatest weight), and as in consequence of such request I have before pointed out the neglect of the magistrates and recommended that such neglect should be noticed by severe reprehension, I feel myself entitled to inquire, before I afford any further opinion, what effect my recommendation has had.

The Magistrates are perfectly aware that their negligence is known to me, they know that I am in communication with the Governor upon the subject of the Police and they must know also, or at least conclude, that I have made representations to you of their neglect—can it be right that they should see that those representations have no effect? I have no hesitation in saying that the judges' opinions on those matters connected with the administration of justice within their own jurisdiction should be conclusive—they are conclusive when delivered from the Bench, and no one would consent to give them except from the Bench unless they were sure to meet with the highest consideration from those to whom they are afforded.

I am sure, my dear Sir John, you will not take these observations amiss—particularly as nothing is more common in England than for a judge to represent to the Lord Chancellor, who appoints the Magistrates, any misconduct of any of those Magistrates which may come before him on the circuit, and I am sure that you will also remember that I have never been offended at your various observations in our conversation on the administration of justice by the Supreme Court, as to the supposed too great lenity in the punishment of criminals, the supposition repeated and alluded to repeatedly (derived however from misrepresentation and from those who had to find an excuse for their own negligence), that the Court held too strict a hand over the Police Magistrates and that they did not dare to perform their duty for fear of the judges, and your observations as to the process of the Court up the country, &c.

Though I have expressed these sentiments merely as my own I know that the other judges participate in them as you may to a great extent be assured by the different charges of those learned persons. Also with respect to the conduct of the Magistrates, particularly of the Senior, though I have confined my statement to a few facts which have lately been the subject of discussion and which indeed have caused all those inquiries, their whole conduct is marked by a degree of indolence, indifference, and incapacity which to me is matter of as much regret as of real astonishment. They are I know utterly ignorant of the Regulations, seldom if ever take the trouble of referring to them, so that poor Mr. Bridgman,[1] aware of this, actually promised, and I believe began to carry his promise into effect, to read them over with the Magistrates.—I am, my dear Sir John, yours very truly,

EDWARD WEST.

To the Honble. Sir John Malcolm, G.C.B.

Within a month of writing this letter, Sir Edward West was dead and buried. And Malcolm, returning from the funeral, sent to the Board of Control his "honest sentiments"[2] on the choice of the next Chief Justice; who "must view him-

[1] Mr. Bridgeman, a lawyer of great promise, had just succeeded Mr. Norton as Advocate-General, and had died suddenly. See Lady West's "Journal," p. 284.

[2] Kaye's "Life," p. 510.

self as an aid to the Company;" and in a letter to his wife he said, "I am now engaged in a battle with the Supreme Court" to prevent "the Government over which I preside being trampled on, not by honest fellows with glittering sabres, but quibbling, quill-driving lawyers." The voice of the swashbuckler rings through it all!

CHAPTER XVI

"In Death too, in the Death of the Just, as the last perfection of a work of Art, may we not discern symbolic meaning? . . . The Confluence of Time with Eternity."—CARLYLE, "Sartor Resartus," Book III.

Lady West's Journal (August and September 1828):—Death of George Forbes; illness and death of Sir Edward West; funeral; widespread manifestations of regret; conclusion of Lady West's "Journal." Death of Lady West—Letter from Sir J. P. Grant—General Order by the Bombay Government on Sir E. West's death—Newspaper appreciations—Sir John Malcolm's despatch—Address of condolence from native inhabitants of Bombay; foundation of Scholarships by them in Sir E. West's memory—The great strength of English love of justice; its importance to India.

FROM LADY WEST'S JOURNAL (*August and September* 1828)

Aug. 4. I am sorry to say Edward has a return of palpitation and nervous feeling, I think in a degree brought on by writing to Sir John Malcolm to decline giving any further private opinion as to the Police and Magistrates unless his first suggestions are attended to.

Aug. 5. Edward received this morning Ana Saab, and Dumderry, a Mahratta, father-in-law to the Peishwa, a good, kind old man. His son lives with the Peishwa, who has, I understand, 10 miles of territory to go about, and keeps a Body Guard and 3000 troops, and has an allowance of 8 lacs of Rupees a year. I was glad to find Ballajee Goclerk [1] had been released from prison by Order of the Court of Directors and came to Poona last year, but Trim-

[1] Probably "Gocla." Bapu Gocla, the gallant commander of the Mahrattas, was killed at the battle of Ashti.

buckjee,[1] to the shame of the English, is still kept in close Prison (2 rooms); the cage that Capt. Nott made is, I hope, not now used. His property was all confiscated, though people try to say it is in trust for his wife and children.

Aug. 6. I am sorry to say that Edward is not very well, he has nervous feelings and palpitation. Though this (Poona) is a most enjoyable Climate, it is not cold enough to brace nerves.

Aug. 7. We are much pleased with the spirit of the Judges at the (Bombay) Sessions, though I think Sir Charles has said what was not necessary about the 7th Regiment, and uselessly offensive to the Government. One man condemned to death for Burglary. Edward had a very civil and conciliatory letter to-day from Sir John Malcolm in answer to his about the Police Magistrates.

Aug. 8. Thank God, all well at Hillington.

Aug. 9. We hear that Mr. George Forbes[2] is very weak and unwell from a Guzerat fever; Edward is feverish and far from well; it makes me a little anxious.

Aug. 10. Edward was so hot in the night I sent for Dr. Ducat, who gave calomel and James' Powder. We heard last evening with deep regret of the death of poor Mr. George Forbes after only 6 days' illness; as a Merchant he was a man of great integrity, a sincere friend, and a great loss to Bombay; to his poor wife and children the loss is irreparable.

Aug. 11. Edward has passed another wretched night, and seems very little better to-day, and his eyes anxious.

Aug. 12. Another dreadful night; Dr. Ducat wishes to bleed him, but first to see some other Medical Man. I am very very anxious; Dr. Brydon has been here, and they have bled my dearest Edward. Dr. Ducat strongly recommends sending for Martin West. I am so frightened, I have written to him and laid a dawk.[3] He cannot be here before Friday night. On this night, Tuesday, he had three

[1] Trimbuckjee was the Peishwa's confidential Minister. Elphinstone insisted on his surrender after the assassination of the Baroda envoy. He was imprisoned at Tannah, in the Island of Salsette, and probably intentionally allowed to escape and to join the Mahratta irregulars before the coming Mahratta War.

[2] Of the great mercantile house of which Sir Charles Forbes had been head.

[3] Relays of bearers.

dozen leeches put on to his right temple; I never saw anyone so patient, so calm, so gentle, so thankful as he is for attention.

Aug. 13. Dearest Edward is so much worse that Dr. Ducat has called in Dr. Thomson of the 4th Dragoons. He takes 3 calomel powders a day, of I suppose 20 grains each, and they cannot get the fever under; he has had an immense blister put on to the back of his neck; dear fellow, he thinks he is very seriously ill, and has asked Dr. Ducat, who cannot deny it. I strive to be and look cheerful when my heart is breaking. We prayed together.

Aug. 14. Dearest Edward at 6 begged to have a sheet of paper and a pencil, and made his Will in 6 lines; such a flattering one to me, and one I hope I shall deserve from the great confidence he has placed in me. He mentioned many things to me about dear Fanny, our property, and serious things which are indelibly engraved on my heart. Dr. Thomson and Dr. Brydon came with Dr. Ducat, and recommended his head to be shaved, and two immense blisters all over the sides of his head.

Aug. 15. The breathing better, but a wretched night, tho' not quite so much fever.

Aug. 16. I prepared Edward to see Martin. He arrived this morning; dear Edward has seen him, and seemed quite pleased at his coming, and talked a little to him. He is always asking after dear little Fanny, but feels too ill to see her. He has been attacked with an incessant and violent hiccough which they cannot stop. He has a very attentive Portuguese Servant; and so is Batt, but I have the comfort of doing everything for him myself; he smiles his thanks so sweetly, and says he likes to see my face. He says little but is, I am sure, aware of his danger—his gentleness, his patience, his resignation, and his will to do everything he is asked is quite beautiful.

Aug. 17 (*Sunday*). The night has been a dreadful one, with hiccough and fever, and his dear mouth so parched. God have mercy upon him, and support me under the awful trial which I fear awaits me. He laid in my arms and his breathing became fainter and fainter, and his dear soul departed at ½ past 8 on Monday morning, August 18th, 1828. I closed his sweet eyes myself, and sat by the Bed and watched his sweet countenance all day. It was so calm and serene. At 6 I was obliged to take my long last kiss, and I wonder that I am alive and in my senses, but God, in his mercy, has wonderfully supported me.

Aug. 19 (*Tuesday*). At 6 this morning the Minute Guns began to fire; each seemed a death blow to me. At 7 I went to Church with my beloved Edward, and saw him put into his Grave. Good God, what a moment—one only longs to be there also. Martin and Sir John Malcolm supported me through the service. How I got Home I scarcely know. An Express was sent down to Bombay and Minute Guns were fired, and I believe I may say no one was ever before so much regretted by the Natives there, or indeed by the Europeans, as, except by a few of Mr. Erskine's Friends, he was universally respected, admired and beloved. The Natives are wishing for Pictures of him to put into the Court House, and various plans to do something and everything to show their feelings towards his beloved Memory. The Archdeacon says he has not self-command enough to preach a Funeral Sermon. The regret here is, I understand, as great amongst all Classes. A Ball was put off; all these marks of compliment and admiration are painfully gratifying to me; I only wish my dearest Edward could have been persuaded of a tenth part of it, but he never fancied he was loved or appreciated. The Court has been like an English Court, and the good he has done must, I hope, remain for years, and the name of West deeply engraven on all hearts, especially those of the Natives for whom he was so deeply interested, and whose advantage he always had so much at heart. His integrity, independence, manliness and spirit was astonishing, notwithstanding all he had gone through. He now hoped to have passed the remainder of his time in quiet, reaping the pleasing fruits of his former exertions, but God has willed it otherwise, and no doubt, I trust, for his happiness, for never was there a better Husband, Father, Master, Relation or Friend. He is buried in the Church in the Centre of the Aisle close to the Altar. I shall remain here till November, the time my dearest Edward intended, and I hope I shall ever do what I think he would have wished me, in every particular.

Aug. 27. I have endeavoured to write down the last dreadful week of my adored Husband's life, there I must stop. The last week I have seemed so lost, and my nerves so shattered, I have scarcely the power to do anything, and seem as if I must close my eyes to the future. I dare not look forward, only back to the six last blessed years of my life. Yesterday was the 6th Anniversary of our Wedding; I feel so alone, so deserted, and quite tremble when I think I have no one to look up to, and to my God I now look for my only happiness and support, and pray that He will be a Father to me and to my poor fatherless Child. I requested Martin to return to Bombay on the 21st. I find quiet and dear Fanny and Batt all I want or can bear as yet. The dear Child asks all day for her Papa and looks for him in his dressing-room, and everywhere; how delighted he would be; he doted upon her. Martin wrote home to ffolkes and Gilbert the dreadful news. I must do so, but have not yet the power. How much I wish there was a picture of him for the natives and myself, and dear Fanny might recollect his face as well as his name.

Aug. 29. Every day I feel more wretched and forlorn. Sir John Malcolm kindly wished to call, but I have begged to be excused seeing him.

Aug. 30. There is a very well drawn up short Sketch of my beloved Edward in Wednesday's *Gazette*, Lady Chambers writes me word, done by Sir Charles at the request of the Editor. The Chambers have felt his loss severely as a Friend, and have a kind sympathy for me in my heavy affliction, and are all that is affectionate and attentive to me and my dear Child.

Sept. 1. A fortnight to-day since my dreadful bereavement. Every day, more and more, I am gratified by the universal regret manifested for the death of my beloved Husband. Even at Damaun.[1] "*25th August* 1828.—In consequence of the melancholy intelligence of the death of the Hon. Sir Edward West, Chief Justice of the Supreme Court of Judicature at Bombay, having reached this yesterday, two battalions of Infantry paraded last evening with reversed arms, and 45 Minute Guns were fired by a park of Artillery, likewise drawn up for the occasion, followed by 3 volleys of Musketry by the Infantry. The Hon. the Governor, as Rigidor da Justica, and his suite, with the whole of the public authorities of this place, both Civil and Military, attended the ceremony in full mourning. It is said that the above honours have been paid as a particular mark of esteem for the deceased."

[1] A Portuguese town, sixty miles from Surat.

Sept. 3 (*Wednesday*). Dear little Fanny had a cold and cough yesterday, which always makes me anxious, especially as Dr. Ducat was obliged to leave this yesterday to see a sick friend at Sholapore, 200 miles off, and may be absent a fortnight. I am not very well myself, so weak.

Sept. 4. Dear Fanny coughed a good deal in the night, but is, thank God, better to-day. I was so unwell, *and am*, that I thought it prudent to see Dr. Brydon.

This is the last entry. Life and Journal ended together.

There is a note on the last page of the "Journal," written by a different hand, and in less faded ink.

"Lady West died a few hours later in giving birth to a son, who did not survive."

The following letter, from Sir J. P. Grant to Capt. Lane, Sir E. West's brother-in-law, shows that Lady West was at once removed to Bombay, and died there in the house of Sir Charles and Lady Chambers.

From SIR JOHN PETER GRANT, *surviving Judge of the King's Court, to* CAPT. LANE.

MONDAY, 17*th Dec.* 1828.

SIR,—Your letter of 17th ulto. only reached Bombay a few days ago—since when I have been absent on a short Excursion.[1]

My much and sincerely lamented Colleague, Sir Edward West, died of a very short and sudden illness at Poonah, a determination of blood to the head,[2] to which I understand he had been occasionally subject.

Lady West's unremitted and anxious attendance on him, and the excess of her grief, were too much for her strength in the situation she was in. Unfortunately she could not at

[1] Sir J. P. Grant had adjourned the Court.

[2] Modern medicine, as is well known, recognises no illness of this nature.

first be persuaded to leave Poonah; and being there alone, her health failing, and no one to press on her the propriety of returning in time to Bombay, she unhappily remained till her physicians were of opinion her only chance was removal, though at a critical period of her pregnancy.

She came to Sir Charles Chambers' House, where she of course received every kindness and attention, but the consequences were such as had been too probable. . . . She died in a few days.

You of course know that Sir Edward and Lady West had one child only, a daughter. The little girl is sole heiress to both Father and Mother. Mr. Martin West, Sir Edward's nephew, is sole executor in this country. The little girl, who is a remarkably fine child, now living under Lady Chambers' care at her House, goes home in the *Mountstuart Elphinstone* which sails on the 28th inst., every provision being made for her being carefully attended to, the Captain having been well known both to Sir Edward and Lady West, and a gentleman who stands very high in the esteem of all who know him, and there being ladies on board also well known to Lady West.[1]

I need not say that the memory of Sir Edward West is much and most deservedly cherished by the inhabitants of this Island[2] as a Judge. As a colleague his death has been an irreparable loss to me, and to both him and to Lady West, my family and myself were growing daily more attached when we so suddenly lost both of them.

I am happy to say that I have enjoyed perfect health since my arrival in India, and have as yet no reason to fear the climate.—I have the honour to be, Sir, your very obedient Servant, J. P. GRANT.

CAPT. LANE.

[1] On coming of age, Fanny West went to Hillington and lived there with her uncle and aunt, Sir W. and Lady Ffolkes; and in later life married Colonel Robert Gregory Wale, 33rd Regiment, son of Sir Charles Wale, K.C.B., Commander of the Reserves at Guadeloupe, and Governor of Martinique until its restoration to the French in 1814. Colonel and Mrs. Wale lived and died at Shelford, in Cambridgeshire. In memory of her parents, Mrs. Wale erected a beautiful monument in Hillington church, and built, at her own expense, the parsonage of Flitcham, in Norfolk.

[2] Island of Bombay.

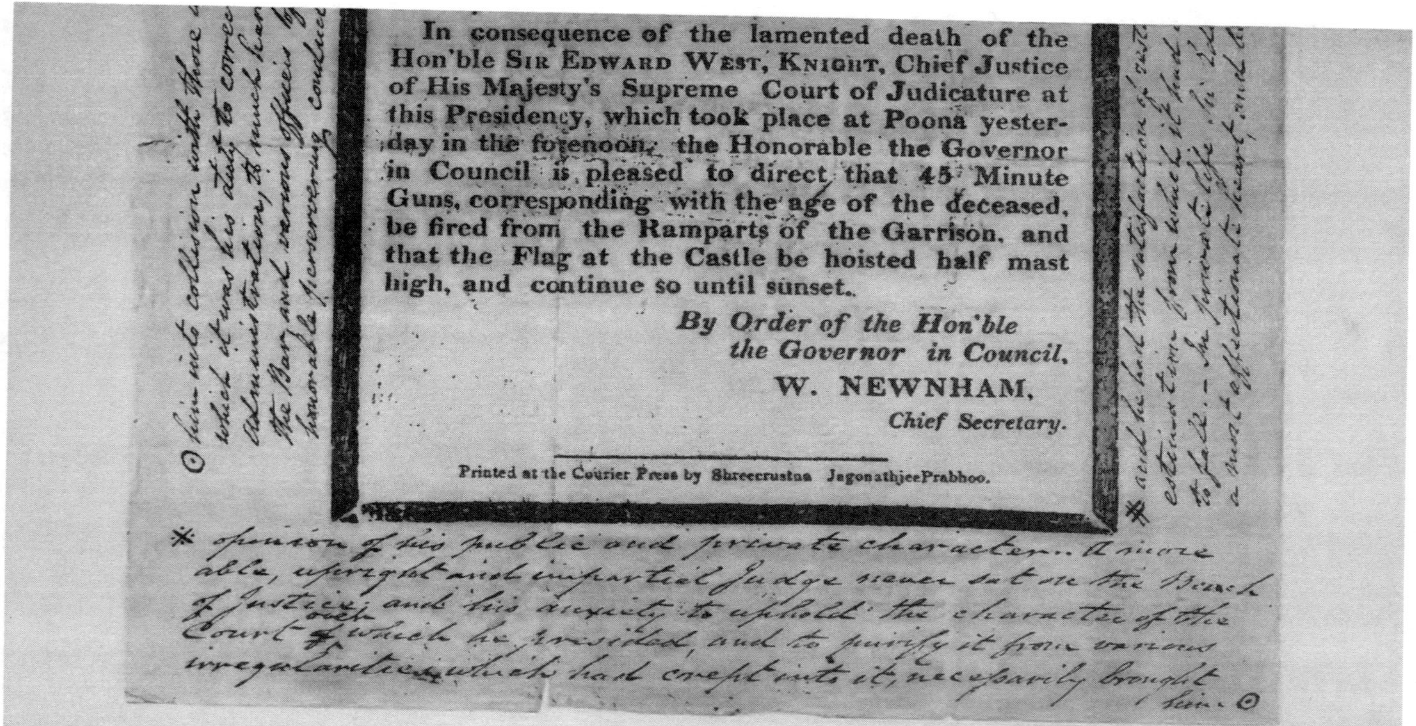

In consequence of the lamented death of the Hon'ble SIR EDWARD WEST, KNIGHT, Chief Justice of His Majesty's Supreme Court of Judicature at this Presidency, which took place at Poona yesterday in the forenoon, the Honorable the Governor in Council is pleased to direct that 45 Minute Guns, corresponding with the age of the deceased, be fired from the Ramparts of the Garrison, and that the Flag at the Castle be hoisted half mast high, and continue so until sunset.

By Order of the Hon'ble
the Governor in Council,
W. NEWNHAM,
Chief Secretary.

Printed at the Courier Press by Shreecrustna Jogonathjee Prabhoo.

* opinion of his public and private character.. A more able, upright and impartial Judge never sat on the Bench of Justice; and his anxiety to uphold the character of the Court over which he presided, and to purify it from various irregularities which had crept into it, necessarily brought him ⊙

General Order by Sir JOHN MALCOLM (*see p.* 314).

Sir Edward West arrived at Bombay in February, 1823, and with Lady West, and his Nephew Edward- lived with us for the first six months after their arrival.. I was also, (as an Alder-man of the Court) associated with Sir Edward on the Bench up to the period of my leaving Bombay for England in March 1824, and was thus enabled to form a correct opinion *

BOMBAY COURIER
EXTRAORDINARY.

TUESDAY, AUGUST 19, 1828.

It is with feelings of the deepest regret we have to announce the Death of the Honourable Sir Edward West Knt. Chief Justice of the Supreme Court of Judicature at this Presidency, which took place at Poonah yesterday in the forenoon. The following General Order by Government, has been issued on the occasion.

BOMBAY CASTLE,---19th August 1828.

...had been benefiting by the irregularities ... subjecting him in the first year of this ... ing opposition from the Government, ... the Court; but which his straight forward ... enabled him triumphantly to overcome, and *

...o the Court to that high place in public ... allowed by his immediate predecessor ... ard West was most amiable, possessing ... nevolent disposition. His education had (See over)

On August 19, 1828, a general order was published by the Bombay Government:—

"In consequence of the lamented death of the Hon. Sir Edward West, . . . which took place in Poona yesterday . . . the Hon. the Governor in Council is pleased to direct that 45 minute guns, corresponding with the age of the deceased, be fired from the ramparts of the garrison, and that the flag of the castle be hoisted half-mast high."

A leader in the *Bombay Gazette*[1] says:—

"We wish to give expression, however inadequate, of our heartfelt sorrow and distress at a loss so unexpected and so serious to the inhabitants of the Presidency. However unworthy our tribute of praise may be of the high reputation of our departed chief magistrate we shall not be lukewarm in our mention of him. . . .

"The materials for forming a just estimate of his character, as it has been exhibited in the execution of his high and important office in this Presidency, are in the hands of every one who has paid any attention to what has been passing before his eyes.

"Upon our arrival in Bombay we found our attention forcibly drawn to the consideration of it by those discussions which filled the *Gazette* under our predecessor, and we were in a more interesting manner induced to contemplate his character by being frequently in court during

[1] *Bombay Gazette*, August 27.

criminal and civil trials. Upon such occasions the force and strength of his mind attracted our attention.

"His energy, zeal, decision, firmness — the hardier qualities which in a climate so debilitating are rarely to be met with—appeared to predominate; and they are qualities which, in whatever country their possessor may be called upon to act, will not be long before they produce a strong sensation on the public mind. With regard to the discussions to which we have alluded, we found ourselves strongly impressed in his favour by discovering that in all those discussions, though sheet after sheet teemed with assertions that Sir Edward West's decision was contrary to abstract justice in such and such particular cases, there was no breath of imputation against his judicial integrity. . . . In these cases in which we have heard Sir E. West's conduct canvassed, we have repeatedly endeavoured to discover what general principle was at stake, and as often have been led to the conviction that, however strenuously those who were affected by his acts might insist upon technical irregularities, or complain of harsh treatment, the public good was the only motive in the mind of the Judge, and that he was prepared, at any hazard, at the risk of his ease, his domestic comfort, his social happiness, to drag those whom he considered offenders to the open face of day, and to secure to the public the inestimable advantage of cheap Justice. Higher praise than this we can give no man, and when the memory of the dissensions, which were the consequence of his boldness and intrepidity, shall have vanished, his character will rest on its true basis—the public esteem and veneration.

"Sir E. West was in person rather below the middle size and well proportioned. His eyes were light grey, and the contour of his head was particularly striking, and gave an elevated and distinguished expression to his face.

"The remark upon seeing him which a casual observer would make would be perhaps that his countenance betrayed a considerable degree of susceptibility. Where his mind was in the least degree excited, his sensations appeared like lightning on his countenance, but we have seen him keep complete mastery of himself under circumstances of the greatest provocation. In the transaction of ordinary business his perfect knowledge of general principles, and that adroitness in detail which is the result of long practice, enabled him to despatch what was brought before him with the most perfect ease and coolness. In his judgments of more important cases, nothing could exceed his anxiety to arrive at a right decision. His language was in general terse and to the point, without any effort at eloquence; and his reasoning logical and conclusive.

"With regard to the native population, he was most anxious to give them the full benefit of English law. We have reason to believe that the native population did him full justice in this respect, and that a most deep and general regret prevails among them at his death."

The *Bengal Hurkaru*, one of the most influential of Anglo-Indian newspapers of the time, reported: "With the deepest regret we have to announce the death of that able and upright Judge Sir E. West. His remains were followed to the grave by the whole European community at Poona, besides a large concourse of natives. British-born subjects have to mourn in the death of Sir E. West the deprivation of one of the most zealous and unflinching defenders of their constitutional rights; the natives, one of their most watchful, zealous, and persevering defenders against oppression and injustice; while British India at large has cause to lament him as one of the ablest and purest administrators of the law who ever conferred honour by his talents and integrity upon the Bench of this country. We trust that some one possessing information and ability for the task will present us with a tribute to his memory more worthy of it than any which our feeble pen could offer."

Malcolm's overland despatch, which was sent off the following October, reached London at the end of January 1829, and was the first announcement of the news in England. In the February number of the *Oriental Herald* Buckingham says: "The prevalence of easterly winds during the past month has prevented the arrival of any late news by ships from India; but an overland despatch has reached the India House, bringing intelligence from Bombay to the 22nd of October, the most material part of which indeed is of a painful and afflicting nature. It appears that that most excellent man and upright judge, Sir Edward West, died sometime early in October" (August), "and that his colleague, Sir Charles Chambers, followed him about the middle of the same month, leaving only one judge, Sir John Grant, on the Bombay Bench.

"The immediate cause, it is said, of the Government" (of Bombay) "sending home this overland despatch was to apprise the Court of Directors of an open rupture between themselves and the Supreme Court of that Presidency, on a point of authority to which they attach the utmost importance.

"We have taken occasion in many previous numbers . . . to show that just in proportion to the subserviency of the English judges in India are they popular with the Company's governments; and, on the other hand, that in proportion to their integrity, impartiality, and independence, are they unpopular in the same quarter. . . . Of the character of Sir C. Chambers we do not remember that we have had reason ever to speak but with respect; and we feel the loss of such a man as one of great importance to India. But of Sir Edward West we have had occasion in almost every number to express ourselves in terms of the highest praise and admiration. No Indian judge of whose public character and conduct we know anything appears to us to have united in himself so completely the clear perception of what was his duty, as it regarded the extension of legal protection to the natives of India, and the firmness necessary to enable him to perform that duty, in spite of all the bland allurements of patronage, the intrigues of secret enemies, or the open threats of power.

"He had all the tenderness of feeling necessary to sympathise with the oppressed and suffering classes of our fellow-subjects in India; and all the strength of nerve to qualify him to stand up openly before the whole world as their protector. In every transaction in which we have watched his proceedings (and we have done so with the jealousy with which we habitually regard the acts of all men holding elevated stations in trust for the public good), we have seen him the friend of the oppressed—the supporter of the weak—the inflexible administrator of justice, without regard to colour, caste, or condition—in short, the Righteous Judge, than which a more dignified office cannot appertain to humanity; and no man deserves more honour and veneration than he who discharges its duties with integrity.

"Sir Edward West was that man. And if ever monument were appropriate tribute from the living to the dead, one of splendid simplicity, conformable to his own pure and unsullied character, ought to be raised on the spot where he breathed his last, where his life was sacrificed to the arduous duties of his elevated profession. For themselves," continued Buckingham, "we congratulate them on having thus sunk sweetly to repose, with all the odour of good deeds breathing incense around their tombs: for when can men die happier —since die they must—than when borne to the chamber of death . . . by those who honour their departure with tears and regrets? For their weeping families the only balm is time and hope. . . . For England, whose honour and renown is so intimately blended with due administration of justice in every corner of her extended realms, our prayer is, May the places thus left vacant by death be filled as adequately as talent, merit, and independence, untainted by any meaner consideration of patronage or profit, can effect."

The Times of January 29 announced the arrival of Malcolm's overland despatch.

An obituary notice in that paper says: "Sir E. West, who is thus lost to India and to his country, was a man of great talents and moral qualities. He is known beyond his profession as the author of the pamphlet on the Nature of Rent, published by him when a Fellow of University College, in which he expounded the same opinions on the subject which were about the same time advanced by Mr. Malthus. . . . In his judicial capacity his conduct was marked by a zeal for justice, and a determination to discountenance oppression, which made him a favourite, we believe, with the natives; though his occasional warmth of temper (justified perhaps by the abuses which he had to control) set him at variance with some of the lawyers of the Presidency."

Round his copy of the Government announcement, Mr. John Stewart, Sir Charles Forbes' brother-in-law, had written the week before:—

21*st Jan.* 1829.

Sir Edward West arrived at Bombay in February 1823, and with Lady West, and his Nephew Edward, lived with us for the first six months after their arrival. I was also (as an Alderman of the Court) associated with Sir Edward on the Bench up to the period of my leaving Bombay for England in March 1824, and was thus enabled to form a correct opinion of his public and private character. A more able, upright and impartial Judge never sat on the Bench of Justice; and his anxiety to uphold the character of the Court over which he presided, and to purify it from various irregularities which had crept into it, necessarily brought him into collision with those who had been benefiting by the irregularities which it was his duty to correct, subjecting him in the first year of his Administration to much harassing opposition from the Government, the Bar, and various officers of the Court; but which his straightforward honourable persevering conduct enabled him triumphantly to overcome, and he had the satisfaction of restoring the Court to that high place in public estimation from which it had been allowed by his immediate predecessors to fall. In private life Sir Edward West was most amiable, possessing a most affectionate heart, and benevolent disposition. His education had been of the first rate order, which with his superior talent rendered him a most instructive and pleasing companion. I had the happiness of enjoying his confidence up to the period of his death, his last letter to me bearing date within a day or two of that lamentable event.

From the period of my leaving India in March 1824 up to the last days of Sir Edward's valuable life, our correspondence never ceased; every ship from India brought voluminous despatches from him; many of his letters being of a strictly confidential nature. J. S.

The natives of Bombay now did a thing entirely without precedent. Hindoos, Parsees, and Mahomedans combined and founded a scholarship in honour of the lost Chief Justice. We learn from the *Bombay Gazette* that, soon after Sir E. West's death, a deputation of the principal Native Merchants and Inhabitants of Bombay proceeded to the house of Sir Charles Chambers, Acting Chief Justice, to present this address of condolence.[1]

To the HONBLE. SIR CHARLES H. CHAMBERS, Kt., *and the* HONBLE. SIR JOHN PETER GRANT, Kt., *judges of His Majesty's Supreme Court of Judicature, Bombay.*

MY LORDS,—We the undersigned Members of the several tribes composing the Native Community, subject to the jurisdiction of His Majesty's Supreme Court of Judicature under the Bombay Presidency, beg leave respectfully to present ourselves before your Honourable Bench for the purpose of offering a last mournful tribute of affection to the memory of your late distinguished Colleague our gracious Chief Justice, the Honble. Sir Edward West.

[1] *Bombay Gazette*, October 1828.

We are conscious that it is a novelty for the people to come forward to address a bench of English Judges on such a subject; it is no less a novelty (actually witnessed by many of us) to be rescued in the short space of twenty-nine years, since the establishment of a regular Court of British law on this Island, from the evils of an inefficient and irregular administration of justice which previously existed. Grateful for such advantages, we resort to those means, which alone are open to a community like ours, to express publicly our sense of them; and indeed we should justly merit the reproach of want of feeling did we *now* silently confine within our own breasts the grief, the unfeigned sorrow, we experience in the event which has deprived us of him, at whose hands those advantages have been so largely extended and confirmed to us. In expressing to your Lordships our sorrow for the death of Sir Edward West, we seek a balm for our sufferings, and would fain hope thereby to alleviate the distress with which you must contemplate your earthly separation from a colleague so able and indefatigable, so undaunted, and so upright.

The time is past when any commendation of ours, or indeed any earthly honours can be of value to him, whom the joys and sorrows of this world no longer affect; and who is therefore equally removed from the reach of human censure and of human applause. But we should deem it an omission of duty, as well as of gratitude, did we not come forward, now that our motives cannot be misconstrued, to mark in the strongest manner the deep sense we entertain of his virtuous administration. The spirit of even-handed justice which prompted his decisions; the unconquerable assiduity and unshaken firmness which he evinced in discharging the functions of his high office; the unshrinking zeal which animated him in making salutary reforms; but above all that high principle of independence and integrity which led him to sacrifice so much of his private happiness to the conscientious performance of his public duties: these, my Lords, are the virtues which have grown upon our gratitude, since every day's succeeding experience teaches us to appreciate their value.

In briefly noticing the most prominent features in the administration of Sir Edward West, we cannot but dwell with grateful delight on the easy access which that humane and honourable judge at all times afforded to the poor and needy part of our countrymen. That he rendered the administration of law less expensive to the Inhabitants of this Presidency, thus throwing open to the poor the avenues of justice, so long barred against them, is not the least solid advantage derived from a career fertile in benefits. But great and salutary as was this reform, it did not satisfy that glowing spirit of philanthropy, ever thoughful to devise, and active to execute what might lessen the distresses or increase the happiness of his fellow-creatures. Scrupulous in the discharge of his high functions as a judge, which alone seemed labour too great even for his energetic mind, he found leisure, and had the condescension to become himself the *advocate of the indigent.*

But amongst the many great favours received at the hands of Sir Edward West, that for which we would chiefly record our gratitude is the manner in which, conjointly with your Lordships, he carried into execution the recent provision of the British Legislature for admitting the Natives of this country to sit on juries. The wise and conciliatory method he took to give effect to the wishes of Parliament, the condescension with which he conferred with every class of the Native community, the prudent deference he paid to all their national and religious feelings, the zeal with which he laboured to overcome difficulties arising out of the multiform constitution of our body, and the solicitude he displayed to set the intent of the enactment in its true light, are fresh in the recollection of us all. To these exertions it is owing that the Natives of Bombay are now in the enjoyment of one of the greatest privileges of freemen.

A knowledge of the virtuous and enlightened character of the late Chief Justice cannot fail to have prevailed throughout a large portion of our countrymen in India; but it has only been permitted to the Inhabitants of this Island to enjoy the immediate fruits of his distinguished judicial administration. However imperfect therefore any further addition may prove to this record of our deep sorrow for his demise and respect for his memory, we beg to announce that we have raised a sum of money which it is designed to make over to the Native Education Society to be vested by them in Government securities for the endowment of one or more scholarships and the distribution of one or more annual prizes, according to the amount of interest realised from the total fund, to be denominated "Chief Justice West's Scholarships and Prizes."

Engaged as the late judge was himself so earnestly in improving the condition of the Natives, we humbly hope that we have devised the most durable and appropriate method of perpetuating the grateful recollection of him among them, and training up our children to the proper discharge of those public duties to which he first showed them the way.

With a firm reliance on the continued favour and kindness of your Lordships, we are, with the greatest respect, my Lords, your Lordships' most obedient and most humble servants.

(Signed by about 140 of the principal Hindoos, Parsees, Mahomedan Merchants, and Inhabitants.)

BOMBAY, 1*st October* 1828.

The address was delivered by Bomanjee Hormusjee.

Sir Charles Chambers in answer said that neither he nor Sir J. P. Grant could receive the address; that a judge should proceed on his course without desire of applause or fear of censure; that it was a novelty to address a court of justice, and that a bad precedent might be established; that if Sir E. West were present he would be the first to approve the judges' determination.

In their private capacities the judges welcomed such a disinterested tribute of admiration to the character and conduct of Sir E. West. They mourned with deep sorrow the loss of so valuable a counsellor and friend, but their loss could not be compared with that of the public; during the short period Sir E. West passed in Bombay his warmest wishes and most ardent prayers were for the improvement and elevation of his native fellow-subjects, and the consciousness of having the approbation of the respectable natives would have supported him in the execution of his arduous duties.

They approved, too, of the proposed mode of perpetuating Sir E. West's memory; "Not," said Sir C. Chambers, "by an inscription on a tablet of marble, which would be confined to a little space and would be soon obliterated by time, but in the more durable monuments of the mind—by associating his name with an admirable institution which is chiefly supported by your liberality. . . .

"The scholarships and prizes which you propose to denominate 'Chief Justice West's Scholarships and Prizes' in the schools of the Bombay Native Education Society, will implant an unwritten but unfading record of his public worth in the breasts of all those who shall derive the inestimable benefits of knowledge from your munificence, and will hand down in the most honourable manner the name of our departed colleague to your latest posterity."

Memories are short in India. Lady West's remark that in Bombay people are buried as soon as dead, "their furniture sold the third day, and they are forgotten on the fourth," had now come true again.

Sir Edward and Lady West, together with this pathetic tribute from the natives—a wreath for their dead friend's grave—were soon forgotten. The schools supported by native generosity became "Elphinstone College," and Bombay handbooks have long informed their readers that the "West" scholarship was founded by Sir Edward West, not by the natives he befriended.

But the loss of Sir E. West at this time was deplorable; a time when in Bombay and its Provinces government by the Company had reached its lowest level; when for two or three years in England a reactionary Board of Control was to be in power, and when even a man of the strength of Lord William Bentinck, beginning his epoch-making work in Bengal, must have been in need of all possible moral support from the sister Presidencies.

But West had not lived in vain. Who can tell what he, and King's Judges such as he was, have done for England in the East. Already natives were flocking to the Presidency towns, to be under the jurisdiction of the King's Courts and out of the reach of the Company's Provincial Courts. "English laws and institutions," said a writer of the time,[1] "are popular with the Hindoos, notwithstanding the pains taken to convince the English public to the contrary. What but this attachment has peopled the towns of Calcutta,

[1] *Oriental Herald*, vol. xvii. p. 427.

Madras, and Bombay, and makes a real property in Calcutta worth twenty years' purchase, when in the Provinces it is not worth five? What but this makes a Hindoo content with an interest of five per cent. for his money when he might receive in the Provinces twenty? The Indians, in short, are thoroughly imbued with a just sense of the advantages of being considered British subjects, and of living under the protection of English law. . . . When the natives living within the pale of English law contrast their own prosperity and security with the poverty, disorder, and anarchy of the Provinces how should they feel otherwise?"

And surely this love of justice by the best of her sons is the only charter by which England holds her vast Empire; the attribute which renders her of all nations fittest for the task. It is not her courage—that she shares with Zulus and Dervishes; not military organisation, for that too she shares with others; but innate love of justice, mercy, and fair play to all men.

This it is that makes England's subject races come to her support. This, more than the sword, has kept down rebellion; this probably more than anything else has kept her, both in Africa and India, almost free from those outbursts of wolfish blood-thirstiness and insane lust which have disgraced European nations in tropical countries.

It may be the highest attribute to which we can attain.

But the history of India, as historians have written it, is the history of war and conquest, of military and diplomatic intrigue. The quieter movements, with their far-reaching consequences, together with the men who have lived for honour and justice, not glory and gold, are soon lost sight of in the deepening twilight of the past.

And though we proclaim in our Commemoration services that "the just shall be had in everlasting remembrance," it remains for ever true that the "growing good of the world is partly dependent on unhistoric acts,"[1] and that things are not so ill with us as they might have been, is largely due to those who have faithfully lived forgotten lives, and rest in neglected tombs.

[1] George Eliot.

CHAPTER XVII

Renewed attack on the King's Court by Sir John Malcolm—Death of Sir C. Chambers—Bitter conflict between remaining Judge Sir J. P. Grant and the Bombay Government—Civil War threatened—Court adjourned—Malcolm's overland despatch—Reaction in England—Two Judges favourable to the Company appointed by Lord Ellenborough—Malcolm leaves India—Sir C. Metcalfe's Minute—Comments on the situation—Eventual change in system of legislature.

THE ablest of the judges being now out of the way, a direct attack on what remained of the King's Court became easier.

Under certain ill-defined conditions[1] the Supreme Court had jurisdiction not only over inhabitants of the island of Bombay, but over those British subjects, European and native, outside its limits, who were connected with Bombay, and who appealed to the Court for protection. Shortly after Sir E. West's death, two writs of *habeas corpus* had been issued by the King's Court, to bring before the judges prisoners who had been "committed by word of mouth" in a Provincial Court "habitually irregular and oppressive."[2] In the first case Sir C. Chambers found "no cause of detention" and dismissed the prisoner. In the second, a poor debtor, wrongly imprisoned, had also been

[1] See Appendix. [2] Sir C. Chambers' speech.

released. A third writ was pending. The relations of an orphan Hindoo boy had appealed to the King's Court for his removal from the custody of an uncle, reported to be ill-treating him.

Had Sir E. West been alive, the case would probably have been regarded as being outside the jurisdiction of the King's Court, and would have been left to the Provincial Court. But Sir C. Chambers and Sir J. P. Grant issued a writ for the examination of the boy. Malcolm, now finding the King's Court on debatable ground, summoned his Council, and with them wrote a letter to the judges to the effect that he had given orders to Company's servants to take no notice of any writs issued by the King's Court to officers of any Provincial Courts, or to native subjects outside the Island of Bombay.

The letter was read aloud in Court, and had the effect the Governor must have expected, and probably desired. The judges were furious, and decided to ignore the communication from the Governor. Sir J. P. Grant pointed out that it was the duty of the King's Judges to issue writs of *habeas corpus*, and bring before the Court for examination all subjects of the King reported to be unlawfully confined, and that if there was loss of life in resisting the writ of the King's Court, responsibility for the murder would rest with those who advised the resistance.

Sir Charles Chambers still more indignantly

addressed the Court. He said that the letter was written in a dictatorial tone by those who had no right to address the King's Court except as suitors. That, although in matters which did not concern the administration of justice, the Court was willing to pay members of the Bombay Government the respect and courtesy due to them, "the East India Company and those who govern their possessions, however absolute over those whom they may consider their subjects, must be told, as they have been told a thousand times before, that in the King's Court they are not entitled to more favour than other suitors."

Within a week of his defiance of the Governor, Sir Charles Chambers had followed the Chief Justice to the grave,[1] and Sir J. P. Grant, with unflinching courage, carried on the contest alone.

The Governor's letter, he said, had "killed his fellow-judge, but it should not kill him."

Addressing the Grand Jury on October 20, after a pathetic allusion to the two empty chairs beside him, Sir J. P. Grant said:—

"Sir Charles Chambers[2] has been removed at a time when I have most need of his honesty, prudence, and the comfort of his society. . . . An impressive testimony has been given by the respectable natives of Bombay to

[1] He died on the morning of October 13, in his thirty-ninth year.

[2] The speech is given in abstract.

the benefits they had received from the integrity and firmness of Sir E. West. In firmness and integrity the colleague I have lost was his equal. Born with a quick perception of all that was beautiful, with an intimate knowledge of literature, he was also a sound lawyer. Bred, educated, and accustomed to live among the gentle and refined, he was on a question of duty as unbending as the sternest, and an imputation on his integrity shook him with a power which only those can estimate whose honour is as pure and as sensitive. Left myself alone to discharge the whole duties of administration of justice in this place, I am duly sensible of the weight that is thrown upon me, but it shall only quicken my vigilance and strengthen my exertions. Placed here by my sovereign to perform the duties of this office, it is not permitted me to judge of my fitness or unfitness. No consideration shall induce me to shrink from the due discharge of my important duties. . . .

"I regret to say that the jail remains in the state in which I found it. There is the same revolting spectacle of men confined in irons for weeks on the testimony, as may happen, of a single false witness, and this because those whose duty it is will not make the jail secure. . . ."[1]

There was nothing now to check Sir John

[1] *Bombay Gazette*, October 1828.

Malcolm's high-handedness. "The opportunity," he wrote, "of striking a blow at these Courts was given me, and to the utmost of my strength I will inflict it."[1]

Sir J. P. Grant had obtained from five brother judges in Madras and Calcutta the opinion that the King's Courts had without doubt power to exercise the jurisdiction of the Court of the King's Bench over all territories subject to the Presidencies where they sit; and a communication to that effect was published in the *Bombay Gazette*.[2] In the next issue appeared an order from Malcolm that any remark on the proceedings of the Court would be punished.

Opinion too in Bombay, even among the Company's servants, was by no means all on the side of the Governor. Sir Thomas Bradford, the Commander-in-Chief,[3] though a member of the Council, was now prepared to assist the remaining King's Judge, and enforce his writ. But Sir John Malcolm, depending possibly on the support he might receive from the reactionary ministry of his former friend the Duke of Wellington, who had already ejected from the Board of Control Charles W. Wynn (though he had been more than once offered the Governor-Generalship), and on the fact that the

[1] Letter, p. 522, "Life." [2] June 24, 1829.

[3] Sir Thomas Bradford had been appointed Commander-in-Chief at Bombay in 1825. He had served in the Peninsula, and had been present at Corunna, and had commanded a Portuguese division at Vittoria.

first news ministers would receive of the events at Bombay would be his own account of it (hastily despatched overland, and carried by his confidential friend, Major Barnwell), had the audacity to make arrangements to attack, capture, and deport the Commander-in-Chief of the King's troops as soon as he attempted to enforce the King's writ.

Civil war in Bombay between King and Company thus became possible. Sir J. P. Grant adjourned the Court and awaited orders from England.

Malcolm in his Report to the Board of Control laid stress on the violence of the judges, and on his own "forbearance"; and Kaye, in his "Life of Malcolm," with biographical fervour, states the case for the Governor. But that another opinion was held by independent Anglo-Indians is shown by an article in the *Bengal Hurkaru*, a paper published in the presidency of which Bentinck, not Malcolm, was governor, and consequently permitted the ordinary freedom of speech.

"It is a weighty responsibility which the Governor takes upon him when he opposes a military force to prevent the service of the King's writ of *habeas*. . . . It is difficult to conceive the extent to which such interference may be carried. It involves the power of defeating altogether the objects for which his Majesty's courts were established. Sir J. P. Grant has conducted himself with that firmness and temperance on the occasion which are worthy of the dignified station he fills. His situation is extremely trying; left alone on the bench, his decrees defied by authority, and a military force arrayed against the Court to oppose the execution of the King's writ. In these arduous circumstances the learned judge has displayed a degree of moderation which has never been exceeded. In order to prevent any effusion of blood, he has ordered the attachment to issue to the government, that they may have it executed. Of course they will not attend to it, and the authority of the Court will be defied; but its dignity will be maintained." [1]

The answer from England then came. Lord Ellenborough,[2] with the approval of the Duke of Wellington's ministry, busy in opposing bills for Catholic relief and the reform of rotten boroughs, decided against the judge, and appointed over his head Mr. Dewar, a friend of the Governor, and a Mr. Seymour. "Two tame elephants," as he said, "to lead the wild one," a confidential communication, which was allowed to appear in the papers to the annoyance of the judge; and afterwards of its sender.

And so reaction towards the old order had for a short time full swing in Bombay. Malcolm returned to England. He had done little to mend

[1] *Bengal Hurkaru*, March 23, 1829.

[2] Afterwards Governor-General of India—"was recalled by the Directors, who disliked his theatrical display."—Hunter, p. 311.

matters in the East, but satiated with his revenge against the "rising spirit of the time," he obtained a seat for a pocket borough, and fought in Parliament a losing battle against reform in England, as well as in India.

At this time Sir Charles Metcalfe, an able and trusted Company's servant, wrote a minute on the King's Courts of the Presidency towns. It is published in his "Papers and Correspondence."[1] This minute probably had an important bearing on the coming change in Indian legislation. Metcalfe, as was only natural, approached the question from the Company's side; and to him the three King's Courts were all encroaching on the Company's rights. All opponents are apt to be spoken of as "encroaching." The most orderly policeman must be considered by a London pickpocket to have a reprehensible habit of "encroaching" on the liberties of more enterprising men. But Metcalfe goes further; speaking of the Bombay Court, the Charter of which he had not seen, he says, "the King's Court does not recognise the existence of any right in the Provincial Court to punish."[2] This, of course, was not so. Sir C. Chambers and Sir J. P. Grant only maintained the right of the King's Court to revise (when appealed to) the irregular decisions of the Company's Provincial Court.

The chief aim of Metcalfe's long minute was to persuade his readers in England that the King's

[1] p. 269.

[2] Idem., p. 278.

Courts were a "hardship" to the natives—that it was a hardship for a native to be "dragged from a distance" and brought before the King's Court. The fact was—as can be easily seen by any one who takes the trouble to study for himself the records of this time—that natives who were "dragged" from the Provinces to the King's Court, under a writ of *habeas corpus*, were generally natives who had been imprisoned illegally by the Provincial Court, and were "dragged" to the King's Court to be liberated.

A Company's magistrate no doubt considered such a proceeding a "hardship"—but it is difficult to believe that the released native held the same opinion—or would have agreed with Metcalfe that "the writs of the King's Court ought not to interfere with the previous decrees of the Provincial Courts."[1]

But even Company's servants—those of them who were not absorbed in money-making—acknowledged the good done by the King's Judges, whose lives were so extraordinarily short at this unhappy period. T. C. Robertson, of the Company's Civil Service, wrote in 1829:[2]—"The King's Court is, like all human institutions, imperfect; but still as a wholesome check upon the Government, and upon the European community in general, it is of incalculable benefit

[1] Metcalfe, Paper, p. 283.
[2] "Remarks on the Civil Government of India," p. 62. 1829.

to the country. This is its proper part, and this it well fulfils." And Macaulay, Secretary of the India Board, unfair to the first King's Judges at Calcutta, as the late Sir James Stephen[1] shows him to have been, speaking in 1833 on the renewal of the Company's Charter, acknowledges that "the Supreme Court has perhaps improved more than any institution in India. The judges have in our time deserved the greatest respect. Their judgment and integrity have done much to mitigate the vices of the system. But you have two supreme powers in India. There is no arbitrator except a Legislature, 15,000 miles off. Such a system is in itself an absurdity in politics. The members of the Indian Government, the Judges of the Supreme Court, call upon you to reform this system."[2]

And reform came. The power to make laws, and to determine points of law for all law courts in every part of British India, was deputed to a new Governor-General of India, with a new Council containing four members, one with legal knowledge, and independent of the Company. While the final word on every Indian question was to be said by Parliament.

In 1834 Macaulay himself became the first legislative member of the Council of India,[3] under Lord William Bentinck as Governor-General.

[1] "Story of Nuncomar," by Sir James Stephen. London, 1885.
[2] Macaulay's Speech on the India Bill, July 1833.
[3] Wilson's "History," ix. p. 359.

CHAPTER XVIII

1828, the year of darkness before dawn—Lord William Bentinck; fearless reformer; difficulties of his task; experiences of his early career—Address of welcome from natives of Madras—Retrenchment—The new Provinces a neglected garden—Widow burning and organised assassination flourishing and increasing; Bentinck's vigorous measures for their suppression — Abolition of Provincial Courts—Treaty with Runjeet Singh—India saved from bankruptcy—Bentinck's return.

THIS record of a gloomy epoch in Indian history seems to call for some slight sketch of the coming dawn.

The year 1828—the year in which West died, and Malcolm trampled on the King's Court—in which maladministration was at its height in India, and the forces of reaction had full swing in England, was also the year in which Heaven sent the first Governor-General of India[1] to heal that sorely-stricken land.

All the wise legislation—all the much-needed reform to which that sorrowful age at last gave birth, are connected with the name of Lord William Bentinck.

When we consider the character of Bentinck, and the work he was able to accomplish, the popular heroes of the Company's administration—its Elphinstones, its Malcolms, and its many hard-

[1] The official title was "Governor-General of Bengal" until 1833, when Bentinck was made "Governor-General of India."

working, state-paper-writing, self-seeking — yet praiseworthy—men, shrink into smaller niches in the great monument of British rule in the East.

Bentinck it was who—partly owing to character, partly in obedience to the call of the time—was destined to gather up scattered threads spun by many a friend of India; by unobtrusive lovers of justice; by dead judges; by honest writers, and weave them together for the good of India and the honour of England.[1]

This he did in consultation with fellow-workers, and with deference to their opinions, though with the moral courage of a Hebrew prophet in a hostile crowd.

Biographers[2] dwell on the hostility he encountered at the beginning of his Governor-Generalship — from the military whose pay he was ordered to reduce—and from civilians whose great incomes he curtailed; and they speak of the fierce attacks made on him by the Anglo-Indian Press—attacks he magnanimously refused to suppress. They do not appear to notice the delight of less interested writers, when news of his coming reached the Presidency towns; and it became known that public opinion in England had forced the Directors of the Company to accept

[1] "The modern history of the British in India, as benevolent administrators ruling the country with a single eye to the good of the natives, may be said to begin with Lord William Bentinck."—Hunter, "The Indian Empire," p. 306. London, 1882.

[2] There is a biography of Bentinck (by Boulger) in the "Rulers of India" Series, and in the "Dict. of Nat. Biography," and many notices of him in the biographies of other Anglo-Indians.

a Governor-General so opposed to their traditions. Nor do biographers seem to notice the widespread approval of his measures when it was found that the new Governor-General was prepared to see things for himself, to consult fellow-workers, and to appoint committees to report on proposed changes, instead of adopting measures evolved from the inner consciousness of an autocratic bureaucracy.

Bentinck at the time of his appointment as Governor-General was no Company's servant. Twenty years before, the Directors had dismissed him with as little ceremony as they would have discharged a dishonest clerk.

In the year 1803, a smart soldier, under thirty years of age, he had been made Governor of Madras. Writing to Lord Wellesley at that time, he declared a "steady and determined resolution to do what was right, uninfluenced by party or prejudice, careless and fearless of the result."[1] That was the keynote of his life. Lord Wellesley spoke of the "truly British spirit, sound judgment, and hereditary integrity" shown by Bentinck—and to Napier he was "A man of resolution, capacity, and spirit; just in his actions, and abhorring oppression." But the course of his five years' Governorship of Madras did not run smoothly. Bentinck was young, and the good metal required some tempering in adversity. The tempering came suddenly.

[1] "Bentinck." "Rulers of India" Series, 1897.

At the fortress of Vellore—some eighty miles from Madras—where there could have been little to occupy soldiers in time of peace, the European officers found work for idle hands in introducing European smartness and attention to pipeclay into native regiments, and in forbidding the use of earrings, caste marks, and distinctive turbans. *Sartor Resartus* had not been written. Still they might have reflected on the symbolism of dress, and have had more sympathy with native feeling and honourable pride. The result of their well-meant efforts was that the soldiers in a crack native regiment—urged to mutiny, possibly by the family of Tippoo Sahib, who were confined in the fortress—refused to obey orders. A deputation from the Sepoys was not allowed a hearing, and the ringleaders were sentenced to 900 [1] lashes each. Bentinck, trusting to the discretion of the Commander-in-Chief, decided that it was impossible to yield to threats, and supported Sir John Cradock's scheme of native army reform.

All at once fanatical patriotism broke loose, and the officers were massacred. The revolt was quickly suppressed. But the Directors were panic-stricken, and both Governor and Commander-in-Chief were recalled with scant courtesy.

In 1822, after serving in the Peninsula, Bentinck was a candidate for the Governor-Generalship. Everybody in India whose opinion was worth having

[1] Wilson's "India," vol. vii. p. 130.

wanted Bentinck back. The *Bengal Hurkaru* (February 22, 1823) says: "It does not appear that the office of Governor-General has been filled. . . . Lord William Bentinck, from his previous habits, his moderation, and known liberality of his views is, if not the ablest, the best suited to the trust of all who have been mentioned."

But Bentinck refused to canvass, or to influence the vote of the Directors, and long before the paragraph was read at Calcutta breakfast-tables, Lord Amherst had been appointed by Lord Liverpool Governor-General of Bengal.

If Bentinck had been chosen, India would probably have been saved the misery of the Burmese War of 1824; and certainly half-a-dozen years of debt and wretchedness, of widow burning and organised assassination, and the course of history would have been changed.

Now at last, in the year 1828, an East Indiaman touches at Madras, on its way to Calcutta, bringing the dismissed Governor of Madras, as the only man in England capable of rescuing India, and of repairing the damaged reputation of the East India Company.

At Madras, we learn from a periodical of the time, 240 natives, many of whom as children Bentinck had saved from starvation, hurried to present him with an address of welcome. It appears that a quarter of a century before this time Bentinck had broken up a disastrous "corner" in rice, and had saved the province of Madras from the worst effects of famine.

The address of these poor natives is not mentioned by Bentinck's biographers, but it is worth quoting:—

To the Rt. Honble. LORD WILLIAM C. BENTINCK.

MY LORD,—When the inhabitants of Madras had the good fortune . . . of being protected by your Lordship, when Governor of this Presidency, they experienced the good effects of your liberal policy, and your pious and charitable disposition towards the poor, and every class of the community, particularly during the dearth of 1803; as, by the exercise of those exalted qualities, the distressed villagers had been all provided with the means of support, and had thus been rescued from an untimely dissolution resulting from starvation and despair, to the utter disappointment of the uncharitable and ambitious hopes of the grain dealers, when rice was ordered to be supplied from Calcutta by your Lordship's command, which was gratuitously distributed to the poor, and sold to others at a moderate rate. Thereby effectually providing a remedy against the inseparable consequences of such an awful visitation.

This act of your Lordship's benevolence not only thus saved many thousands of lives, but contributed to the security of the public revenues, the result of a wise policy. For had not your Lordship then pitied the miserable state of the country, and provided the dying population with means of support, the environs of Madras, and the countries dependent thereon, would have been totally deserted, and thereby the resources of Government must have suffered most materially.

These considerations excited our admiration and gratitude in no small degree, and have impressed us with no less attachment for your Lordship's amicable virtues. . . . That God may be with you wherever you are, protecting your Lordship against all dangers is the fervent wish of your most grateful servants.

Signed by 240 natives.

Lord William Bentinck was evidently much gratified, and returned an affectionate answer.

Arrived at Calcutta, Bentinck inquired on his own account into all matters connected with the government of India, and appointed military and civil committees to report on possible reductions.

The military pay, the least extravagant of the charges on the Company, was at once reduced by order of the Directors; Bentinck had no choice in the matter—the orders were peremptory.

For this, and for the reduction of the incomes of civil servants, he was fiercely attacked, and misrepresented in newspapers he could have suppressed, and whose editors he could have banished. But a natural dignity of mind, and love of fair play to opponents, prevented interference on his own behalf. The situation was accepted, and even personal abuse, which would have crushed smaller men, was allowed to continue. In the Upper Provinces, Europeans even "withheld from him the courtesies of civilised society—almost the common dues of humanity. When his barge grounded no help was afforded; when he halted no one attended his receptions."[1]

But reform went on. By the reduction of the extravagant salaries of civil servants a large sum was saved—although even after that reduction, and after the issuing of an order that Company's officials should not receive presents, the incomes

[1] Keene's "History of India," ii. 106.

of 400 civil servants amounted to nearly a million sterling.

Fiercely criticised as he was, Bentinck always received the support of those who were capable of recognising his greatness and his integrity.

When a communication from the Council to European Merchants was published, to the effect that their land might be used for other purposes than indigo growing, and when an official notice appeared in the newspapers that "suggestions, tending to promote any branch of national industry, to improve commercial intercourse, to amend defects in existing establishments, to encourage the diffusion of useful knowledge," would be welcome, the announcement was received with enthusiasm.

The editor of the *Bengal Hurkaru*[1] wrote: "We most sincerely congratulate the community on the new order of things which is indicated in the novel and gratifying spectacle of a Governor of India inviting useful suggestions from all classes, as to the physical improvement of the country, and the moral and political advancement of its people; and on the termination of that exclusive system which has so long been the bane of British India.

"Had India always been governed in that spirit which the two notices of the Governor-General indicate, instead of those narrow views which have formed the basis of Indian legislation,

[1] March 25, 1829.

she would have exhibited now a very different aspect to that which she actually presents—an aspect tending more to the honour of the conquerors, and to the happiness of the conquered, and to the value and security of our possessions. But a new era is dawning upon India. . . ."[1]

The *Hurkaru* went on to show the introduction of capital and skill—and the improvement in the condition of the Ryots to have been chiefly due to interlopers—indigo planters and others, who have been treated by the Company as aliens, subject to banishment "whenever the caprice of a vindictive ruler might will it."

While financial reform was proceeding, Bentinck, on his own responsibility, and with little support from the Directors, set to work to cope with the hideous custom of native widow burning.

Although, as has been shown,[2] the Company had been continually told by competent judges that the custom could be suppressed with little difficulty, no Governor-General had attempted the task.

Suttee, in spite of some local decrease, had increased in Bengal under the Company's rule. The necessary licence for a human sacrifice, granted by the Company, was looked upon as a sanction of the custom, so that in Bengal alone the licensed widow burnings amounted to six hundred a year.

Previous Governor-Generals had refused to

[1] The *Hurkaru* was right—a new era was dawning upon India.
[2] Chapter vi.

interfere, from the supposed danger of hurting the prejudices of the high-caste sepoys. But Lord W. Bentinck took the commonsense course of finding out for himself what the opinion of the sepoy was, and discovered that — although the sepoy, in common with the rest of mankind, was not without prejudices — he was not in favour of so horrible a rite. He found, too, that the much-abused ex-Peshwa had forbidden suttee at Poona, and that the best Brahmins were against it. And so in 1829 throughout Bengal, and in the following year in Madras and Bombay, the burning of a Hindoo widow was made a crime, and the custom died with scarcely a struggle.

Another of Bentinck's most important measures was the suppression of bands of native assassins.

The unhappy period with which this history deals had been as favourable to their ugly calling as to that of fraudulent native tax-gatherers or promoters of suttee. The Mahratta wars had broken up the rule—such as it was—of native princes, but the Company had failed to establish good government in its stead.

The newly-acquired Provinces of India had become like a neglected garden, from which the old gardeners had been discharged; and in which the skill of the new gardeners chiefly lay in strengthening the fence, and in receiving wages.

And what on God's earth is more pitiable than a neglected garden—one on which much care has been spent, and for which good men have toiled—overgrown with noxious weeds—dark, dank, unwholesome. Rare flowers, choice shrubs, choked by elder, docks, and nettles—rotting wood—broken pottery—rusting metal—green slime on gravelled paths—and all around the stifling atmosphere of rank decay! Pleasanter far waste land or open heath, where the rude forces of Nature reign, than such a garden. Better it were to break down the fence and let Nature have her way; to let deer and cattle trample down the poisonous weeds; open up glades and lawns, admit the lost sunshine again into the dark places, and bring back the picturesque old forest land!

Among the noxious weeds which flourished during that unhappy period was the barbarous crime of organised assassination for plunder.

Indigenous in all lands since the time of Cain, the crime of murder had grown rapidly in India with the growth of the Company's territory. By the year 1830 it had assumed ghastly proportions. "In that year," writes Colonel Meadows Taylor,[1] "and for some years previously, thuggee seemed to have reached a frightful pitch of audacity, and the British Government" (of the Company) "could no longer remain indifferent to an evil of such enormous and increasing magnitude."

The government of the Company had, how-

[1] "Confession of a Thug" (Ameer Ali), Colonel Meadows Taylor, C.S.I., of the Thug Suppression Pepartment, xii. London, 1839.

ever, managed to remain indifferent for some years, while assassins—Mahometan and Hindoo—preyed on innocent people, and numbered by thousands, hunted like wolves in packs through the length and breadth of the land—from Bengal to Bombay, from Cape Comorin to the foot of the Himalayas.

Their success was appalling. Quietly and without bloodshed they garrotted or poisoned parties of travellers on every main road. Stripping their victims, they buried them with extraordinary rapidity in graves already prepared by their scouts; and, free from all suspicion on the part of the Company's magistrates, they carried on their diabolical trade even within sight of the Company's cantonments.

The history of the Thugs[1] reveals an extraordinary phase of human nature. Every virtue seems to have its caricature in a vice. Good men recognising the fact that they are in the hands of a Higher Providence, accept with thanks their appointed lot; and their resignation to the will of Heaven is looked upon as a virtue. Those suffering from the neglect of laws of health, or from over-indulgence in food and drink, are also apt to

[1] The native name for these assassins was "Thug," literally "a dishonest person." "Pronounced Tug slightly aspirated" (M. Taylor), now often spelt Thag. The old word is here retained, for it is difficult for a mere student of Indian history to follow the modern varieties of Anglo-Indian spelling. For instance Datura, the Latin word for thorn apple, a poisonous plant still used by Thugs ("Datūra id est Stramonium." Gerard's "Herbal," 1638), now suffers a sea-change on its return passage to India, and becomes in the same volume of a work on crime in India "dhatura," "dhâtura," and "dhátura."

ascribe their distress to the "Will of Heaven" to which they are "resigned." Here both virtue and reasoning seem a little impaired. But never was "Heaven's will" made the excuse for worse deeds than it was by the Thugs.

A devout Indian assassin, feeling some remorse as he stands over his hundredth innocent victim, who had trusted him with his friendship and his life, would console himself by the reflection, "All things are predestined. It was Heaven's will that these poor people should die. I and my brave companions are but instruments in the hands of Providence, whom we thank for our success in so profitable and exciting a calling." To such base uses was the virtue of resignation applied in India.

The passion for garrotting, like other vices—and happily like many virtues—grew by exercise; and a Thug found it difficult to forsake a vice of which he had even become proud. When enlisted as a sepoy, he would use his few days' leave to join a Thug band—"You English," said a Thug to Colonel Meadows Taylor,[1] "are passionately devoted to sporting. Days and months are passed in its excitement. A tiger, a buffalo, or a hog, rouses your utmost energies for its destruction. You risk your lives in its pursuit. How much higher game is a Thug's?" And Ameer Ali, an informer who had turned king's evidence, and whose disclosures were all verified, confessing to 719

[1] Colonel Meadows Taylor in "Confessions," p. 2. 1893.

murders, exclaimed: "Ah, sir, if I had not been in prison twelve years the number would have been a thousand."

India thus seems to have possessed two entirely opposed creeds, each pushed to its furthest extreme; that of the Thug, to whom no life is sacred—that of the Brahmin, to whom all life, even that of poisonous flies and mosquitoes, is sacred. Both beliefs disastrous to human life!

Like many systematic criminals engaged in hazardous adventures, the Thugs were grossly superstitious, and at the mercy of every possible omen. Few birds there were, or four-footed beasts, which did not furnish portents, to be religiously obeyed.[1] Most omens (as usual) were unfavourable. A kite screaming on the wing was a warning. If heard just before daybreak, it put to flight the whole gang. Two large owls answering each other, had almost the same effect; while the continued hooting of a small owl on the left, was propitious.

The cry of a hare crossing the road broke up an expedition, and all travellers in the power of the gang were allowed to proceed unhurt.

The "lamentation" of a pack of jackals, or the wailing of a wolf, meant disaster; but a single jackal crossing from the right was a good omen. While if a dog shook its head, all plans were postponed for the day.

[1] James Hutton, "Popular Account of Thugs and Dacoits." 1857.

A snake crossing the road during an expedition had to be killed, and sacrifices were made.

A crow perched on any animal, dead or alive, was a bad omen; but the Great Sarus Crane on the left was an order to proceed—as was also the Blue Jay crossing from left to right.

And so we are reminded of Horace's charming Ode to Galatea:—

> Impios parrae recinentis omen
> Ducat et praegnans canis aut ab agro
> Rava decurrens lupa Lanuvino
> Fetaque vulpes.
>
> Rumpat et serpens iter institutum,
> Si per obliquum similis sagittae
> Terruit mannos: ego cui timebo
> Providus auspex.
>
> . . . .
>
> Sis licet felix ubicunque mavis.
>
> . . . .
>
> Teque nec laevus vetet ire picus
> Nec vaga cornix.[1]
>
> HORACE, Ode iii. 27.

and of the continuity of all human history.

[1] Let the omen of a chattering bird guide the wicked,
And a cur with young, or grey wolf cantering down the hill,
Or a vixen.

And let a snake startling the horses as it shoots across the road,
Spoil their journey just begun,

To one for whom I care I will be
A watchful augur

. . . .

May you, Galatea, be happy in any place you choose,

. . . .

And let no woodpecker screaming on the left hinder you;
Nor stray crow.

The attention of the Company had been continually called to the Thugs, and some arrests had been made by its more energetic servants; but Thuggee, like Suttee, had nothing to do with 10 per cent. dividends on India Stock, and little notice had been taken, except to warn sepoys, going home on leave, against the danger.

Even in 1831, Major Sleeman[1] of the Bengal Army, whom Bentinck had made political agent in the Central Provinces, was at first inclined to discredit some disclosures which had been obtained by his senior colleague, Mr. F. C. Smith, from an informer. But when, as an object-lesson, thirteen bodies of murdered men had been exhumed near his own tent, sickened at the sight, he stopped further excavations, and armed with special powers bestowed on him by Bentinck, set to work to exterminate the gang.

Informers obtained in the Central Provinces, on condition that their lives were spared, freely denounced their companions, some of whom, apprehended at a distance, gave information on the same terms of gangs further off. And so the circle widened until it was found that the ghastly crime extended over the whole of India; and the disinterment of victims showed that not a day passed without its accompanying murder. "Few,"

[1] Afterwards Sir William Sleeman, well known for his energy in suppressing the Thugs.

wrote Colonel Meadows Taylor, "who were in India in 1832, will ever forget the excitement which the discovery occasioned in every part of the country. It was utterly discredited[1] by the magistrates of many districts."

The able officers appointed by Bentinck for the suppression of the assassins did their work well. Many hundreds of arrests were made. Hunter gives the number as 1562. Wilson at about 2000; while in some tables furnished by Captain Reynolds, the superintendent of the department, the number of arrests between 1830 and 1837 amounted to more than 3000.[2] By the end of 1837, about 1500 Thugs had been hanged, imprisoned, or transported to Penang; while 483 had been accepted as "informers." One item, "In jail —not yet tried, 936," incidentally gives an insight into the state of the Company's Provincial Courts; and two others, "Escaped from jail, 11," and "Died in jail, 36,"[3] throw some light on the state of the jails themselves.

When we consider that, in addition to those arrested, 1800 notorious assassins were still at large when Captain Reynolds wrote, and of course many whose names were not known, it becomes quite impossible ever to make any kind of guess at the amount of human life

[1] It always had been.
[2] See also James Hutton, "Popular Account of Thugs," p. 92. 1857.
[3] James Hutton gives 208 (up to the year 1840) as the number of those who died a natural death before sentence was passed.

and property destroyed during this terrible period.[1]

And in many other ways reform went on. The conquered races rose in honour and self-respect, in knowledge of science and literature. Natives were admitted to posts previously held by highly salaried Europeans; to the advantage of the native, and to the diminution of the expenditure.

The collection of the land revenue was everywhere vastly improved, and the barbarous "settlement" of the Deccan, arranged with some unction in the time of Elphinstone, was entirely revised, the land taxes reduced, and the depopulation of the Deccan arrested.

The hopeless Provincial Courts of Appeal and Circuit—"notorious for delay and uncertainty of verdict"—whose judgments the dead judges of the King's Court of Bombay had often tried to reverse, were abolished, and their civil business was transferred to courts with native judges. No war of importance was waged; but a treaty was made with Runjeet Singh, the Lion of the Punjab, and with the Amirs of Scind.

Still, modest in estimating the result of his measures, Bentinck, like Sydney Smith, ap-

[1] Although the Thug bands were broken up, there is no doubt that frequent murder by poisoning remained. As late as 1888 Dr. Lyons, Analyst to the Government, had to deal with no less than 360 cases of poisoning in one year, and in Bombay alone. He shows in his Report that poisoning was a "very common crime in India,' and difficult to discover, and that poisons were and are within reach of all.—General Hervey, "Some Records of Crime," p. 70. 1896.

pears from the following interesting entry in the "Journal" of Sir Charles Bunbury,[1] to have been not quite convinced that India was at that time the better for British sovereignty:—

"*London, Nov.* 30, 1835.—I dined at Holland House; the party consisted of Miss Fox,[2] Sydney Smith, Mr. Rogers, Mr. Cutlar Ferguson, . . . besides Lord and Lady Holland and Mr. Allen. There was much agreeable conversation; Sydney Smith very entertaining. . . . An animated discussion upon India, chiefly between Mr. Ferguson and Mr. Smith, Lord Holland and Mr. Allen occasionally taking part. Sydney Smith contended that the English Government in India was not preferable to that of native princes, and quoted the opinions of Lord William Bentinck and Captain Burnes on his side; Mr. Ferguson maintained the contrary. Lord Holland's frank good-humoured manner, readiness to talk, and fund of agreeable anecdote, gave a very pleasant tone to the conversation."

Bentinck carried out his measures with perfect courage, and often in the face of scorn and hatred. He lived a life of simplicity, free from ostentation and vanity, at a time when extravagance and Oriental profusion were at their height. He left India in 1835 revered by all classes, even by those

[1] The "Life of Sir Charles James Fox Bunbury, Bart.," edited by Mrs. Henry Lyell. London, 1906.

[2] The Hon. Caroline Fox, rightly described by Sydney Smith as an "Aged Angel."

who had opposed him. Although he had reduced the extortionate land taxes, he had changed an annual deficit of a million into a surplus of two million a year, and had saved India from bankruptcy.

But from England later on came a discordant note. When Bentinck, after his great work was finished, was standing for Glasgow, Charles Greville, clerk to the Privy Council, made the following entry in his "Journal":—

"Lord William Bentinck has published an address to the Electors of Glasgow. It is by no means well done, and a very silly address in many respects. He is a man whose success in life has been greater than his talents warranted, for he is not right headed, and has committed some great blunder or other in every public station in which he has been placed; but he is simple in his habits, popular in his manners, liberal in his opinions, and magnificently hospitable. These qualities are enough to ensure popularity."—"Greville Memoirs," Feb. 12, 1836.

Greville's unexpected comment comes as a shock. But when we reflect that Bentinck was Greville's uncle, that kith and kin stand too near us to be seen in true perspective; so that even a prophet is apt to be first recognised and honoured among strangers rather than among his own kinsfolk, it becomes easier to understand his criticism.

Greville too was notoriously cynical, one to

whom no Lancelot was brave. There may, of course, be some foundation for Greville's comment. If so, it points to the truth of a remark made by Bishop Creighton—who was a judge of both qualities—that character is of greater importance than intellect.

But the reorganisation of India was carried out by a master hand; the Company took credit for Bentinck's work; and the signing of the great charter was again postponed.

The short-lived King's Judges had done their work; and it remains.

The wells of Granada, skilfully dug by forgotten Moors, still flow for Spanish children. Of these wells Dean Stanley wrote: "So it is with the good deeds of those who have gone before us. Whatever there has been of charity, of high-minded justice, of saintly devotion, these still feed the stream of moral fertilisation which will run on when the place knows them no more, even when their names have perished."

APPENDIX

NOTES FROM THE COMPANY'S CHARTERS

SIR WILLINGHAM FRANKLIN, brother of the great leader of Arctic exploration, and friend of Sir Edward West, kept a journal during his very short life as a King's Judge at Madras. In this journal, lent to the Author by the judge's grandson, Mr. Willingham Rawnsley, there are notes of important points in the Company's Charters. The following extracts are from these notes:—

Sir Willingham Franklin says, I find the Charters of Incorporation to be of ye following date—according to ye "collection of Charters & Statutes relating to ye East India Company."

31 *Dec.* 1600. First Charter. Title "Governor & Company of Merchants of London trading to ye East Indies."

31 *May* 1609. Second Charter.

3 *April* 1661. Third Charter. In this ye Governors & Council are authorized to exercise Civil & Criminal Jurisdiction in the s[d] Factories according to ye laws of England. May seize & send home Englishmen sailing in Indian or English Vessels in East Indies, or residing there without ye Company's licence.

27 *Mar.* 1669. Grants the Port & Island of Bombay to The East India Company to be held by them as of ye Manor of Greenwich in Perpetuity at a Fee Farm Rent of £10 per Ann. The General Court of Proprietors, or the Governor and Committee may make Laws for ye good Government of ye Island, and its Inhabitants, and impose punishments to taking away Life and Member, so that they be *consonant to Reason, & not repugnant but as*

near as may be agreeable to the Laws of England. The Governor and Company shall have ye same Powers in ye Island as in ye other Plantations of ye Company.

16 *Dec.* 1674. St. Helena given in Perpetuity to ye Company.

5 *Oct.* 1677. Fourth General Charter. Authorized to coin money, not to be named after coin current in ye King's Dominions.

9 *Aug.* 1683. Power of declaring Peace and War with ye Heathen Nations—*Sovereign Power still reserved to ye King when he shall think fit to interpose*—Power is given to the Company to appoint Judges who are to *determine according to Equity and good Conscience and the Laws and Customs of Merchants.*

12 *April* 1686. Sixth Charter. Powers to appoint Admirals & Captains and raise Seamen and Soldiers to make war on any Indian Prince, and exercise martial law on ye other side of the Cape of Good Hope—Reserving to the King ye Power of revoking ye Grant. Power also given to ye Company to coin money usually coined by ye Princes of India, agreeable to ye standards of those Princes in Weight and Fineness.

7 *Oct.* 1693. Seventh Charter. Ye former Charter having in strictness of Law been forfeited, a new Charter is granted on ye Conditions to adhere to Regulations promulgated under ye Great Seal.

5 *Sept.* 1698. Charter granted to Second East India Company. "English Company trading to ye East Indies" to establish Courts of Justice consisting of a Person skilled in Civil Law and two Merchants.

22 *July* 1702. The union of the Queen Anne Old Company and the New Company. To be completed at the End of 7 years.

29 *Sept.* 1708. The Consolidated Company to be called "The United Company of Merchants of England trading to the East Indies."

24 *Sept.* 1726. Charter of George I. erects Court of Mayor & Aldermen at Madras, Calcutta, and Bombay, for 10 miles round Courts of Record. Mayor's Court had nothing to do with Criminal prosecutions. Governor & Council to hold Quarter

Sessions for punishment of Persons accused of Crimes in *ye same manner as in England*.

37 George III. c. 142. A New Charter gives Power to His Majesty to establish a Recorder's Court at Madras & Bombay in the place of ye Mayor's Court. *All ye Stat: Law does not extend to ye East Indies. It is difficult to ascertain what Statutes do apply.*

8 *Jan.* 1753. Charter Recites Surrender of Charters 1726 & 1727.

17 *Sept.* 1757. Charter states ye Commencement of Hostilities ag[t] ye Nabob of Bengal. A Moiety of ye plunder to be given to ye Captors, and ye other Moiety reserved for ye King, who gives it to ye Company.

14 *Jan.* 1758. Booty is given to ye East India Company when their Troops or Seamen alone obtain it. If it be got by ye conjoint efforts of ye Company's and His Majesty's Forces, the distribution shall be as his Majesty shall direct.

26 *Mar.* 1774. Charter. Recites an Act passed in ye 13th of George III., empowering ye King to create in Bengal a Court of Civil, Criminal, Ecclesiastical, & Admiralty Jurisdiction with 4 Judges. May admit advocates, and attorneys without licence. *Persons employed directly or indirectly by ye Company made amenable to Court. Natives also when they have agreed to submit their Contracts to the Supreme Court.* Persons complained against are to be summoned by the Sheriff. I believe an attachment issues if they do not. Afterwards ye Charter says if the Party so summoned shall not appear, the Court may issue a writ & arrest.

24 George III. c. 25. (The Act which establishes ye Board of Control) declares all British subjects answerable to all Courts of Justice of Competent Jurisdiction to try offences committed in India. Receiving presents to be deemed Extortion, and to be punished as such.

33 George III. c. 52, sec. 151. Governor-General in Council may appoint Justices of the Peace for ye Presidencies.

Sec. 153. Proceedings of Justices of ye Peace

may be removed into ye Supreme Courts of ye Presidencies, under ye same conditions as in England.

37 George III. c. 142. May erect a Recorder's Court at Madras and Bombay. Recorder to be ye President, and 3 Aldermen to sit with him. Court to be a Civil, Criminal, Ecclesiastical, and Admiralty one. Jurisdiction of these Courts not to extend to Revenue matters. In Civil matters between natives to determine as a native Court would do. No action to be brought ag[t] ye judges of ye Provincial Courts for Judicial Acts. May proceed by information after notice. Appeals may be made from the Regulations of the Governors & Councils of Madras & Bombay.

39 & 40 George III. King may erect a Supreme Court, and ye powers of the Recorder's Court to be transferred to it. Transportation to be made to New South Wales in cases of Persons not Natives of India.

INDEX

Y

Z